...ish Verbs M...

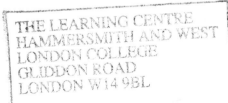

David Brodsky

Spanish VERBS MADE Simple(r)

University of Texas Press   Austin

Requests for permission to reproduce material from this work should be sent to
Permissions, University of Texas Press, P.O. Box 7819, Austin, TX 78713-7819.

⊚ The paper used in this book meets the minimum requirements of
ANSI/NISO Z39.48-1992 (R1997) (Permanence of Paper).

Library of Congress Cataloging-in-Publication Data
Brodsky, David, 1950–
    Spanish verbs made simple(r) / David Brodsky.— 1st ed.
        p.   cm.
    Summary: "Provides rules for conjugating all classes of Spanish verbs, includ-
ing irregular verbs. Includes discussion of the uses of the subjunctive and the
difference between the verbs *ser* and *estar*"—Provided by publisher.
    Includes bibliographical references.
    ISBN 0-292-70677-4 (hardcover : alk. paper) — ISBN 0-292-70653-7 (pbk. :
alk. paper)
1. Spanish language—Verb.   2. Spanish language—Textbooks for foreign
speakers—English.   I. Title: Spanish verbs made simple.   II. Title.
    PC4271.B76   2005
    468.2'421—dc22

2004024713

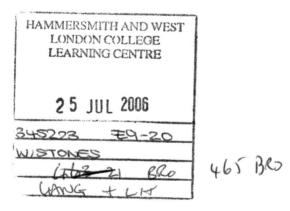

For Daniel, Michael, and Beatriz

Contents

Preface

The fundamental aim of this book is to provide:

(a) easily understood—yet comprehensive—tools to recognize and learn the patterns that govern the large majority of "irregular" verbs in Spanish; and
(b) clear and systematic illustrations of the use of all of the principal Spanish verb forms, with particular emphasis placed on the subjunctive.

It is intended for both the relatively new student grappling with the apparent complexities of Spanish verbs, as well as for the more advanced student seeking to "perfect" his or her understanding.

The book is divided into three parts, which to a certain extent are independent:

Part I provides a description of the various verb tenses and forms, the emphasis being on establishing rules for the more than 90 percent of irregular verbs whose irregularities are entirely "predictable". Emphasis is also given to the stress accent patterns of the various forms, which play a critical role in the Spanish verbal system.

Chapter 8 highlights one of the major differences between the Spanish language of Spain and that of the Americas, namely the contrasting use of personal pronouns (and verb forms) corresponding to "you". Chapter 9 provides an overall summary of verb forms and presents 35 general models (or *classes*) into which all Spanish verbs can be placed.

Part II illustrates the use of the various verb tenses and forms, with particular emphasis given to the subjunctive and its use in *"if . . . then"* clauses. Chapter 11 is devoted to the distinctions in use between *ser* and *estar,* which many students find to be the most confusing element of the Spanish verbal system.

Annexes: By reviewing **Annex A,** the student can become familiar with the various classes of verb "irregularities" and their unifying features. Complete conjugations are presented for each of the 35 model verbs, as well as for various subclasses including those displaying purely orthographic changes. Verb classes are nested, so that one can easily see that a verb like *colgar* (sub-class 4B-2) is identical in form to the basic model *mostrar* (class 4B), apart from regular orthographic modifications which are highlighted in the conjugations, and described in detail in Part I of the text. *Mostrar* itself is clearly identified as following a very regular pattern—a vowel change (e.g., *muestro*) in the 9 conjugations where the stress accent falls on the initial syllable.

Annex B provides an alphabetical index of more than 4,800 verbs, showing for each verb its class model and, where applicable, sub-class, e.g.,

verb	class (sub-class)	number
prevenir	venir (convenir)	32-1
prever	ver (prever)	14-1
primar	cantar	1
pringar	cantar (pagar)	1-2
priorizar	cantar (cazar)	1-4
privar	cantar	1

Thus one can determine at a glance that: (a) *primar* and *privar* follow the model of the (perfectly regular) verb *cantar;* (b) *pringar* and *priorizar* also follow the model of *cantar,* but with orthographic modifications as per the sub-models *pagar* and *cazar;* (c) *prevenir* follows the model of *venir,* with the same modifications as the sub-model *convenir;* and (d) *prever* follows the basic model *ver,* and is itself a sub-model for certain modifications, as shown in Annex A.

A more advanced student will have the option of reading the book either sequentially or "à la carte". A student at a more elementary level may find it preferable to concentrate initially on those chapters dealing with the indicative—both forms and uses—before passing on to the subjunctive. In this case the suggested order of chapters would be the following:

chapter	topic
1–4	indicative verb forms
6	compound verb forms
8	second person pronouns: *tuteo* and *voseo*
9	summary and presentation of verb classes
10	uses of indicative
11	*ser* versus *estar*
7	orthographic modifications
5	subjunctive and imperative forms
12	uses of subjunctive

Spanish Verbs Made Simple(r)

Introduction

The structure of Spanish verbs is not difficult to comprehend for a native English speaker, as most of the forms parallel or are very close in meaning to those employed in English. This basic similarity is at times obscured, however, by the lack of uniformity in naming the various verb forms. Consider, for example, some of the names variously applied to the two verb forms represented by *I took* and *I have taken:*

I took	I have taken
preterite	present perfect
past	past perfect
simple past	compound past
past definite	past definite
past indefinite	past indefinite

To emphasize the close correspondence between English and Spanish verb forms, we have chosen to use names which are simple to remember and convey the essential nature of the verb form in question, even if some grammarians might not always consider them the most appropriate.

One seeming major difference between Spanish and English verb systems is that Spanish employs two "moods": the *indicative* and the *subjunctive*. The mood of the verb does not refer (at least directly) to that of the speaker but rather to the type of statement he or she is making. The indicative can be thought of as the "normal" verb mood (or mode), while the subjunctive is used in a number of special circumstances—in connection with orders, desires, uncertainty, etc. Contrary to what many might think, the subjunctive also exists in English, though its existence generally passes unnoticed since subjunctive and indicative verb forms in Modern English are almost always the same. But a sentence like

I insist that he *be* punished.

provides an illustration that there is at times a difference between the two.

In Spanish the subjunctive is an essential element of the verb system and it is virtually impossible to have a meaningful conversation without using it. For this reason we will devote a substantial portion of Part II to a discussion of its use.

In addition to the indicative and subjunctive, there is a third verbal "mood"—the imperative ("Go!" "Run!" etc.). In Spanish some forms of the imperative are distinct, while others (including all negative imperatives) use subjunctive forms.

For any English verb there are essentially only five "simple" forms:

infinitive	(to) write
present	write(s)
past	wrote
past participle	written
present participle	writing

All other verb forms are *compound* ones created from the simple ones using various auxiliaries or "helping" verbs (e.g., *I was writing, I will write, I would have written*). For Spanish, there are *eleven* simple verb forms—the five English ones, plus:

indicative	subjunctive	imperative
imperfect	present	present
future	imperfect	
conditional		

Each Spanish verb thus has associated with it 47 basic "simple" conjugations, e.g., for the verb *cantar* ("to sing"):

infinitive	cantar
present indicative	canto, cantas, canta, cantamos, cantáis, cantan
simple past	canté, cantaste, cantó, cantamos, cantasteis, cantaron
imperfect	cantaba, cantabas, cantaba, cantábamos, cantabais, cantaban
past participle	cantado
present participle	cantando
future	cantaré, cantarás, cantará, cantaremos, cantaréis, cantarán
conditional	cantaría, cantarías, cantaría, cantaríamos, cantaríais, cantarían
present subjunctive	cante, cantes, cante, cantemos, cantéis, canten
imperfect subjunctive[1]	cantara, cantaras, cantara, cantáramos, cantarais, cantaran
imperative	canta, cantad (*you:* singular and plural)

---

[1] As we shall see in Chapter 5, there is a second form of the imperfect subjunctive (*cantase, cantases,* etc.) which in many cases can be used interchangeably with the first.

There are in addition a number of *compound* verb forms, most having close English counterparts.

The Spanish future and conditional tenses are each equivalent to very specific English *compound* forms (*I will write, I would write*). For the imperfect tense, there is no one-to-one correspondence with a specific English verb form, which probably is why among the various indicative verb forms it often causes the greatest difficulty.

The table below illustrates basic English equivalents for the simple and principal compound Spanish *indicative* verb forms. In each case the name in bold type (e.g., **simple past**) is the name by which the form will be referred to throughout the text; for several of the forms common alternative names are shown in parentheses.

SIMPLE FORMS (INDICATIVE)

infinitive	*To live* is *to love.*
present	He *writes* in the book.
simple past (preterite)	He *wrote* a book about Shakespeare (in 1974).
imperfect	When I *was* young I *played* baseball every day.
	When the phone rang I *was leaving* the house.
future	Some day I *will write* a book about Shakespeare.
conditional	If I were not so lazy, I *would write* a book about Shakespeare.
present participle/ gerund[2]	I saw your brother *crossing* the street.
	I am *writing* a book about Shakespeare.
past participle	The book, *written* in the Middle Ages, is now in the British Museum.

COMPOUND FORMS (INDICATIVE)

compound past (present perfect)	He *has written* a number of best-sellers.
past perfect (pluperfect)	By the age of 30, he *had written* a number of best-sellers.
future perfect	By the time I retire, I *will have worked* 40 years.
conditional perfect (past conditional)	I *would have done* it, if only I had had the chance.

---

[2] In English the present participle and gerund have the same form but fulfill different grammatical functions (e.g., "the man running" versus "running is healthy"). The Spanish *gerundio* fulfills some but not all of the functions of both the English gerund and present participle. This is discussed in Chapter 10.

Verb Classes

Spanish has three basic classes of verbs:

1. -*ar* verbs	can**tar**	"to sing"
2. -*er* verbs	com**er**	"to eat"
3. -*ir* verbs	sub**ir**	"to climb"

The -*ar* verbs are by far the most numerous.

DISTRIBUTION OF SPANISH VERBS

-*ar*	-*er*	-*ir*
85%	7%	8%

They are also the most dynamic, in the sense that the vast majority of verbs created in the post-Latin period have taken this ending, e.g.,

espiar	"to spy"
esquiar	"to ski"
robar	"to rob"
escanear	"to scan"
telefonear	"to telephone"
xerografiar	"to photocopy"
chatear	"to chat" (in common use but without "official" approval)

Endings of the -*er* and -*ir* verbs are *nearly* always the same, differing for only three of the 47 simple conjugations (present indicative 1p and 2p, and imperative 2p).[3]

Stress Accent

As in English, each word in Spanish is pronounced with a stressed or accented syllable. The place of the stress accent plays a critical role in Spanish, particularly

---

[3] Throughout the text we will use the notation *1s, 1p, 2s, 2p, 3s, 3p* to refer to "first person singular", "first person plural", etc.

in the verbal system. This is illustrated by the following examples, where the stressed syllable is shown in bold:

a•mo	Te amo.	"I love you."
a•**mo**	Te amó.	"He loved you."
can•te	¡Cante la canción!	"(You, *usted*) sing the song!"
can•**te**	Canté la canción.	"I sang the song."
ter•**mi**•no	termino	"I finish"
ter•mi•**no**	terminó	"he finished"
ter•mi•no	término	"term", "limit"
ma•**mas**	Todas las mamás son invitadas.	"All the mothers are invited."
ma•mas	Todas las mamas son invitadas.	"All the breasts are invited."

The syllable on which the stress[4] falls is determined according to the following general rule:

> **In the absence of a *written* accent mark, words ending in**
> **(a) a consonant other than *n* or *s* are stressed on the last syllable;**
> **(b) *n, s,* or a vowel are stressed on the next-to-last syllable.**
> **When the *stress* accent does not fall on the "expected" syllable, it is marked by placing a *written* accent mark (*tilde,* in Spanish) over the vowel in the stressed syllable. The letter *y* is treated as a consonant.**

It is thus necessary to distinguish between the *stress* accent, which every word has, and the *written* accent which only occurs when the *stress* accent does not fall on the "expected" syllable.

The above rule does not cover the very tricky issue of vowel combinations, which can be pronounced either as part of separate syllables or as elements of a *diphthong*. This issue will be addressed in Chapter 7.

Irregular Verbs

In Spanish, as in most languages, a "Murphy's law of verbs" seems to hold:

1. Regular verbs are infrequently used.
2. Frequently used verbs are irregular.

---

[4] We will use the terms *stress* and *stress accent* interchangeably.

There is actually a simple explanation apart from that of Sr. Murphy: frequently used verbs simply have much greater capacity to resist the constant pressure to become uniform. Consider, for example, the English verb *to crow*, whose historical past tense was *crew:*

> Then began he to curse and to swear, saying, I know not the man. And immediately the cock *crew*. (Matthew 26:74, King James Version)

> And, as the Cock *crew*, those who stood before The Tavern shouted— "Open then the Door!" (*Rubáiyát of Omar Khayyám*)

Yet the verb was so infrequently used that most people assumed, or were easily convinced, that the past tense must be *crowed* and so it has become.

> Then he began to invoke a curse on himself and to swear, "I do not know the man." And immediately the cock *crowed*. (Revised Standard Version)

The verb *to mow* (old past tense *mew*) had a similar experience, while the much more commonly used verbs *to know, to blow, to grow* have been able to resist such uniformizing tendencies and still have "irregular" past tenses: *knew, blew, grew*.

Of course if one goes back far enough in the history of English (and its predecessors) one will discover that most irregular verbs are really quite regular, following archaic patterns that have become obscured by several thousand years of gradual phonetic (and other) changes. In Spanish a similar situation prevails, but with one important advantage: *more than 90 percent of (seemingly) irregular verbs follow easily understood and readily remembered patterns*. Recognizing and learning these patterns is a far more efficient way to learn Spanish verbs than simply attempting to memorize what may at first seem like almost random irregularities.

In Spanish, a fundamental distinction can be made between verbs having regular simple past tenses—whose irregularities in other tenses, if any, generally follow *predictable* patterns—and those with irregular simple past tenses, which generally have *unpredictable* irregularities in other forms as well.

Basically regular verbs are those with regular simple past tenses and include verbs that
  (a) are (perfectly) regular;
  (b) are predictably regular;
  (c) are irregular in the first person singular present, but otherwise (largely) predictable;
  (d) have mixed patterns.
Fundamentally irregular verbs are those with irregular simple past tenses.

Those in the second group are "fundamentally" irregular not only because they tend to have more than one irregularity, but also because of the nature of the past tense irregularity itself: the pattern of accentuation is different and in most cases there is a vowel change (e.g., infinitive *poder* → simple past *pude*).

The 17 *fundamentally irregular* verbs are:

ser/estar	to be	*ir*	to go
haber/tener	to have	*poder*	to be able (can)
andar	to walk	*poner*	to put
caber	to fit	*querer*	to want
dar	to give	*saber*	to know
decir	to say	*traer*	to bring, carry
hacer	to do, make	*venir*	to come
-ducir	(*conducir, producir, seducir*, etc.)		

Apart from *caber* and *andar*, all would likely appear on any list of the 25 most important Spanish verbs.[5] It is also interesting to note that the majority correspond to *English* irregular verbs.

We will use the nomenclature "perfectly regular", "predictably regular", "basically regular", and "fundamentally irregular", in accordance with the above schema.

Personal Pronouns

One of the major differences between the Spanish spoken in Spain and that spoken in the Americas concerns the pronouns used for the second person ("you"), and in some cases the verb forms used in the second person as well. This will be considered in Chapter 8. Until that point we will consider only the "standard" forms:

	singular		plural	
1st person	*yo*	"I"	*nosotros/nosotras*	"we"
2nd person	*tú*	"you"	*vosotros/vosotras*	"you"
3rd person	*él/ella*	"he/she"	*ellos/ellas*	"they"
	usted	"you"	*ustedes*	"you"

---

[5] *Caber* owes its place on the list due to the close association, dating back to Latin, of its form with that of *saber*. *Andar* is the sole survivor of a group of regular verbs which attempted to develop irregular simple past tenses in Old Spanish times.

It should also be noted that, like Latin and most other Romance languages,[6] Spanish generally does not use personal pronouns unless there is a specific need for emphasis or, in the case of third person pronouns, to identify the subject with greater precision:

Voy a hacerlo.	"I am going to do it."
Yo voy a hacerlo.	"*I* am going to do it."
Él está ausente pero *ella* está aquí.	"*He* is absent but *she* is here."

Additional Observations

1. Real Academia Española

At various points in the text we will make reference to the Real Academia Española (RAE). Since 1714 the RAE has been charged with the responsibility to "fix the words and expressions of the Castilian language in their greatest propriety, elegance and purity."[7] The RAE thus functions in a role similar to that of the Académie Française with regard to French, but with the important difference that the RAE has to take into account the views of 21 other national academies of Spanish,[8] whereas—at least in principle—the Académie Française rules unchallenged in the Francophone world. The RAE's excellent online site contains not only the entire text of its *Diccionario de la lengua española*,[9] but also the complete conjugations for *all* Spanish verbs.

2. Definitions and Dictionaries

Brief definitions (one or two words) are given for most of the verbs presented in the text, either the first time they appear or at a later stage. These definitions are meant to be suggestive only and are in no manner a substitute for fuller definitions to be found in a dictionary. As early as possible, one should try to use a Spanish-Spanish dictionary, preferably one with examples. Outstanding (and perhaps unique) in its class is the VOX *Diccionario para la enseñanza de la lengua española*, which is specifically designed for non-native speakers. Apart from good

---

[6] French being the principal exception.

[7] From the RAE's online description of its *origen y fines* (<www.rae.es>, July 2004): "fijar las voces y vocablos de la lengua castellana en su mayor propiedad, elegancia y pureza."

[8] Including the Academia Puertorriqueña de la Lengua Española and the Academia Norteamericana de la Lengua Española.

[9] The 22nd edition (2001) as well as all preceding editions dating back to 1726.

examples, it offers a feature found surprisingly rarely in Spanish dictionaries, pronunciations of individual words. The RAE's dictionary, while authoritative, does not have examples (or pronunciations). The "Rolls Royce" of Spanish dictionaries is the two-volume *Diccionario de uso del español* by María Moliner, frequently referred to simply as *Moliner.* A CD-rom version is available and includes conjugations of individual verbs.

3. Prepositions Accompanying Verbs

Just as in English we *insist **on*** something and *laugh **at*** somebody, Spanish verbs are often associated with specific prepositions. Thus, corresponding to the two English examples, in Spanish one generally says *insistir **en*** and *reírse **de***. When learning the definition of an individual verb, it is a good idea to learn at the same time the associated preposition(s).

4. Historical References

At various stages in the text references are made to the historical development of Spanish and its relation to other Romance languages and Latin. While many are limited to footnotes, there are also several extended historical and methodological notes. The motivation for all such references is to help provide answers to the "why" questions which occur to many students—e.g., why do some verbs have vowel changes (*yo **cuento***) but only in certain conjugations (*nosotros **contamos***) and tenses (*yo conté*)?

PART I

FORMS OF VERBS

CHAPTER 1
Present, Simple Past, Imperfect, Participles

Present Tense (Indicative)

The present tense is formed by adding the following endings to the verb *stem* or *root*, i.e., the infinitive minus the final *-ar, -er,* or *-ir.*

-ar verbs	*-er* verbs	*-ir* verbs
-o	-o	-o
-as	-es	-es
-a	-e	-e
-amos	-emos	-imos
-áis	-éis	-ís
-an	-en	-en

Thus,

infinitive	can•tar	co•mer	su•bir
	(to sing)	(to eat)	(to raise, climb)
1s	**can•to**	co•mo	su•bo
2s	**can•tas**	co•mes	su•bes
3s	**can•ta**	co•me	su•be
1p	can•ta•mos	co•me•mos	su•bi•mos
2p	can•táis	co•méis	su•bís
3p	**can•tan**	co•men	su•ben

where the stressed syllable is shown in bold.
   Note that:

(1) For all three singulars and for the third person plural, the stress accent is on the stem (root) syllable, while for the first and second person plurals it is on the post-stem syllable. Among regular verbs, non-uniform stress patterns occur for the present indicative, present subjunctive, and imperative. All other tenses have uniform stress patterns for all six conjugations.

(2) In the second person plural a written accent is required for all three classes: *áis, éis, ís.* The first two are pronounced as diphthongs.

(3) The endings for the -er and -ir verbs differ only for the first and second person plural.

Irregularities for the present indicative—predictable and otherwise—are presented in Chapter 2.

Simple Past Tense

The *simple* past tense for regular verbs is formed by adding the following endings to the verb stem:

	-*ar* verbs	-*er* and -*ir* verbs
1s	-é	-í
2s	-aste	-iste
3s	-ó	-ió
1p	-amos	-imos
2p	-asteis	-isteis
3p	-aron	-ieron

	cantar	*comer*	*subir*
1s	can•**té**	co•**mí**	su•**bí**
2s	can•**tas**•te	co•**mis**•te	su•**bis**•te
3s	can•**tó**	co•**mió**	su•**bió**
1p	can•**ta**•mos	co•**mi**•mos	su•**bi**•mos
2p	can•**tas**•teis	co•**mis**•teis	su•**bis**•teis
3p	can•**ta**•ron	co•**mie**•ron	su•**bie**•ron

The simple past tense endings for -er and -ir verbs are identical. This is no random occurrence: of the 47 simple verb forms, -er and -ir verbs have 44 in common, the only discrepancies being the two already noted in the present (1p and 2p) plus the imperative (2p).

Regarding pronunciation and orthography:

(1) In all cases the stress accent is on the post-stem syllable, which necessitates a written accent for the first and third person singulars—apart from the one-syllable verb *ver* (the other one-syllable verbs—*ser, ir,* and *dar*—have irregular simple past tenses).

(2) For the singulars and the third person plural, the stress accent is moved forward compared to the present tense, e.g.,

	present	simple past
1s	**co**•mo	co•**mí**
2s	**co**•mes	co•**mis**•te
3s	**co**•me	co•**mió**
3p	**co**•men	co•**mie**•ron

It is important to put the stress on the correct syllable in order to avoid confusion with other tenses:

can•**tó** (3s, simple past)   **can**•to (1s, present indicative)

can•**té** (1s, simple past)   **can**•te (1s/3s, present subjunctive)

(3) for -*ar* and -*ir* verbs, the first person plural has identical forms for the *present* and *simple past*:

Llegamos muy tarde.	"We *arrive* very late."
	"We *arrived* very late."
Subimos la montaña.	"We *climb* the mountain."
	"We *climbed* the mountain."

For -*er* verbs there is no such potential confusion:

Comemos muy tarde.	"We *eat* very late."
Comimos muy tarde.	"We *ate* very late."

Irregularities for the simple past are presented in Chapter 3. For -*er* and -*ir* verbs whose stem ends in a vowel (e.g., *caer, construir, reír*), there are certain regular orthographic modifications (Chapter 7).

Imperfect (Indicative)

The following endings are added to the verb stem:

	-*ar* verbs	-*er* and -*ir* verbs
1s	-aba	-ía
2s	-abas	-ías
3s	-aba	-ía
1p	-ábamos	-íamos
2p	-abais	-íais
3p	-aban	-ían

1s	can•ta•ba	su•bí•a
2s	can•ta•bas	su•bí•as
3s	can•ta•ba	su•bí•a
1p	can•tá•ba•mos	su•bí•a•mos
2p	can•ta•bais	su•bí•ais
3p	can•ta•ban	su•bí•an

The imperfect has a *uniform* stress pattern, as all six forms are stressed on the post-stem syllable. A written accent is required for:

(1) the first person plural for *-ar* verbs
(2) all six conjugations for the *-er* and *-ir* verbs, in order to maintain *-i* and
     -a as distinct vowels.

Irregularities

The imperfect is the most "perfect" of all Spanish verb forms, as there are only three verbs having irregular imperfects: *ser, ir,* and *ver.*

	ser	*ir*	*ver*
1s	era	iba	veía
2s	eras	ibas	veías
3s	era	iba	veía
1p	éramos	íbamos	veíamos
2p	erais	ibais	veíais
3p	eran	iban	veían

The imperfect for *ver* would be entirely regular if the infinitive were **veer*[1] (which was in fact the case in "Old" Spanish) rather than *ver.* The imperfects for *ser* and *ir* are direct continuations of irregular Latin forms.

Past Participle

The following ending is added to the verb stem:

-ar verbs	*-er* and *-ir* verbs
-ado	-ido

---

[1] An asterisk (*) placed immediately before a particular verb form indicates that the form is not a correct one.

Thus,

	infinitive	past participle
-*ar* verbs	cantar	can·**ta**·do
	dar	dado
	hablar	hablado
-*er* verbs	comer	co·**mi**·do
	beber	bebido
	morder	mordido
-*ir* verbs	subir	su·**bi**·do
	cumplir	cumplido
	vivir	vivido

Under certain circumstances, a written accent is added to the vowel of the past participle ending:

> **Rule.** If an -*er* or -*ir* verb has a stem ending in -*a, -e,* or -*o,* then the ending of the past participle has a written accent (-*ído* rather than -*ido*). For all other cases in which the stem ends in a vowel, no change is made.

Examples:

caer	caído
leer	leído
roer	roído
oír	oído

compared to

crear	creado	*not* *creádo
loar	loado	*not* *loádo
evaluar	evaluado	*not* *evaluádo
criar	criado	*not* *criádo
construir	construido	*not* *construído

This rule reflects a particularity of the Spanish orthographic system, which distinguishes between "strong" and "weak" vowels (Chapter 7).

Of the 14 irregular past participles, eleven are found among the "basically regular" verbs, three among the fundamentally irregular ones (italicized).

infinitive	past participle	*not*	
abrir	abierto	*abrido	"opened"
cubrir	cubierto	*cubrido	"covered"
decir	dicho	*decido	"said"
escribir	escrito	*escribido	"written"
freír	frito	[see below]	"fried"
hacer	hecho	*hacido	"done"
imprimir	impreso	[see below]	"printed"
morir	muerto	*morido	"died"
poner	puesto	*ponido	"placed", "put"
resolver[2]	resuelto	*resolvido	"resolved"
romper	roto	*rompido	"broken"
ver	visto	*vido	"seen"
volver	vuelto	*volvido	"turned"
pudrir	podrido	*pudrido	"rotted", "putrefied"

These generally represent the continuation of "strong" Latin past participles which had the ending (-*TUS* or -*SUS*) connected directly to the root without an intervening vowel. As a result of their truncated form, irregular Spanish past participles (apart from *podrido*)[3] are stressed on the stem syllable, as compared to regular past participles, whose stress is on the post-stem syllable:[4]

di·cho   **ro·**to   **vuel·**to   *versus*   can·**ta·**do   co·**mi·**do   su·**bi·**do

Compound verbs generally have the same irregularities (*descubierto, impuesto, absuelto, disuelto,* etc.). Exceptions include *bendecir* and *maldecir* ("to bless", "to curse"), which have regular past participles (*bendecido, maldecido*),[5] and *corromper* ("to corrupt"), whose regular past participle is *corrompido*.

The RAE accepts the regular form *freído* alongside *frito* as a past participle for *freír,* but *frito* is far more common. For *imprimir* it accepts either *impreso* or *imprimido;* however, for *comprimir* ("to compress"), *deprimir* ("to depress"),

---

[2] Although the verb *solver* exists, it is rarely used. Thus one *resolves* a Spanish mystery rather than *solving* it.

[3] *Pudrir* used to be *podrir:* the stem vowel *-o* changed to *-u* in all 47 forms except the past participle. The old infinitive *podrir* still exists alongside *pudrir.*

[4] For *abrir, cubrir,* and *ver* the past participles are stressed on what is in fact the *original* stem syllable, as each of these verbs subsequently "lost" a syllable: *ab(e)rir, cub(e)rir* and *v(e)er.*

[5] The forms *bendito* and *maldito* exist but are used only as adjectives: *el agua bendita* ("holy water").

exprimir ("to *express*"), and *reprimir* ("to *repress*") only the regular forms *comprimido, deprimido, exprimido,* and *reprimido* are accepted.[6]

Satisfacer, which is essentially a compound form of *hacer,*[7] has *satisfecho* as past participle. Apart from *reescribir,* compounds of *escribir* omit the "helping" initial -*e* and thus have past participles ending in -*scrito*:[8]

inscribir	inscrito
suscribir	suscrito
transcribir	transcrito

Important observation:
No -*ar* verb has an irregular past participle.

Present Participle (*Gerundio*)

The Spanish present participle (*gerundio*) is formed by adding the following ending to the verb stem:

-*ar* verbs	-*er*/-*ir* verbs
-ando	-iendo

Thus,

	infinitive	present participle
-*ar* verbs	cantar	can·**tan**·do
	dar	dando
	hablar	hablando
-*er* verbs	comer	co·**mien**·do
	beber	bebiendo
	morder	mordiendo
-*ir* verbs	subir	su·**bien**·do
	cumplir	cumpliendo
	vivir	viviendo

---

[6] For *proveer*—a compound formed using the "old" form *veer* of *ver*—both *provisto* and the regular *proveído* are acceptable.

[7] Like many words in Spanish (e.g., *higo* "fig"), *hacer* changed its initial *f* to *h*.

[8] The RAE also accepts the "old" forms ending in -*scripto* for all -*scribir* verbs apart from *escribir*, *rescribir*, *reescribir*, and *manuscribir*, and these are still found with some frequency in certain regions (notably Argentina and Uruguay): *inscripto, suscripto, transcripto*, etc.

This verb form is called *gerundio* in Spanish because it was derived from the Latin *gerund*; many English-language books on Spanish call it the *present participle* because its use more closely parallels that of the English present participle. In English, of course, the present participle and gerund both have the same *-ing* form.

There is essentially only one irregular present participle:

poder	pudiendo	*not*	*podiendo

Other apparent regularities are all of the predictable type and fall into three categories:

(1) *-ir* verbs with stem vowels *-e* or *-o* have the stem vowel changed to *-i* and *-u*, respectively:

sentir	sintiendo	*not*	*sentiendo
medir	midiendo	*not*	*mediendo
dormir	durmiendo	*not*	*dormiendo

[See "La regla milagrosa (extended)" in Chapter 9.]
Exceptions:
  (a) **oír** [see below]
  (b) "regular" present participle [9]

   discernir   discerniendo

(2) for *-er* and *-ir* verbs whose stem ends in a vowel, the *-i* in *-iendo* is changed to *-y*, a normal orthographic change (Chapter 7):

infinitive	present participle	*not*
caer	cayendo	*caiendo
leer	leyendo	*leiendo
traer	trayendo	*traiendo
construir	construyendo	*construiendo
huir	huyendo	*huiendo
oír	oyendo	*oiendo

---

[9] Also *cernir* and *hendir*—although the RAE prefers the forms *cerner* and *hender*—and *concernir*. Like *discernir* these were originally *-er* verbs and behave throughout their conjugations as *-er* diphthong verbs. *Concernir* is a "defective" verb used only *impersonally*, e.g.,

A mí no me *concierne* este asunto.   "This matter is of no *concern* to me."

The only forms which exist are the infinitive, participles, and third person (singular and plural).

Also:

ir	**y**endo	****i**endo

(3) *-er* and *-ir* verbs whose stem ends in a *palatalized* consonant—either *ñ* or *ll*—omit the *-i-* from *-iendo* (Chapter 7):

infinitive	present participle	*not*
tañer	tañ**e**ndo	**tañ**i**endo
bullir	bull**e**ndo	**bull**i**endo

CHAPTER 2

Irregularities: Present Tense

Present-tense (indicative) irregularities—real and apparent—can be divided among the following categories. Verbs shown in bold are those we have defined as *fundamentally irregular,* i.e., having irregular simple pasts.

"Predictable" irregularities

1. *Diphthong* in verbs having stem vowel -*e* or -*o*
   A. *e → ie*
   B. *o → ue*
2. *Umlaut (e → i)* for -*ir* verbs having stem vowel -*e*
3. First person singular ending in -*zco*
   A. (Most) infinitives ending in -*cer* (e.g., *conocer*)
   B. (All) infinitives ending in -*ucir* (e.g., **producir,** *lucir*)
4. Verbs ending in -*uir* add -*y* except before -*i*

"Unpredictable" irregularities[1]

5. "To be"	***ser, estar***
6. Other first person singulars ending in **-oy**	***ir, dar***
7A. First person singular ending in **-e**	***haber, saber***
7B. First person singular with *umlaut (a → e)*	***caber***
8. First person singular ending in **-go,** other persons without -g (*hago,* *haces,* *hace,* etc.)	***decir, hacer,*** *caer,* ***traer,*** *oír,* ***poner,*** *salir,* ***tener,*** *valer,* ***venir***

Verbs with "mixed" patterns

9. *Ver, adquirir, jugar, argüir* (and *discernir*)

Purely orthographic changes

Orthographic changes will be treated in Chapter 7.

Predictable Irregularities

1. Diphthong in Verbs Having Stem Vowel -*e* or -*o*

A large number of verbs display the following change in stem vowel in four of the six grammatical persons—the three singulars and the third person plural.

---

[1] By coincidence there are 17 verbs with irregular present tenses and the same number with irregular simple past tenses. Thirteen verbs are in both groups.

A. *e → ie*   pronounced like "ye" in *yet*[2]
B. *o → ue*   pronounced like "we" in *wet*
             (sometimes more like "wei" in *weight*)

These are known as the *diphthong* verbs. Some examples, with the stressed syllable highlighted in bold:

	e → ie		*o → ue*	

-*ar* verbs

	pensar (to think)		*mostrar* (to show)	
1s	pienso	**pien·**so	muestro	**mues·**tro
2s	piensas	**pien·**sas	muestras	**mues·**tras
3s	piensa	**pien·**sa	muestra	**mues·**tra
1p	pensamos	pen·**sa·**mos	mostramos	mos·**tra·**mos
2p	pensáis	pen·**sáis**	mostráis	mos·**tráis**
3p	piensan	**pien·**san	muestran	**mues·**tran

-*er* verbs

	perder ("to lose")		*mover* ("to move")	
1s	pierdo	**pier·**do	muevo	**mue·**vo
2s	pierdes	**pier·**des	mueves	**mue·**ves
3s	pierde	**pier·**de	mueve	**mue·**ve
1p	perdemos	per·**de·**mos	movemos	mo·**ve·**mos
2p	perdéis	per·**déis**	movéis	mo·**véis**
3p	pierden	**pier·**den	mueven	**mue·**ven

-*ir* verbs

	sentir ("to feel")		*dormir* ("to sleep")	
1s	siento	**sien·**to	duermo	**duer·**mo
2s	sientes	**sien·**tes	duermes	**duer·**mes
3s	siente	**sien·**te	duerme	**duer·**me
1p	sentimos	sen·**ti·**mos	dormimos	dor·**mi·**mos
2p	sentís	sen·**tís**	dormís	dor·**mís**
3p	sienten	**sien·**ten	duermen	**duer·**men

---

[2] At the beginning of a word or syllable, the *ie* diphthong in much of the Spanish-speaking world is pronounced either like the "s" in *pleasure* or the "*j*" in *judge,* while after a consonant the "ye" sound is maintained. This has only very limited effect on the verbal system, where virtually all *ie* diphthongs are preceded by a consonant, the principal exceptions occurring in *errar* and *erguir.*

We note the following *fundamentally* important pattern:

The diphthong occurs only in *stressed* syllables, i.e., in those conjugations where the stress accent falls on the stem (root) of the verb.

We shall subsequently see that this pattern holds for all of the 47 simple conjugations and thus provides a remarkably simple way to remember which conjugations have diphthongs and which do not.

How to Determine (and Remember) Whether a Verb Is a Diphthong Verb

The historical note presented as an appendix to this chapter shows that whether a Spanish verb diphthongs or not is generally dependent on the *quantity* (short or long) of the vowel in its corresponding Latin root. While this is of little practical assistance to those whose Latin is a bit rusty, there fortunately exists an alternative method which is applicable in the large majority of cases:

General rule:
  -*ar* and -*er* verbs:
    If the stem vowel of *any* associated noun or adjective has diphthonged, then it is almost certain that the verb has diphthonged as well.
  -*ir* verbs:
    (i) There are only three commonly employed verbs with stem vowel -*o*—*dormir, morir,* and *oír*—of which the first two diphthong.
    (ii) For verbs with stem vowel -*e, la regla milagrosa* presented in the following section provides a sure method for determining those which diphthong.

For -*ar* and -*er* verbs the general rule is illustrated below with regard to a number of verbs in common use:

infinitive		noun/adjective		1s
e → ie				
acertar	(to get/guess right)	cierto	(certain)	acierto
alentar	(to encourage)	aliento	(breath)	aliento
apretar	(to squeeze)	aprieto	(predicament)	aprieto
arrendar	(to rent)	arriendo	(rent)	arriendo
atravesar	(to cross)	travieso	(mischievous)	atravieso
calentar	(to heat)	caliente	(hot)	caliento
cegar	(to blind)	ciego	(blind)	ciego
cerner	(to sift, blossom)	cierne	(blossoming)	cierno

cerrar	(to close)	cierre	(snap, clasp)	cierro
cimentar	(to lay foundations)	cimiento	(foundation)	cimiento
comenzar	(to commence)	comienzo	(commencement)	comienzo
desmembrar	(to dismember)	miembro	(member)	desmiembro
despertar	(to awake)	despierto	(awake)	despierto
desterrar	(to exile)	tierra	(land)	destierro
emparentar[3]	(to become related)	pariente	(relative)	empariento
empezar	(to begin)	pieza	(piece)	empiezo
encomendar	(to entrust)	encomienda	(commission)	encomiendo
enmendar	(to amend)	enmienda	(amendment)	enmiendo
ensangrentar	(to bloody)	sangriento	(bloody)	ensangriento
errar	(to err)	yerro	(error)	yerro[4]
fregar	(to scrub)	friega	(rubdown)	friego
gobernar	(to govern)	gobierno	(government)	gobierno
herrar	(to shoe a horse)	hierro	(iron)	hierro
manifestar	(to manifest)	manifiesto	(manifest)	manifiesto
merendar	(to snack)	merienda	(snack)	meriendo
negar	(to deny)	reniego	(curse)	niego
pensar	(to think)	pienso	(fodder)	pienso
plegar	(to fold)	pliegue	(crease)	pliego
quebrar	(to break)	quiebra	(bankruptcy)	quiebro
regar	(to irrigate)	riego	(irrigation)	riego
segar	(to reap)	siega	(reaping)	siego
sembrar	(to sow)	siembra	(sowing)	siembro
sentar	(to seat)	asiento	(seat)	siento
serrar	(to saw)	sierra	(mountain range)	sierro
sosegar	(to calm)	sosiego	(tranquillity)	sosiego
tender	(to extend/stretch)	tienda	(tent, shop)	tiendo
tentar	(to feel/touch)	tiento	(touch, feeling)	tiento
tropezar	(to stumble)	tropiezo	(stumble)	tropiezo

o → ue

acordar	(to remember)	acuerdo	(accord)	acuerdo
acostar	(to put to bed)	cuesta	(slope)	acuesto
almorzar	(to lunch)	almuerzo	(lunch)	almuerzo

---

[3] *Emparentar* can also be conjugated without diphthongs.
[4] The initial *ie* is written *ye* (Chapter 7) : *yerro, yerras, yerra, erramos, erráis, yerran.*

apostar	(to bet)	apuesta	(bet)	apuesto
avergonzar	(to shame)	vergüenza	(shame)	avergüenzo
clocar	(to cluck)	clueco	(broody, decrepit)	clueco
colgar	(to hang)	cuelgacapas	(hatrack)	cuelgo
consolar	(to console)	consuelo	(consolation)	consuelo
contar	(to count, to tell)	cuenta	(bill, account)	cuento
degollar	(to behead)	degüello	(beheading)	degüello
doler	(to hurt)	duelo	(mourning)	duelo
encontrar	(to meet)	encuentro	(encounter)	encuentro
esforzar	(to strengthen)	esfuerzo	(effort)	esfuerzo
forzar	(to force)	fuerza	(force)	fuerzo
hollar	(to tread on)	huella	(trace)	huello
moler	(to mill)	muela	(millstone, molar)	muelo
mostrar	(to show)	muestra	(sample)	muestro
poblar	(to populate)	pueblo	(town)	pueblo
probar	(to prove/try)	prueba	(proof)	pruebo
recordar	(to remember)	recuerdo	(memory)	recuerdo
renovar [5]	(to renovate)	nuevo	(new)	renuevo
resolver	(to resolve/solve)	resuelto	(resolute)	resuelvo
rodar	(to roll)	rueda	(wheel)	ruedo
rogar	(to request)	ruego	(request)	ruego
soltar	(to loosen)	suelto	(loose)	suelto
soñar	(to dream)	sueño	(sleep, dream)	sueño
torcer	(to twist)	tuerto	(one-eyed)	tuerzo [6]
trocar	(to barter)	trueque	(exchange)	trueco
volar	(to fly)	vuelo	(flight)	vuelo
volcar	(to capsize)	vuelco	(overturning)	vuelco
volver	(to turn)	vuelta	(return)	vuelvo

Also three "weather" verbs used only in the third person singular:

helar	(to freeze)	hielo	(ice)	hiela	(it is freezing)
nevar	(to snow)	nieve	(snow)	nieva	(it is snowing)
tronar	(to thunder)	trueno	(thunder)	truena	(it thunders)

---

[5] *Innovar* does not diphthong: *yo innovo.*

[6] See Chapter 7 for an explanation of the (regular orthographic) change of the ending to *-zo.*

Compound verb forms almost always follow the same pattern, e.g.,

infinitive	1s	
absolver	absuelvo	"to absolve"
aprobar	apruebo	"to approve"
comprobar	compruebo	"to verify", "to check"
concertar	concierto	"to harmonize", "to arrange"
contender	contiendo	"to contend", "to contest"
entender	entiendo	"to understand"
demoler	demuelo	"to demolish"
desenvolver	desenvuelvo	"to unwrap", "to evolve"
envolver	envuelvo	"to wrap up", "to involve"
revolver	revuelvo	"to mix", "to turn over", "to revolve"
remover	remuevo	"to remove", "to stir"

with the following major exceptions:[7]

pretender	pretendo	"to try to", "to aspire to"
interrogar[8]	interrogo	"to interrogate"

There exist a much smaller number of verbs with no associated commonly used diphthonged nouns or adjectives which nevertheless are diphthonged, including:

infinitive	1s	
ascender	asciendo	"to ascend"
cocer	cuezo[9]	"to cook"
confesar[10]	confieso	"to confess"
costar	cuesto	"to cost"
defender[11]	defiendo	"to defend"
descender	desciendo	"to descend"
encender	enciendo	"to light"
heder	hiedo	"to stink"

---

[7] *Aterrar* is essentially two separate verbs: a diphthong verb like *desterrar* when its meaning has to do with *tierra* ("to cover with earth", "to demolish", "to land"); a regular verb when it relates to *terror* ("to frighten", "to terrify").

[8] Similarly, *abrogar, arrogar, derogar, prorrogar, subrogar* are conjugated without diphthongs.

[9] See Chapter 7 for an explanation of the (regular orthographic) change of the ending to *-zo*.

[10] *Profesar* does not diphthong: *yo profeso*.

[11] *Ofender* does not diphthong: *yo ofendo*.

hender	hiendo	"to crack", "to split"
morder	muerdo	"to bite"
oler	huelo	"to smell"
perder	pierdo	"to lose"
restregar	restriego	"to scrub", "to rub"
reventar	reviento	"to burst"
soler	suelo	"to be accustomed to"
sonar	sueno	"to sound", "to ring"
temblar	tiemblo	"to tremble"
tostar	tuesto	"to toast", "to roast"
verter	vierto	"to pour", "to spill"

as well as

| llover | llueve | "it rains" (used only in third person singular) |

2. Umlaut (*e → i*) for *-ir* Verbs Having Stem Vowel *-e*

The situation with regard to *-ir* verbs with stem vowel *-e* is more complex, yet in some respects far simpler. More complex, since there is not one but two possible "irregularities": while some verbs *diphthong*, others display a *different* pattern of vowel alternation (*e → i*) which we will call *umlaut*.[12]

	diphthong		umlaut	
	sentir (to feel)		**pedir** (to request)	
1s	siento	**sien·to**	pido	**pi·do**
2s	sientes	**sien·tes**	pides	**pi·des**
3s	siente	**sien·te**	pide	**pi·de**
1p	sentimos	**sen·ti·mos**	pedimos	**pe·di·mos**
2p	sentís	**sen·tís**	pedís	**pe·dís**
3p	sienten	**sien·ten**	piden	**pi·den**

---

[12] *Umlaut*, since the shift *-e* to *-i* occurred because of a (now disappeared) "y" in the following syllable, analogous to the process of umlaut which occurred in the Germanic languages (including English—e.g., when a verb was created from the adjective *full*, the vowel was umlauted, hence *to fill*). The term generally used to describe this process in Romance languages is *metaphony*, a word the French created by translating German "umlaut" into Classical Greek ("um" = *meta*, "laut" = *phony*).

For umlaut verbs the stem vowel -*e* is raised to -*i* in the four conjugations in which the stress accent falls on the stem syllable, i.e., in exactly the same conjugations where diphthong verbs have diphthongs.

While having two separate patterns of vowel variation, -*ir* verbs with stem vowel -*e* are nonetheless simpler than their -*ar* and -*er* counterparts because virtually *all* of them [13] display one variation or the other, and there is a simple rule for determining which "regular irregularity" they follow:

La regla milagrosa

-*ir* verbs with stem vowel -*e* have diphthongs or umlauts as follows:

Diphthong (model *sentir*):	*if the stem vowel is followed by -r or -nt*
Umlaut (model *pedir*):	all other cases
Exceptions:	*servir* (umlaut)
	venir (diphthong)

Examples:

DIPHTHONG (MODEL *SENTIR*)[14]

infinitive	1s	
adherir	adhiero	"to adhere"
arrepentir(se)[15]	me arrepiento	"to repent"
convertir	convierto	"to convert"
digerir	digiero	"to digest"
discernir	discierno	"to discern", "to distinguish"
erguir[16]	yergo	"to raise", "to lift up"
herir	hiero	"to wound"
hervir	hiervo	"to boil"
ingerir	ingiero	"to ingest"
mentir	miento	"to lie"
referir	refiero	"to refer"
requerir	requiero	"to require", "to request"
sentir	siento	"to sense", "to feel", "to regret"
sugerir	sugiero	"to suggest"

[13] The single exception being *sumergir*, a former -*er* verb, which neither diphthongs nor umlauts.

[14] *Venir* has an additional irregularity and will be considered at a later stage (number 8).

[15] The (*se*) indicates that the verb is used only *reflexively*; see Chapter 10.

[16] *Erguir* allows either diphthong (*yergo*) or umlaut (*irgo*) forms, although the former are more common. The initial *ye*- in place of *ie*- is a regular orthographic change (Chapter 7).

UMLAUT (MODEL *PEDIR*)

infinitive	1s	
ceñir	ciño	"to fit (tightly)"
colegir	colijo	"to collect", "to deduce"
comedir(se)	me comido	"to control oneself", "to be courteous"
competir	compito	"to compete"
concebir	concibo	"to conceive"
constreñir	constriño	"to constrain"
derretir	derrito	"to melt"
desleír	deslío	"to dissolve", "to dilute"
elegir	elijo	"to elect"
embestir	embisto	"to assail", "to attack"
expedir	expido	"to send", "to issue"
freír	frío	"to fry"
gemir	gimo	"to moan"
henchir	hincho	"to fill", "to stuff"
impedir	impido	"to prevent", "to impede"
medir	mido	"to measure"
pedir	pido	"to request"
regir	rijo	"to rule", "to govern"
reír	río	"to laugh"
rendir	rindo	"to render", "to give up", "to defeat"
reñir	riño	"to quarrel"
repetir	repito	"to repeat"
seguir	sigo	"to follow", "to continue"
servir	*sirvo*	"to serve"
teñir	tiño	"to dye", "to tint"
vestir	visto	"to clothe"

The -j in *colijo, elijo,* and *rijo* is a regular orthographic change, as is the -g in *sigo* (see Chapter 7). While *concebir* and *regir* are "umlauted" in the normal way, for the closely related *recibir* ("to receive") and *dirigir* ("to direct") the umlaut propagated itself throughout the entire verb, thus converting them into completely regular verbs with stem vowel -i in all 47 conjugations. Verbs ending in -eír have a written accent throughout their present conjugations to maintain the independent pronunciation of the stem vowel, i.e., to avoid a diphthong with the following vowel.

	reír "to laugh"	**freír** "to *fry*"
1s	río	frío
2s	ríes	fríes
3s	ríe	fríe
1p	reímos	freímos
2p	reís	freís
3p	ríen	fríen

Compound verbs generally follow the same patterns. For example:

DIPHTHONG

infinitive	1s	
conferir	confiero	"to confer", "to bestow"
inferir	infiero	"to infer", "to cause"
preferir	prefiero	"to prefer"
transferir	transfiero	"to transfer"
interferir	interfiero	"to interfere"
asentir	asiento	"to assent"
consentir	consiento	"to consent", "to coddle"
presentir	presiento	"to have a presentiment or premonition of"
advertir	advierto	"to notice", "to warn"
divertir	divierto	"to amuse", "to divert oneself"
invertir	invierto	"to invest", "to invert"
pervertir	pervierto	"to pervert", "to corrupt"
subvertir	subvierto	"to subvert"

UMLAUT

infinitive	1s	
corregir	corrijo	"to correct"
despedir	despido	"to bid farewell", "to dismiss"
investir	invisto	"to invest" (with a responsibility)
conseguir	consigo	"to obtain", "to attain"
perseguir	persigo	"to pursue", "to persecute"
proseguir	prosigo	"to continue", "to proceed"
refreír	refrío	"to refry"
sonreír	sonrío	"to smile"

3. First Person Singular Ending in -*zco*

These fall into two general categories: (A) verbs ending in -*cer;* (B) verbs ending in -*(d)ucir.*

A. (Most) Infinitives Ending in -*cer*

Many of these are descendants of Latin "inceptive" verbs[17] where an ending -SCERE was added to "normal" verbs to indicate the beginning of an action or process, e.g.,

| FLORERE | "to bloom or blossom", i.e., *to flower* |
| FLORESCERE | "to begin to bloom or blossom", i.e., *to flourish* |

Over time many such verbs were created referring to the process itself, not necessarily only to its beginning. Eventually they were created from adjectives and nouns as well (e.g., *noble → ennoblecer*).

In Spanish the descendants of these verbs all have an -*zco* ending in the first person singular, while the other persons are "normal".

	crecer (to grow)	*conocer* (to know, be familiar with)
1s	crezco	conozco
2s	creces	conoces
3s	crece	conoce
1p	crecemos	conocemos
2p	crecéis	conocéis
3p	crecen	conocen

Examples:

FORMED DIRECTLY FROM VERBS			
infinitive	1s	3s	
adormecer	adormezco	adormece	"to put to sleep"
conocer	conozco	conoce	"to know"
crecer	crezco	crece	"to grow"
establecer	establezco	establece	"to establish"
fallecer	fallezco	fallece	"to die"
guarnecer	guarnezco	guarnece	"to garnish", "to reinforce"
merecer	merezco	merece	"to merit"
nacer	nazco	nace	"to be born"

---

[17] Their more formal name is *inchoative* verbs.

obedecer	obede**zc**o	obedece	"to obey"
ofrecer	ofre**zc**o	ofrece	"to offer"
pacer	pa**zc**o	pace	"to pasture", "to graze"
padecer	pade**zc**o	padece	"to suffer"
parecer	pare**zc**o	parece	"to appear", "to seem"
perecer	pere**zc**o	perece	"to perish"
permanecer	permane**zc**o	permanece	"to stay", "to remain"
prevalecer	prevale**zc**o	prevalece	"to prevail"

DERIVED FROM ADJECTIVES OR NOUNS

adj./ noun	infinitive	1s	3s	
agrado	agradecer	agrade**zc**o	agradece	"to be grateful for"
mañana	amanecer	amane**zc**o	amanece	"to dawn"
bello	embellecer	embelle**zc**o	embellece	"to embellish"
blanco	emblanquecer	emblanque**zc**o	emblanquece	"to whiten"
pobre	empobrecer	empobre**zc**o	empobrece	"to impoverish"
negro	ennegrecer	ennegre**zc**o	ennegrece	"to blacken"
noble	ennoblecer	ennoble**zc**o	ennoblece	"to ennoble"
rico	enriquecer	enrique**zc**o	enriquece	"to enrich"
viejo	envejecer	enveje**zc**o	envejece	"to age"
claro	esclarecer	esclare**zc**o	esclarece	"to illuminate"
favor	favorecer	favore**zc**o	favorece	"to favor"
oscuro	oscurecer	oscure**zc**o	oscurece	"to darken/obscure"

Due to the popularity of these verbs, several Spanish verbs ending in -*cer* but which are not by origin "inceptive" have adopted the -*zco* ending for the first person singular, notably:

infinitive	1s	3s	
complacer	compla**zc**o	complace	"to please"

Not all -*cer* verbs have -*zco* endings. The principal exceptions are:

infinitive	1s	3s	
cocer	cuezo	cuece	"to cook"
coercer	coerzo	coerce	"to coerce"
ejercer	ejerzo	ejerce	"to exercise"
mecer	mezo	mece	"to rock"
torcer	tuerzo	tuerce	"to twist"
vencer	venzo	vence	"to vanquish"

The *-zo* ending (rather than *-co*) is a regular orthographic change occurring when the soft *c* sound occurs before *-o* (Chapter 7). We have previously seen that *cocer* and *torcer* are diphthong verbs, hence the vowel change *-o* → *-ue*. We can formulate the following general rule:

> **General rule for -cer verbs:**
> (a) Two-syllable verbs are regular (type *vencer*).
> **Exceptions:** *crecer* + those with stem vowel *-a* (*nacer, pacer, placer, yacer*).[18]
> (b) Verbs of three or more syllables have first person singular *-zco* (type *conocer*).
> **Exceptions:** *coercer, ejercer.*[19]

Historical Note In the other Romance languages the inceptive class of verbs also experienced exponential growth, as a large number of existing verbs were replaced by inceptive ones and many new ones were created from adjectives or nouns.[20] This process was so widespread that, via Old French, it became the basis for the *-ish* endings of *English* verbs, e.g.,

> **abolish, accomplish, blemish, brandish, cherish, demolish, embellish, establish, finish, flourish (from** FLORESCERE**), furbish, furnish, garnish, impoverish, languish, nourish, perish, polish, ravish, relinquish, replenish, tarnish, vanish, etc.**

The popularity of the *-ish* ending in English was such that it was extended to a number of verbs which in neither Latin nor the Romance languages had been inceptive: e.g., *admonish, diminish, distinguish, famish, publish, vanquish.*

---

[18] *Yacer* ("to lie") is in a class by itself, offering three possibilities for the first person singular: *yazco, yazgo,* or *yago.*

[19] One could thus formulate the rule: verbs of three or more syllables have 1s *-zco,* except those ending in *-ercer.*

[20] In French one of the three principal groups of verbs consists entirely of "inceptive" verbs (those conjugated like *finir* "to finish"), while in Italian the majority of *-ire* verbs have inceptive elements in their conjugations (e.g., *non capisco,* "I don't understand").

B. (All) Infinitives Ending in -ucir

These are all composites of -ducir ("to lead") and -lucir ("to shine"). Largely due to the influence of the -cer verbs, they also adopted -zco endings for the first person singular:

	conducir (to drive)	*lucir* (to shine)
1s	conduzco	luzco
2s	conduces	luces
3s	conduce	luce
1p	conducimos	lucimos
2p	conducís	lucís
3p	conducen	lucen

Similarly:

infinitive	1s	3s	
aducir	aduzco	aduce	"to adduce"
deducir	deduzco	deduce	"to deduce"
inducir	induzco	induce	"to induce"
introducir	introduzco	introduce	"to introduce"
producir	produzco	produce	"to produce"
reducir	reduzco	reduce	"to reduce"
seducir	seduzco	seduce	"to seduce"
traducir	traduzco	traduce	"to translate"
deslucir	desluzco	desluce	"to tarnish", "to discredit"
enlucir	enluzco	enluce	"to plaster", "to polish"
entrelucir	entreluzco	entreluce	"to show through"
relucir	reluzco	reluce	"to shine", "to excel"
traslucir	trasluzco	trasluce	"to be translucent", "to reveal"

4. Verbs Ending in -uir Add -y Except before -i

Apart from those ending in -guir, all verbs ending in -uir undergo a "predictable" change:

> **-uir verbs (apart from -guir)**
> A -y is inserted after the -u for the three singulars and the third person plural, i.e., whenever the normally following letter is *not* an -i.

	huir (to flee)	*construir* (to construct)
1s	huyo	construyo
2s	huyes	construyes
3s	huye	construye
1p	huimos	construimos
2p	huís	construís
3p	huyen	construyen

The logic of the rule is that a -*y* is effectively present in *all* conjugations but is absorbed by a following -*i* (the combination *yi* not normally being permitted in Spanish orthography).

Other verbs following the same pattern include:

atribuir	(to attribute)	concluir	(to conclude)
constituir	(to constitute)	destituir	(to deprive, to dismiss)
destruir	(to destroy)	diluir	(to dilute)
disminuir	(to diminish)	distribuir	(to distribute)
excluir	(to exclude)	imbuir	(to imbue)
incluir	(to include)	influir	(to influence)
instituir	(to institute)	obstruir	(to obstruct)
restituir	(to restitute)	sustituir	(to substitute)

For verbs ending in -*guir* (e.g., *distinguir, seguir*) the -*u* is not a "real" *u* but simply an orthographic device (Chapter 7) for marking a "hard" "G" sound before the front vowel -*i*, analogous to the -*u* in English *guilt* and *guitar*.

We will see in number 8 below that the verb *oír* ("to hear") follows a similar pattern.

Unpredictable Irregularities

We will begin with the verb (or rather *verbs*) that almost certainly cause the most problems for students of Spanish—the equivalents of the English verb *to be*.

5. Ser/estar

"to be"	*ser*	*estar*		
1s	soy	estoy	soy	es•**toy**
2s	eres	estás	e•res	es•**tás**
3s	es	está	es	es•**tá**

1p	somos	estamos	so·mos	es·**ta**·mos
2p	sois	estáis	sois	es·**táis**
3p	son	están	son	es·**tán**

The difficulty is of course not with the conjugations but rather with determining which of the two verbs to use in any given situation, a topic to be explored in Chapter 11. For *estar* it is important to note that—in contrast to regular verbs—the stress is uniformly on the post-stem syllable; thus it is es·**tás** not *es·tas.

6. Other First Person Singulars Ending in *-oy: ir, dar*

In addition to *ser* and *estar*, there are two other verbs whose first person singular ends in *-oy: ir* and *dar*.

	ir (to go)	*dar* (to give)
1s	**voy**	**doy**
2s	vas	das
3s	va	da
1p	vamos	damos
2p	vais	dais
3p	van	dan

Thus, apart from *ver* ("to see"), all one-syllable Spanish verbs have first person singulars ending in *-oy*, along with *estar*.[21] *Vais* and *dais* do not have the usual second person plural written accent because they have only one syllable.

7A. First person singular ending in *-e: haber, saber*
7B. First person singular with umlaut (*-a* → *-e*): *caber*

Haber and *saber* are the only Spanish verbs which have a first person singular present ending of *-e*. Due to *haber*'s frequent use as an *auxiliary* verb, its form was drastically shortened at the Vulgar Latin stage, which is why only the second person plural has a regular form. In contrast, the present tenses of both *saber* and *caber* are regular apart from the first person singular.

---

[21] The "natural" form of *estar* would have been the one-syllable *star. A "helping" e- was added—as it was to all words beginning with s + *consonant* (e.g., *español, especial, esnob, espagueti*). This also accounts for the uniform stress of *estar* on the post-stem syllable.

In the conjugations below, irregular forms are italicized.

	haber (to have)	*saber* (to know)	*caber* (to fit)
1s	**he**	**sé**	**quepo**
2s	**has**	sabes	cabes
3s	**ha**	sabe	cabe
1p	**hemos**	sabemos	cabemos
2p	habéis	sabéis	cabéis
3p	**han**	saben	caben

While the vowel in *quepo* is irregular, the *qu-* is not—it is a regular orthographic change required to maintain a "hard" *c* sound (see Chapter 7). The written accent in *sé* is purely orthographic and serves to distinguish it from the reflexive pronoun *se*.

8. First Person Singular Ending in *-go*

decir, hacer, caer, **traer**
oír, **poner,** salir
tener, valer, **venir**

These are verbs with irregular first person singular ending *-go*, where the *-g* does not appear in the other grammatical persons. Four of these verbs (*decir, oír, tener, venir*) have other apparent present tense irregularities—marked below in italics—but all are of the "predictable" type. The ten verbs can be divided into three groups, as shown in the following lists.[22]

	decir (to say)	*hacer* (to do)
1s	**digo**	**hago**
2s	*dices*	haces
3s	*dice*	hace
1p	decimos	hacemos
2p	decís	hacéis
3p	*dicen*	hacen

---

[22] In addition to these ten verbs, there are several others which "optionally" show this characteristic. *Roer* ("to gnaw") and *raer* ("to wear away") offer multiple possibilities: *roigo, royo,* or the regular *roo; raigo* or *rayo*. *Asir* ("to grasp") presents only the conjugation with *-go* (*asgo*), but in practice this form is avoided (as are other forms of the verb in which an "extraneous" *-g* appears).

Apart from the irregular first person singular, *decir* follows the pattern of umlauting *-ir* verbs with stem vowel *-e* (number 2 above) in accordance with *la regla milagrosa*.

	caer (to fall)	*traer* (to bring)	*oír* (to hear)
1s	**caigo**	**traigo**	**oigo**
2s	caes	traes	*oyes*
3s	cae	trae	*oye*
1p	caemos	traemos	oímos
2p	caéis	traéis	oís
3p	caen	traen	*oyen*

Apart from the irregular first person singular, *caer* and *traer* have regular present conjugations. *Oír* follows the same pattern as the *-uir* verbs (number 4 above): *-y* is inserted following the stem vowel *-o* in those conjugations where the following letter is *not* an *-i*.

	poner (to put)	*salir* (to exit)	*valer* (to be worth)
1s	**pongo**	**salgo**	**valgo**
2s	pones	sales	vales
3s	pone	sale	vale
1p	ponemos	salimos	valemos
2p	ponéis	salís	valéis
3p	ponen	salen	valen

	tener (to have)	*venir* (to come)
1s	**tengo**	**vengo**
2s	*tienes*	*vienes*
3s	*tiene*	*viene*
1p	tenemos	venimos
2p	tenéis	venís
3p	*tienen*	*vienen*

Apart from the irregular first person, *tener* and *venir* display regular diphthong patterns (*venir* representing one of the two exceptions to *la regla milagrosa*).

Compounds of these ten verbs generally have the same irregularities:

infinitive	1s	
bendecir	bendigo	"to bless"
contradecir	contradigo	"to contradict"
desdecir	desdigo	"to retract", "to be unworthy of"
maldecir	maldigo	"to curse"
predecir	predigo	"to predict"
deshacer	deshago	"to undo", "to destroy"
satisfacer	satisfago	"to satisfy"
decaer	decaigo	"to decay", "to weaken"
recaer	recaigo	"to fall back (or on)", "to relapse"
atraer	atraigo	"to attract"
contraer	contraigo	"to contract"
detraer	detraigo	"to detract", "to remove"
extraer	extraigo	"to extract"
sustraer	sustraigo	"to subtract", "to remove"
desoír	desoigo	"to disregard"
entreoír	entreoigo	"to hear vaguely"
componer	compongo	"to compose", "to repair"
deponer	depongo	"to depose", "to lay aside"
exponer	expongo	"to expose", "to explain"
imponer	impongo	"to impose"
oponer	opongo	"to oppose"
posponer	pospongo	"to postpone"
presuponer	presupongo	"to presuppose", "to budget"
proponer	propongo	"to propose", "to propound"
suponer	supongo	"to suppose"
yuxtaponer	yuxtapongo	"to juxtapose"
sobresalir	sobresalgo	"to protrude"
equivaler	equivalgo	"to be equal"

abstener(se)	me abstengo	"to abstain", "to refrain"
contener	contengo	"to contain"
detener	detengo	"to detain", "to stop", "to arrest"
entretener	entretengo	"to amuse", "to entertain"
mantener	mantengo	"to maintain", "to keep"
obtener	obtengo	"to obtain"
retener	retengo	"to retain"
sostener	sostengo	"to support", "to sustain"
contravenir	contravengo	"to contravene"
convenir	convengo	"to agree", "to be suitable"
intervenir	intervengo	"to intervene"
prevenir	prevengo	"to forewarn", "to prevent"
reconvenir	reconvengo	"to reproach"

Mixed Patterns

9. *Ver, jugar, adquirir, argüir* (and *discernir*)

In the present tense *discernir* behaves as a normal *-ir* verb with diphthong (model *sentir*). The conjugations for the other four are:

	ver (to see)	*jugar* (to play)	*adquirir* (to acquire)	*argüir* (to argue)
1s	**veo**	juego	adquiero	arguyo
2s	ves	juegas	adquieres	arguyes
3s	ve	juega	adquiere	arguye
1p	vemos	jugamos	adquirimos	argüimos
2p	veis	jugáis	adquirís	argüís
3p	ven	juegan	adquieren	arguyen

As noted in Chapter 1, by origin *ver* was a two-syllable word, as its Old Spanish form was *veer*. In the infinitive and most of its conjugations it has lost one of the *e*'s but the original form remains in the first person singular present (and throughout the imperfect indicative and present subjunctive). The second person plural lacks the usual written accent (*veis*, not **véis*) since it has only one syllable. Compound forms of *ver*—*prever* and *entrever*—require written accents on those forms for which *ver* has only one syllable:

prevés (2s), prevé (3s), prevéis (2p), prevén (3p)

Jugar comes from the same Latin word that produced English *joke,* and it has lived up to its name: the three singulars and the third person plural have a diphthong *-ue* instead of the expected stem vowel *-u*.[23] *Adquirir* was at an earlier stage *adquerir,* with a completely regular conjugation following the model of *sentir.* When it subsequently evolved to *adquirir,* the conjugations with diphthongs were left unchanged.

Argüir adheres to the following formula (throughout all 47 conjugations):

except before *-i*
(i) add *-y* (like *construir*);
(ii) *-gü* → *-gu*

Appendix
The Origins of Spanish Diphthongs

In Latin, each of the five vowels (*a, e, i, o, u*) had a short and a long variant which differed only (or primarily) in the length of articulation, not in the fundamental nature of the sound. A similar situation prevailed in English until the so-called "Great Vowel Shift", which occurred between the times of Chaucer and Shakespeare, during the course of which all of the English long vowels changed the fundamental nature of their sound.[24]

In the evolution from Latin to Spanish, the "short" versions of *e* and *o* generally became diphthongs when they were in *stressed* syllables, while they remained unchanged when they were in *unstressed* syllables. The "long" versions remained unchanged regardless of location. This pattern carried through to the verbal system, so that, in general, verbs whose stem vowel *-e* and *-o* come from a short Latin vowel are diphthong verbs, while those which come from a long Latin vowel are not.

The varying pattern of diphthongs of Latin *e* and *o* represents one of the principal features which distinguish the different Romance languages. This can be illustrated by looking at the contrasting treatment accorded by Spanish, French, Italian, and Portuguese to the Latin verbs TENERE, MOVERE, SENTIRE, and DORMIRE. The conjugations for the third person singular ("he has", "he moves", etc.) are shown below, with those displaying diphthongs highlighted in bold.

---

[23] In principle, Latin JOCARI should have evolved to **jogar,* not *jugar.* Viewed from this perspective, the 9 conjugations with *-ue* (4 in the present indicative, 4 in the present subjunctive and 1 in the imperative) are actually "regular" diphthongs of an *-ar* verb with stem vowel *-o,* while the remaining 38 conjugations (including the infinitive) are "irregular"!

[24] Which is why today English "long *a*" corresponds to Spanish *e,* "long *e*" to Spanish *i.*

I.		Spanish	French	Italian	Portuguese
open syllable					
e	tener	**tiene**	**tient**	**tiene**	tem
o	mover	**mueve**	**meut**	**muove**	move
closed syllable					
e	sentir	**siente**	sent	sente	sente
o	dormir	**duerme**	dort	dorme	dorme

Apart from Spanish, a critical element was whether the vowel was located in an *open* or *closed* syllable—i.e., whether the syllable ended in a vowel or a consonant. Expanding the comparison to include Catalan (spoken in northeastern Spain) and Occitan (also known as Provencal, spoken in southern France), the following pattern emerges.

II. *diphthong or no?* X = yes, O = no

	short E		short O	
type of syllable	open	closed	open	closed
Spanish	X	X	X	X
French	X	O	X	O
Italian	X	O	X	O
Portuguese	O	O	O	O
Catalan	O	O	O	O
Occitan	O	O	O	O

Portuguese, Catalan, and Occitan did not diphthong at all. French and Italian diphthonged, but only in open syllables. Only Spanish diphthonged in *both* open and closed syllables. It is not easy to come up with an explanation, or explanations, which can account for this diversity, particularly since the three diphthonging languages were noncontiguous in their formative years.

In "old" Spanish, French, and Italian, for all verbs which diphthonged there was a marked contrast between the diphthong of the 1s-2s-3s-3p forms, on the one hand, and the "pure" vowel of the 1p-2p forms. In both French and Italian, the large majority of diphthong verbs succumbed to the pressures to become "regular", leaving only a very few verbs which today display the original contrast. Spanish was not immune to such pressures, and while the majority of diphthong verbs were able to resist, a number succumbed. In most such cases, it was the "pure vowel" form which was victorious, leading to the following modern *regular* verbs (without diphthongs):

	"old" 1s	modern 1s	
entregar	entriego	entrego	"to deliver"
prestar	priesto	presto	"to lend"
pretender	pretiendo	pretendo	"to try to", "to aspire to"

templar	tiemplo	templo	"to temper"
vedar	viedo	vedo	"to veto"
aportar	apuerto	aporto	"to contribute"
confortar	confuerto	conforto	"to comfort"
derrocar	derrueco	derroco	"to overthrow"
sorber	suerbo	sorbo	"to suck", "to sip"

Less frequently, the diphthong forms prevailed, producing the following modern regular verbs (with diphthongs in *all* 47 conjugations):[25]

	"old" 1p	modern 1p	
adiestrar	adestramos	adiestramos	"to train"
diezmar	dezmamos	diezmamos	"to decimate"
amueblar	amoblamos	amueblamos	"to furnish"
deshuesar	desosamos	deshuesamos	"to bone"

The visible effects of Spanish's greater propensity to diphthong extend well beyond the verbal system, as the following comparison of six common nouns shows:

	Spanish	Italian	Portuguese	French
hundred	ciento	cento	cento	cent
wind	viento	vento	vento	vent
feast	fiesta	festa	festa	fête[26]
bridge	puente	ponte	ponte	pont
death	muerte	morte	morte	mort
fate	suerte	sorte	sorte	sort

---

[25] For each of these verbs, the "old" (mixed diphthong pattern) forms still exist but are rarely used: *adestrar, dezmar, amoblar, desosar.*

[26] Until the early eighteenth century written as *feste* (origin of English *feast*).

CHAPTER 3
Irregularities: Simple Past Tense

Simple past tense irregularities can be divided among the following categories:

"Predictable" irregularities
    1. *Umlaut* for -*ir* verbs having stem vowel -*e* or -*o:* e →i *or* o →u

"Unpredictable" or "fundamental" irregularities
    2. One-syllable verbs: **ser, ir, dar**
    3. Verbs with stem vowel → -*u:* **poner, poder, estar, tener, andar, haber, saber, caber**
    4. Verbs with stem vowel → -*i:* **hacer, venir, querer**
    5. Verbs with post-stem consonant -*j:* **decir, traer, -ducir**

Purely orthographic changes
    Orthographic changes for the simple past (and other tenses) will be treated in Chapter 7.

Predictable Irregularities

1. *Umlaut* for -*ir* Verbs Having Stem Vowel -*e* or -*o*

Essentially all -*ir* verbs with stem vowel -*e* or -*o* have umlauts in the stem vowel of the third person simple past, singular and plural:

    e →i

    o →u

This applies both to verbs which *umlaut* in the present tense (type *pedir*) and those which *diphthong* (types *sentir* and *dormir*):

	sentir	*pedir*	*dormir*
1s	sentí	pedí	dormí
2s	sentiste	pediste	dormiste
3s	*sintió*	*pidió*	*durmió*
1p	sentimos	pedimos	dormimos
2p	sentisteis	pedisteis	dormisteis
3p	*sintieron*	*pidieron*	*durmieron*

Exceptions (i.e., regular simple past):

	3s	3p
discernir[1]	discernió	discernieron
oír[2]	oyó	oyeron
sumergir	sumergió	sumergieron

Note that verbs which diphthong in the present tense (types *sentir* and *dormir*) do not do so in the past tense, since for "regular" verbs the stress in the past tense *never* falls on the stem syllable.

Unpredictable Irregularities

2. One-Syllable Verbs

Of the four one-syllable verbs in Spanish,[3] all but *ver* have irregular simple pasts:

	ser	*ir*	*dar*	*ver* (regular)
1s	*fui*	*fui*	di	vi
2s	fuiste	fuiste	diste	viste
3s	*fue*	*fue*	dio	vio
1p	fuimos	fuimos	dimos	vimos
2p	fuisteis	fuisteis	disteis	visteis
3p	fueron	fueron	dieron	vieron

Several points require comment:

(i) The simple past conjugations for *ser* and *ir* are identical, and clearly originate from an altogether different verb.[4]

---

[1] Also *cernir, hendir,* and *concernir.* As noted in Chapter 1, throughout their conjugations these "mixed pattern" verbs behave like -*er* diphthong verbs.

[2] The -*i* between vowels "regularly" becomes -*y* in *oyó* and *oyeron* (see Chapter 7).

[3] Excluding verbs with a root diphthong—e.g., *huir, fiar*—which can be pronounced with either one or two syllables.

[4] The simple past for *ser* comes directly from Latin, where the verb *to be*—as in English—took elements from different sources. *Ir* abandoned its original Latin past tense, the first person singular in particular being somewhat impractical (*ii,* pronounced i·i). The subsequent merger between the past tenses of the two verbs was facilitated by their natural similarity in meaning; e.g.,

A. Last night I *was* at the library.

B. Last night I *went* to the library.

(ii) *Ser* and *ir* have regular endings apart from the first and third person singular.

(iii) The endings for *dar* are those of a regular *-er/-ir* verb—i.e., *dar* would have a regular simple past tense if the infinitive were *der or *dir rather than *dar*.

(iv) Unlike regular simple past tenses, there are no written accents on the first and third person singulars, as these have only one syllable.[5]

3. Verbs with Stem Vowel → *u*

There are eight verbs which have an irregular stem vowel -*u* in the simple past tense.

	poner	*poder*	*estar*	*tener*
1s	puse	pude	estuve	tuve
2s	pusiste	pudiste	estuviste	tuviste
3s	puso	pudo	estuvo	tuvo
1p	pusimos	pudimos	estuvimos	tuvimos
2p	pusisteis	pudisteis	estuvisteis	tuvisteis
3p	pusieron	pudieron	estuvieron	tuvieron

	andar	*haber*	*saber*	*caber*
1s	anduve	hube	supe	cupe
2s	anduviste	hubiste	supiste	cupiste
3s	anduvo	hubo	supo	cupo
1p	anduvimos	hubimos	supimos	cupimos
2p	anduvisteis	hubisteis	supisteis	cupisteis
3p	anduvieron	hubieron	supieron	cupieron

Note that:

(i) The stress accent falls on the stem syllable for the first and third person singulars, representing a major contrast with regular past tenses. The other four conjugations, as for regular verbs, are stressed on the post-stem syllable.

---

[5] Until 1952 these forms had written accents (*fuí, fué, dí, dió, ví, vió*), and it is not uncommon to encounter such forms well after this date. Written accents are required for the corresponding forms of the compound verb *prever* (*preví, previó*) since they have more than one syllable.

	irregular	regular (-ar)	regular (-er/-ir)
1s	*tu·ve*	can·té	su·bí
2s	tu·vis·te	can·tas·te	su·bis·te
3s	*tu·vo*	can·tó	su·bió
1p	tu·vi·mos	can·ta·mos	su·bi·mos
2p	tu·vis·teis	can·tas·teis	su·bis·teis
3p	tu·vie·ron	can·ta·ron	su·bie·ron

(ii) The endings of the four conjugations with "normal" (post-stem) stress are identical to those of regular -er/-ir verbs, while the first and third person singular endings are those of regular -ar verbs (without the written accent):

	poner, etc.	-ar verbs	-er and -ir verbs
1s	**-e**	**-é**	-í
2s	**-iste**	-aste	**-iste**
3s	**-o**	**-ó**	-ió
1p	**-imos**	-amos	**-imos**
2p	**-isteis**	-asteis	**-isteis**
3p	**-ieron**	-aron	**-ieron**

(iii) For *saber* and *caber,* the stem consonant is -p rather than -b. This goes back to the original Latin forms of these verbs (cf. English *insipid* and *capture*).[6]

4. Verbs with Stem Vowel → i

Three verbs have an irregular stem vowel -i:

	hacer	*venir*	*querer*
1s	hice	vine	quise
2s	hiciste	viniste	quisiste
3s	*hizo*	vino	quiso
1p	hicimos	vinimos	quisimos
2p	hicisteis	vinisteis	quisisteis
3p	hicieron	vinieron	quisieron

---

[6] The Latin verb SAPERE, from which *saber* is derived, meant "to taste" and is the origin of English *savor*. Latin *p* between vowels became a *v* sound in the western Romance languages, written with a *v* in French (*savoir*) but with a *b* in Spanish, while retaining the original pronunciation in Italian (*sapere*). Due to other phonetic factors, the past tense of *saber* and *caber*—as well as the present subjunctive—retained the original *p*.

Comments (i) and (ii) for -*u* stems, with reference to stress and endings, are equally applicable here. The *z* in *hizo* is a regular orthographic change (see Chapter 7) to preserve the "soft" *c* sound before -*o*. The consonant in *querer* changes from -*r* to -*s* for reasons that go back to the earliest days of Latin, and is analogous to the contrast in English *query* and *quest*.

5. Verbs with Post-stem Consonant -*j*

Decir, traer, and the -*ducir* verbs have an irregular -*j* immediately following the stem vowel. The third person plural "loses" the -*i* which normally is the first element of the ending -*ieron* (Chapter 7):

	decir	*traer*	*-ducir*
1s	dije	traje	conduje
2s	dijiste	trajiste	condujiste
3s	dijo	trajo	condujo
1p	dijimos	trajimos	condujimos
2p	dijisteis	trajisteis	condujisteis
3p	*dijeron* (**not** *dijieron)	*trajeron*	*condujeron*

Comments (i) and (ii) for -*u* stems, with reference to stress and endings, apply here as well.

Note that other -*ucir* verbs (*lucir*), as well as all -*cer* verbs (*conocer*), have regular past tenses: *lucí, conocí,* etc.

CHAPTER 4

Future and Conditional Tenses

The future and conditional tenses are formed by adding the following endings to the *infinitive:*

		future	conditional
	1s	-é	-ía
	2s	-ás	-ías
	3s	-á	-ía
	1p	-emos	-íamos
	2p	-éis	-íais
	3p	-án	-ían
cantar	1s	can·ta·**ré**	can·ta·**rí**·a
	2s	can·ta·**rás**	can·ta·**rí**·as
	3s	can·ta·**rá**	can·ta·**rí**·a
	1p	can·ta·**re**·mos	can·ta·**rí**·a·mos
	2p	can·ta·**réis**	can·ta·**rí**·ais
	3p	can·ta·**rán**	can·ta·**rí**·an
comer	1s	comeré	comería
	2s	comerás	comerías
	3s	comerá	comería
	1p	comeremos	comeríamos
	2p	comeréis	comeríais
	3p	comerán	comerían
subir	1s	subiré	subiría
	2s	subirás	subirías
	3s	subirá	subiría
	1p	subiremos	subiríamos
	2p	subiréis	subiríais
	3p	subirán	subirían

Points to note:

(1) The endings are the same for all three classes of verbs: *-ar, -er, -ir.*
(2) In all six conjugations, the stress falls on the stem + 2 syllable. In the future tense this necessitates a written accent for all conjugations

except the first person plural, in the conditional tense for all conjugations.

(3) The -*í* in the conditional is pronounced as a separate vowel, not as a diphthong with the following -*a*.

(4) The endings for the future tense are essentially equal to the *present* tense of *haber* minus the (unpronounced) *h*.

he	$\rightarrow$		é	
has	$\rightarrow$		ás	
ha	$\rightarrow$		á	
hemos	$\rightarrow$		emos	
habéis	$\rightarrow$	(ab)eis	$\rightarrow$	éis
han	$\rightarrow$		án	

(5) The endings for the conditional tense are *identical* to those of the *imperfect* tense of *haber* (and of all other -*er*/-*ir* verbs).[1]

We will see below that facts (4) and (5) did not arise by coincidence but instead reflect the historical development of these verb forms.

Irregularities

Twelve verbs truncate the infinitive stem to which the (normal) future and conditional endings are added. Ten of these are "fundamentally irregular" verbs, the exceptions being *salir* and *valer*.

infinitive	modified form	future 1s	conditional 1s
haber	hab(e)r	habré	habría
saber	sab(e)r	sabré	sabría
caber	cab(e)r	cabré	cabría
poder	pod(e)r	podré	podría
querer	quer(e)r	querré	querría
poner	pon(e)r $\rightarrow$ pon**dr**	pondré	pondría
tener	ten(e)r $\rightarrow$ ten**dr**	tendré	tendría
venir	ven(i)r $\rightarrow$ ven**dr**	vendré	vendría
salir	sal(i)r $\rightarrow$ sal**dr**	saldré	saldría
valer	val(e)r· $\rightarrow$ val**dr**	valdré	valdría
decir	d(ec)ir	diré	diría
hacer	ha(ce)r	haré	haría

[1] Thus, these endings added to the verb *stem* of -*er*/-*ir* verbs give the *imperfect*, while added to the *infinitive* (for -*ar* verbs as well) they give the *conditional*.

In the second group above a "helping" -*d* has been added, analogous to the -*d* in English *thunder* (Middle English *thunre*). Composite verbs having one of these verbs as a base (*convenir, deshacer,* etc.) normally have the same irregularities in the future and conditional tenses, although those of *bendecir* and *maldecir* are regular (*bendeciré,* etc.). [2]

Appendix
Historical and Methodological Note

The Latin future tense died without leaving a trace in the successor Romance languages. [3] The main reason for its disappearance was that phonetic developments during the post-Classical period had created confusions between it and other verb tenses.

A new Romance future tense arose as a refinement of a construction which had already existed in classical Latin, i.e., the combination of the verb *to have* (or "have to") with another verb to convey an idea of what will happen (or has to happen) in the future. Thus, Cicero wrote to his friend Atticus:

DE RE PUBLICA NIHIL HABEO AD TE SCRIBERE
"Of public matters I have nothing to write you."

The meaning of this differs very little from the straightforward future:

"Of public matters I *will write* nothing to you."

Similarly, *I have to go to Rome tomorrow* is not too distant in meaning from *I am going* (will go) *to Rome tomorrow.*

The modern form of the Romance future arose from the custom of placing the verb "to have" (present tense) after the infinitive. Thus

escribir + (h)e	→	escribiré
escribir + (h)as	→	escribirás
escribir + (h)a	→	escribirá
escribir + (h)emos	→	escribiremos
escribir + (hab)éis	→	escribiréis
escribir + (h)an	→	escribirán

Classical Latin had no single verb form corresponding to the notion of a "future in the past" (e.g., *he said he **would write** a letter the next day*). The Romance development of the

---

[2] For *predecir, contradecir,* and *desdecir* there is disagreement: the *RAE* says that their futures and conditionals are like those of *decir* (*prediré, contradiré, desdiré*), while according to *Moliner* they are like those of *bendecir* (*predeciré, contradeciré, desdeciré*).

[3] Apart from *placebo*—directly from the Latin "I *will* please."

future tense led naturally to the development of a future *in the past* by replacing the present of the verb *haber* with the imperfect. Thus, the natural progression in meaning was:

I told you that I *had* a letter *to write.*   →   I told you that I *had to write* a letter.

→   I told you that I *would write* a letter.

In Spanish and most of the other Romance languages the *conditional* tense—originally limited to the past—was thus formed through a fusion of the infinitive with the imperfect of the verb *haber.*

escribir + (hab)ía	→	escribiría
escribir + (hab)ías	→	escribirías
escribir + (hab)ía	→	escribiría
escribir + (hab)íamos	→	escribiríamos
escribir + (hab)íais	→	escribiríais
escribir + (hab)ían	→	escribirían

Even after eliminating the *hab-,* conditionals (and futures) can be very long, particularly for the first person plural. *Escribiremos* and *escribiríamos,* for example, have five and six syllables respectively. While this is a tolerable situation for verbs not used with great frequency (especially in these tenses), twelve more commonly used verbs were successful in shedding an additional syllable, as we have seen above.

CHAPTER 5

Subjunctive and Imperative

Present Tense

The present subjunctive endings for *all* verbs are:

	-ar verbs	*-er* and *-ir* verbs
1s	-e	-a
2s	-es	-as
3s	-e	-a
1p	-emos	-amos
2p	-éis	-áis
3p	-en	-an

For most verbs these endings are added to the normal verb stem, i.e., the infinitive minus the final *-ar, -er,* or *-ir.* The present subjunctives for the standard verbs (*cantar, comer, subir*) are shown below; for comparison the present *indicative* is also shown.

-ar verbs	subjunctive	indicative
1s	cante	canto
2s	cantes	cantas
3s	cante	canta
1p	cantemos	cantamos
2p	cantéis	cantáis
3p	canten	cantan

-er verbs	subjunctive	indicative
1s	coma	como
2s	comas	comes
3s	coma	come
1p	comamos	comemos
2p	comáis	coméis
3p	coman	comen

-ir verbs	subjunctive	indicative
1s	suba	subo
2s	subas	subes
3s	suba	sube
1p	subamos	subimos
2p	subáis	subís
3p	suban	suben

It can be observed that:

(1) The *-ar* verbs form their present subjunctive by uniformly replacing the post-stem vowel of the present indicative with *-e.*

(2) The *-er* and *-ir* verbs form their present subjunctives by uniformly replacing the post-stem vowel with *-a* (or *ái* for the second person plural of *-ir* verbs).

(3) The first and third person singulars have identical forms for the present subjunctive.

(4) The stress pattern for the present subjunctive is identical to that of the present indicative.

The alternation of vowels, $a \rightarrow e$ for *-ar* verbs and $e/i \rightarrow a$ for *-er* and *-ir* verbs, comes straight from Latin. It creates potential problems for the beginning student, since a verb form with post-stem vowel *-e* could theoretically be *either* the indicative of an *-er/-ir* verb *or* the subjunctive of an *-ar* verb. Similarly, a verb form with post-stem vowel *-a* could be the indicative of an *-ar* verb or the subjunctive of an *-er/-ir* verb. There are in fact a small number of couplets where (in some conjugations) the subjunctive of one is the indicative of the other, e.g.,

	sentar ("to seat")	*sentir* ("to feel")
sientas	indicative, 2s	subjunctive, 2s
sientes	subjunctive, 2s	indicative, 2s
siente	subjunctive, 1s/3s	indicative, 3s

Irregularities in the Present Subjunctive

The general situation can be summarized as follows:

1. Verbs with *regular* present indicatives have *regular* present subjunctives.

2. Verbs with *predictably irregular* present indicatives have *predictably irregular* present subjunctives (and hence are not really irregular).

3. Of the verbs which have *unpredictably irregular* present indicatives, four—*ser, ir, haber,* and *saber*—have *unpredictably irregular*

present subjunctives. The remainder have *predictably irregular* *present subjunctives.*

4. The "mixed pattern" verbs offer a mixture of patterns.
5. Present subjunctives are subject to the general rules governing regular orthographic changes (Chapter 7).

Verbs with Predictably Irregular Present Indicatives

For convenience we repeat the four groups of predictable present indicative irregularities:

1. *Diphthong* in verbs having stem vowel -*e* or -*o*
   A. *e* → *ie*
   B. *o* → *ue*
2. *Umlaut* (*e* → *i*) for -*ir* verbs having stem vowel -*e*
3. First person singular ending in -*zco*
   A. (Most) infinitives ending in -*cer* (e.g., *conocer*)
   B. (All) infinitives ending in -*ucir* (e.g., *producir, lucir*)
4. Verbs ending in -*uir* add -*y* except before -*i*

Group #1: Verbs Which Diphthong in the Present Indicative

Here there is an important difference between the -*ar* and -*er* verbs on the one hand, and the -*ir* verbs on the other:

(a) -*ar* and -*er* verbs have diphthongs in the present subjunctive under exactly the same conditions as in the present indicative—the three singulars and the third person plural. The first and second person plural are completely regular.

(b) -*ir* verbs have the same diphthongs but *also* have *umlaut* (*e* → *i*, *o* → *u*) for the first and second person plurals.[1]

	-*ar* verbs		-*er* verbs	
	pensar	*mostrar*	*perder*	*mover*
1s	piense	muestre	pierda	mueva
2s	pienses	muestres	pierdas	muevas
3s	piense	muestre	pierda	mueva
1p	pensemos	mostremos	perdamos	movamos
2p	penséis	mostréis	perdáis	mováis
3p	piensen	muestren	pierdan	muevan

[1] With the exception of *discernir* and associated verbs, which, as noted previously, behave throughout their conjugations as -*er* diphthong verbs.

	-ir verbs		
	sentir	*dormir*	
1s	*sienta*	*duerma*	**diphthong**
2s	*sientas*	*duermas*	**diphthong**
3s	*sienta*	*duerma*	**diphthong**
1p	sintamos	durmamos	**umlaut**
2p	sintáis	durmáis	**umlaut**
3p	*sientan*	*duerman*	**diphthong**

Group #2: -*ir* Verbs Which Umlaut in the Present Indicative

These verbs also have umlaut in the present subjunctive, but in this case the umlaut extends to *all* six conjugations.

	pedir
1s	pida
2s	pidas
3s	pida
1p	pidamos
2p	pidáis
3p	pidan

Group #3: Verbs with First Person Singular -*zco* in the Present Indicative

These verbs use the first person present indicative singular (minus the final -*o*) as the stem to which the regular subjunctive endings are added:

	crecer	*conocer*	**lucir**	**conducir**
1s present indicative	*crezco*	*conozco*	*luzco*	*conduzco*
subjunctive stem	crezc-	conozc-	luzc-	conduzc-
1s	crezca	conozca	luzca	conduzca
2s	crezcas	conozcas	luzcas	conduzcas
3s	crezca	conozca	luzca	conduzca
1p	crezcamos	conozcamos	luzcamos	conduzcamos
2p	crezcáis	conozcáis	luzcáis	conduzcáis
3p	crezcan	conozcan	luzcan	conduzcan

Group #4: Verbs Which Add -y to the Present Stem Except before -i

Like Group #3, these verbs use the first person present indicative singular (minus the final -o) as the stem to which the regular subjunctive endings are added. In other words, the -y is added to all six conjugations of the present subjunctive, in conformity with the general rule of *add -y except before -i,* since the following letter in all six cases is -a.

	huir	*construir*
1s present indicative	*huyo*	*construyo*
subjunctive stem	huy-	construy-
1s	huya	construya
2s	huyas	construyas
3s	huya	construya
1p	huyamos	construyamos
2p	huyáis	construyáis
3p	huyan	construyan

Verbs with Unpredictably Irregular Present Indicatives

Four of these verbs are unpredictable in the present subjunctive as well, while the other 13 are predictably irregular.

Ser, ir, haber, and saber

The present subjunctive is formed by adding the regular subjunctive endings to an irregular subjunctive stem.

	ser	*ir*	*haber*	*saber*
1s present indicative	*soy*	*voy*	*he*	*sé*
subjunctive stem	se-	vay-	hay-	sep-
1s	sea	vaya	haya	sepa
2s	seas	vayas	hayas	sepas
3s	sea	vaya	haya	sepa
1p	seamos	vayamos	hayamos	sepamos
2p	seáis	vayáis	hayáis	sepáis
3p	sean	vayan	hayan	sepan

All Others

The others form their present subjunctive stem from the first person present indicative—minus the final -*o* or -*oy*—in a manner analogous to that of verbs of type *crecer* and *huir*.

	estar	*dar*	*caber*	*decir*
1s present indicative	estoy	doy	quepo	digo
subjunctive stem	est-	d-	quep-	dig-
1s	esté	dé	quepa	diga
2s	estés	des	quepas	digas
3s	esté	dé	quepa	diga
1p	estemos	demos	quepamos	digamos
2p	estéis	deis	quepáis	digáis
3p	estén	den	quepan	digan

For *dar*, the written accents for 1s and 3s (*dé*) are purely orthographic and are meant to distinguish them from the preposition *de*, while the one-syllable *deis* requires no written accent. *Estar* maintains the stress (and written accent) pattern of the indicative.

	hacer	*caer*	*oír*
1s present indicative	hago	caigo	oigo
subjunctive stem	hag-	caig-	oig-
1s	haga	caiga	oiga
2s	hagas	caigas	oigas
3s	haga	caiga	oiga
1p	hagamos	caigamos	oigamos
2p	hagáis	caigáis	oigáis
3p	hagan	caigan	oigan

	traer	*poner*	*salir*
1s present indicative	traigo	pongo	salgo
subjunctive stem	traig-	pong-	salg-
1s	traiga	ponga	salga
2s	traigas	pongas	salgas
3s	traiga	ponga	salga
1p	traigamos	pongamos	salgamos
2p	traigáis	pongáis	salgáis
3p	traigan	pongan	salgan

	tener	*valer*	*venir*
1s present indicative	tengo	valgo	vengo
subjunctive stem	teng-	valg-	veng-
1s	tenga	valga	venga
2s	tengas	valgas	vengas
3s	tenga	valga	venga
1p	tengamos	valgamos	vengamos
2p	tengáis	valgáis	vengáis
3p	tengan	valgan	vengan

Mixed Pattern Verbs: *ver, jugar, adquirir, argüir, discernir*

Ver constructs its present subjunctive using a subjunctive stem derived from the irregular first person singular present indicative *veo*. *Jugar* and *adquirir* repeat their diphthongs from the present indicative (three singulars and third person plural).

	ver	*jugar*	*adquirir*
1s present indicative	veo	juego	adquiero
subjunctive stem	ve-		
1s	vea	juegue	adquiera
2s	veas	juegues	adquieras
3s	vea	juegue	adquiera
1p	veamos	juguemos	adquiramos
2p	veáis	juguéis	adquiráis
3p	vean	jueguen	adquieran

The *-gu* in place of *-g* for *jugar* is a normal orthographic change to maintain the "hard" *g* sound (see Chapter 7).

Argüir follows the rule established in Chapter 2:

except before *-i*
(i) add *-y* (like *construir*);
(ii) *-gü* → *-gu*

Discernir has diphthongs in the expected conjugations but no umlauts.

	argüir	*discernir*
1s present indicative	*arguyo*	*discierno*
subjunctive stem	*arguy-*	
1s	arguya	discierna
2s	arguyas	disciernas
3s	arguya	discierna
1p	arguyamos	discernamos
2p	arguyáis	discernáis
3p	arguyan	disciernan

Subjunctive: Imperfect Tense

There are two distinct forms of the imperfect subjunctive which, subject to certain qualifications (see Chapter 12), can be used interchangeably. In both cases, the endings are added to the imperfect subjunctive stem, defined as follows:

imperfect subjunctive stem = simple past 3p, *minus* final -ron

This rule applies without exception to all verbs, regular or irregular.

infinitive	simple past 3p	imperfect subjunctive stem
cantar	cantaron	canta-
comer	comieron	comie-
subir	subieron	subie-
sentir	sintieron	sintie-
pedir	pidieron	pidie-
dormir	durmieron	durmie-
ser, ir	fueron	fue-
dar	dieron	die-
poner	pusieron	pusie-
poder	pudieron	pudie-
estar	estuvieron	estuvie-
tener	tuvieron	tuvie-
andar	anduvieron	anduvie-
haber	hubieron	hubie-
saber	supieron	supie-
caber	cupieron	cupie-
hacer	hicieron	hicie-
venir	vinieron	vinie-

querer	quisieron	quisie-
decir	dijeron	dije-
traer	trajeron	traje-
(con)ducir	(con)dujeron	(con)duje-

Verbs undergoing an orthographic modification in the simple past 3p (see Chapter 7) display the same modification in the imperfect subjunctive, e.g.,

leer	leyeron	leye-
construir	construyeron	construy-

The two imperfect subjunctives are then formed by adding one or the other of the following sets of endings:

	Imperfect Subjunctive (I)	Imperfect Subjunctive (II)
1s	-ra	-se
2s	-ras	-ses
3s	-ra	-se
1p	-ramos	-semos
2p	-rais	-seis
3p	-ran	-sen

Several examples:

	cantar		*subir*	
	Form I	*Form II*	*Form I*	*Form II*
1s	can·ta·ra	can·ta·se	su·bie·ra	su·bie·se
2s	can·ta·ras	can·ta·ses	su·bie·ras	su·bie·ses
3s	can·ta·ra	can·ta·se	su·bie·ra	su·bie·se
1p	can·tá·ra·mos	can·tá·se·mos	su·bié·ra·mos	su·bié·se·mos
2p	can·ta·rais	can·ta·seis	su·bie·rais	su·bie·seis
3p	can·ta·ran	can·ta·sen	su·bie·ran	su·bie·sen

	tener		*sentir*	
	Form I	*Form II*	*Form I*	*Form II*
1s	tuviera	tuviese	sintiera	sintiese
2s	tuvieras	tuvieses	sintieras	sintieses
3s	tuviera	tuviese	sintiera	sintiese
1p	tuviéramos	tuviésemos	sintiéramos	sintiésemos
2p	tuvierais	tuvieseis	sintierais	sintieseis
3p	tuvieran	tuviesen	sintieran	sintiesen

Note that:

(a) As in the indicative imperfect, all six conjugations are stressed on the *post-stem* syllable; this necessitates a written accent for the first person plural.

(b) The second form differs from the first only in that the *-ra* has been replaced by *-se*.

(c) For verbs of the *sentir/dormir* and *pedir* types, the stem is umlauted *uniformly* throughout all six conjugations, reflecting the umlaut in the third person simple past.

(d) For 2s, 3s, and 3p, the only difference between the imperfect subjunctive (Form I) and the future indicative is the syllable on which the stress falls (marked by a written accent in the future):

	imperfect subjunctive		future (indicative)	
2s	cantaras	can·**ta**·ras	cantarás	can·ta·**rás**
3s	cantara	can·**ta**·ra	cantará	can·ta·**rá**
3p	cantaran	can·**ta**·ran	cantarán	can·ta·**rán**

Imperative

Imperative statements are direct orders or commands:

you	Get out!
we	Let's go!

In Spanish, "you" commands can involve *tú* (2s), *vosotros* (2p), *usted* (3s), and *ustedes* (3p), so that there are thus five grammatical persons in which the imperative is possible (all except the first person singular).

There are separate imperative forms for the *second* person (singular and plural) only; for *nosotros, usted,* and *ustedes* the present subjunctive tense is used. For *all* negative imperative statements (*Don't go!*) the present subjunctive is used:

form of imperative	*nosotros*	*tú*	*vosotros*	*usted*	*ustedes*
positive	subjunctive	*imperative*	*imperative*	subjunctive	subjunctive
negative	subjunctive	subjunctive	subjunctive	subjunctive	subjunctive

The imperatives for all verbs having regular—or predictably irregular—present indicatives are formed as follows:

tú:	present indicative minus final -s
vosotros:	infinitive with final -r replaced by -d

Examples:

infinitive	indicative tú	vosotros	imperative tú	vosotros
cantar	cantas	cantáis	canta	cantad
pensar	piensas	pensáis	piensa	pensad
mostrar	muestras	mostráis	muestra	mostrad
comer	comes	coméis	come	comed
perder	pierdes	perdéis	pierde	perded
mover	mueves	movéis	mueve	moved
subir	subes	subís	sube	subid
pedir	pides	pedís	pide	pedid
sentir	sientes	sentís	siente	sentid
dormir	duermes	dormís	duerme	dormid
huir	huyes	huís	huye	huid

Note that:

(1) The stem vowel diphthongs (*pierde*), umlauts (*pide*), or adds a -y (*huye*) whenever the corresponding form in the present indicative does.

(2) The second person plural imperative for -er and -ir verbs differs (*comed* vs. *subid*), thus constituting the third and final difference among the 47 different simple forms for these verbs (along with the present indicative 1p and 2p).

(3) The *tú* form of the imperative is stressed on the stem syllable, the *vosotros* form on the post-stem syllable (**can·ta**, can·**tad**), as in the present indicative. Unlike the present indicative, however, no written accent is required for the *vosotros* form since it ends with a -d (*cantáis* versus *cantad*).

(4) Verbs with regular orthographic changes in the present indicative have identical changes in the corresponding form of the imperative (see Chapter 7).

Of the 17 verbs having (unpredictably) irregular present indicatives, 8 are entirely regular in the imperative, as are the 5 "mixed pattern" verbs.

infinitive	indicative		imperative	
	tú	*vosotros*	*tú*	*vosotros*
estar	estás	estáis	está	estad
dar	das	dais	da	dad
saber	sabes	sabéis	sabe	sabed
caber	cabes	cabéis	cabe	cabed
caer	caes	caéis	cae	caed
oír	oyes	oís	oye	oíd[2]
traer	traes	traéis	trae	traed
valer	vales	valéis	vale	valed

mixed pattern

ver	ves	veis	ve	ved
jugar	juegas	jugáis	juega	jugad
adquirir	adquieres	adquirís	adquiere	adquirid
argüir	arguyes	argüís	arguye	argüid
discernir	disciernes	discernís	discierne	discernid

The remaining 9 verbs with irregular present indicatives have irregular one-syllable imperatives in the singular but regular forms in the plural:

infinitive	indicative		imperative	
	tú	*vosotros*	*tú*	*vosotros*
ser	eres	sois	**sé**	sed
ir	vas	vais	**ve**	id
haber	has	habéis	**he**	habed
decir	dices	decís	**di**	decid
hacer	haces	hacéis	**haz**	haced
poner	pones	ponéis	**pon**	poned
salir	sales	salís	**sal**	salid
tener	tienes	tenéis	**ten**	tened
venir	vienes	venís	**ven**	venid

Note that:

(a) *Sé* has a written accent to distinguish it from the reflexive pronoun *se*. As a result, its form is identical to the first person singular present of *saber* ("I know").

---

[2] *Oíd* requires a written accent to preserve its two-syllable pronunciation: o•**íd**.

(b) *Ve* ("go!") is identical to *ve* ("see!"), the regular imperative of *ver*.

(c) For *tener* and *venir*, there are no diphthongs of the stem vowel (*ten* not **tien*), despite the fact that it is stressed.

(d) One-syllable imperatives ending in -*n* (*pon, ten, ven*) require a written accent when they appear in compound verbs, since they are then multi-syllable words ending in -*n* and stressed on the final syllable.

infinitive	imperative 2s	imperative 2p
componer	compón	componed
obtener	obtén	obtened
revenir	revén	revenid

Appendix

Future Subjunctive

While rarely used, the future subjunctive is found on occasion in official documents and in certain fixed expressions of the type "what will be will be" (see appendix to Chapter 12). Given the rarity of its use—and its general omission from texts—a frequent reaction upon encountering it is to mistake it for an imperfect subjunctive with a typographical error.

The future subjunctive is formed using the *stem of the imperfect subjunctive*, to which the following endings are added:

1s	-re
2s	-res
3s	-re
1p	-remos
2p	-reis
3p	-ren

For the verb *ser*, which is by far the most common one encountered:

future subjunctive	imperfect subjunctive I	II
fuere	fuera	fuese
fueres	fueras	fueses
fuere	fuera	fuese
fuéremos	fuéramos	fuésemos
fuereis	fuerais	fueseis
fueren	fueran	fuesen

CHAPTER 6
Compound Verb Forms

All compound verb tenses are formed with *haber* as an auxiliary verb:

verb form   =   (form of) *haber*   +   past participle

INDICATIVE	
compound past	present
past perfect	imperfect
past anterior (rare)	simple past
future perfect	future
conditional perfect	conditional

SUBJUNCTIVE	
compound past subjunctive	present subjunctive
past perfect subjunctive	imperfect subjunctive

Compound Past

The *compound past* is formed using the *present* tense of the auxiliary verb *haber* with the past participle.

1s	he cantado	he subido	I have sung/climbed
2s	has cantado	has subido	you have sung/climbed
3s	ha cantado	ha subido	he/she/it has sung/climbed
1p	hemos cantado	hemos subido	we have sung/climbed
2p	habéis cantado	habéis subido	you have sung/climbed
3p	han cantado	han subido	they have sung/climbed

Methodological Note for Those with Background in French

Note the following differences (advantages) compared to the French *passé composé*:

(i) The Spanish compound past uses only one auxiliary verb (*haber*) whereas the French *passé composé* uses two (*avoir* and *être*), depending on the verb and/or situation.

(ii) The Spanish compound past is *invariable,* i.e., it does not change according to the gender of the noun or of a preceding direct object (cf. French *je suis descendu(e)* and *la monnaie que je vous ai donné(e)*.

Past Perfect (Pluperfect)

The Spanish *pluscuamperfecto,* like its English counterpart, refers to situations existing prior to a fixed point in the past. It is formed analogously to the compound past, except that the present tense of *haber* is replaced by the imperfect.

haber (present) + past participle → compound past
haber (imperfect) + past participle → past perfect

había cantado	I	*had sung*
habías cantado	you	"
había cantado	he/she	"
habíamos cantado	we	"
habíais cantado	you	"
habían cantado	they	"

Past Anterior

This marks a past event immediately preceding another past event and is formed using the simple past of *haber* as the auxiliary verb. The past anterior is rarely used in modern speech (or writing), generally being substituted by the simple past or past perfect.

hube cantado	I	*had (just) sung*
hubiste cantado	you	"
hubo cantado	he/she	"
hubimos cantado	we	"
hubisteis cantado	you	"
hubieron cantado	they	"

Future Perfect

The future perfect consists of the future of the auxiliary verb *haber* plus the past participle.

habré subido	I	*will have climbed*
habrás subido	you	"
habrá subido	he/she	"
habremos subido	we	"
habréis subido	you	"
habrán subido	they	"

Conditional Perfect

The conditional perfect is formed by the conditional of the auxiliary verb *haber* plus the past participle.

habría subido	I	*would have climbed*
habrías subido	you	"
habría subido	he/she	"
habríamos subido	we	"
habríais subido	you	"
habrían subido	they	"

Compound Past Subjunctive

This is analogous in its formation to the indicative compound past, with the present subjunctive of the auxiliary *haber* used in place of the present indicative.

haya subido	. . . (that) I	*have climbed*
hayas subido	. . . (that) you	*have climbed*
haya subido	. . . (that) he/she	*has climbed*
hayamos subido	. . . (that) we	*have climbed*
hayáis subido	. . . (that) you	*have climbed*
hayan subido	. . . (that) they	*have climbed*

Past Perfect Subjunctive

This is analogous in formation to the indicative past perfect, with the imperfect subjunctive of *haber* used in place of the imperfect indicative. As there are two forms of the imperfect subjunctive, there are likewise two forms of the past perfect subjunctive.

hubiera subido / hubiese subido	. . . (that) I	*had climbed*
hubieras subido / hubieses subido	. . . (that) you	"
hubiera subido / hubiese subido	. . . (that) he /she	"
hubiéramos subido / hubiésemos subido	. . . (that) we	"
hubierais subido / hubieseis subido	. . . (that) you	"
hubieran subido / hubiesen subido	. . . (that) they	"

CHAPTER 7
Orthographic Modifications

More than half of all Spanish verbs that "look" irregular are actually perfectly regular verbs whose irregular appearance is due to a series of *orthographic changes* which obey very precise rules. These can be divided into the following categories:

Letter changes
1. Consonant changes depending on nature of following vowel
2. Initial *ie* → *ye, ue* → *hue: errar, oler, erguir*
3. Unstressed *-i* between vowels → *-y*
4. *i + i* → *i: reír*
5. (a) Verbs with *-ll* and *-ñ* omit first element of following *-ie* or *-io*
   (b) *Irregular* verbs with *-j* omit first element of following *-ie*

Additional written accents
6. *-er* and *-ir* verbs with stem ending in *-a, -e,* or *-o*
7. Verbs with two vowels in *stem: reinar* (reino) vs. *reunir* (reúno)
8. *-uar* and *-iar* verbs: *adecuar* (adecuo) vs. *actuar* (actúo); *cambiar* (cambio) vs. *enviar* (envío)

Letter Changes

1. Consonant Changes Dependent on Following Vowel

A large number of Spanish verbs display (for certain conjugations) one of the following changes in the consonant which follows the stem vowel:

c	→	*z*
c	→	*qu*
g	→	*gu*
g	→	*j*
gu	→	*g*
gu	→	*gü*
qu	→	*c*
z	→	*c*

For example, for the verb *cazar* ("to hunt", cognate with English *chase*):

	present	simple past	present subjunctive
1s	cazo	cacé	cace
2s	cazas	cazaste	caces
3s	caza	cazó	cace
1p	cazamos	cazamos	cacemos
2p	cazáis	cazasteis	cacéis
3p	cazan	cazaron	cacen

While these consonant alternations give *cazar*—and other verbs displaying such variations—the appearance of an irregular verb, they are in fact entirely normal *orthographic* changes subject to very well defined rules.

Basic Principles

In English, the letter -*c* can have either a "hard" sound (*cat, comb, cut*) or a "soft" sound (*cell, cider*). The basic rule is that:

before	-*c* is pronounced
back vowels (-*a*, -*o*, -*u*)	hard
front vowels: (-*e*, -*i*)	soft

Question: What happens when a "hard" -*c* finds itself placed before a front vowel -*e* or -*i*?

Answer: It changes to a -*k*.

This in fact explains the origin of -*k* in many English words which previously were written with -*c*, including:

keen, keep, kerchief, kettle, key, kill, kin, kind, king, kiss, kitchen, kite, kitten

A similar *orthographic* change explains the -*gu* in several English words in place of the original -*g*:

guess, guest, guilt

The orthographic consonant changes in Spanish verbs represent exactly the same process, albeit on a larger—and more systematic—basis: in Spanish there are *five* sounds which have alternative spellings depending on the nature of the vowel (front or back) which follows. These are:

(i) hard "C" (**K**), spelled with -*c* or -*qu*
(ii) soft "C"—(*θ*), pronounced as "th" in parts of Spain, as "s" elsewhere— spelled with -*c* or -*z*
(iii) hard "G" (**G**), spelled with -*g* or -*gu*
(iv) "GW"—as in *Gwendolyn* (**GW**)—spelled with -*gu* or -*gü*
(v) "H" as in *Halloween* (**H**)—spelled with -*g* or -*j*

As the table below illustrates, the written form for the first four of these sounds is *always* determined *uniquely* by the nature of the vowel which follows. For **H** there is a well-defined rule for back vowels but before front vowels there is ambiguity.

LETTERS USED TO REPRESENT 5 "MULTI-FORM" SOUNDS

sound	back vowels (A, O, U)	front vowels (E, I)
K	c	qu
θ	z	c
G	g	gu
GW	gu	gü
H	j	j *or* g

Some examples:

	back vowels			front vowels	
	A	O	U	E	I
K	c va**ca**	c **co**sa	c **cu**rso	qu **que**mar	qu **qui**nce
θ	z re**za**r	z bra**zo**	z **zu**mo	c **ce**na	c **ci**nco
G	g lle**ga**r	g ami**go**	g **gu**sano	gu **gue**rra	gu **gui**tarra
GW	gu **agua**	gu anti**guo**	—	gü antig**üe**dad	gü ling**üi**sta
H	j **Ja**pón	j ro**jo**	j **ju**sto	j, g **je**fe li**ge**ro	j, g **ji**rafa **gi**gante

The General Rule for Verbs

For verbs whose stems end with one of the following five consonants (or consonant groups)—*c, g, gu, qu,* or *z*—an orthographic change is required to *preserve the regularity* of the pronunciation *whenever* the post-stem vowel changes from back to front (or vice versa).

Such a shift in the nature of the post-stem vowel occurs in the present indicative, simple past, and present subjunctive, as follows:

	-*ar* verbs	-*er* verbs	-*ir* verbs
present indicative	—	1s	1s
simple past	1s	—	—
present subjunctive	all 6	all 6	all 6

Verbs undergoing these orthographic modifications thus display such changes in precisely 7 of the 47 conjugations, though the pattern differs between -*ar* verbs on the one hand, and -*er*/-*ir* verbs on the other.

There are ten categories of verbs subject to such modifications; in the table below, each verb serves as a model for others undergoing the same changes.

	-*ar*	-*er*	-*ir*
-*c*	tocar	vencer	fruncir
-*g*	pagar	coger	dirigir
-*gu*	averiguar	—	distinguir
-*qu*	—	—	delinquir
-*z*	cazar	—	—

verb type	consonant sound	modification
1. tocar	[K]	c → qu
2. pagar	[G]	g → gu
3. averiguar	[GW]	gu → gü
4. cazar	[θ]	z → c
5. vencer	[θ]	c → z
6. coger	[H]	g → j
7. fruncir	[θ]	c → z
8. dirigir	[H]	g → j
9. distinguir	[G]	gu → g
10. delinquir	[K]	qu → c

Some of these groups are large—there are more than *150* verbs like *tocar*—while others are far smaller, *delinquir* being in many dictionaries the only member of its class.

Note that verbs with consonant -*j* never undergo orthographic modification since -*j* is compatible with both front *and* back vowels: thus while the **H** sound in *coger* ("to catch") is modified before back vowels, the same sound in *tejer* ("to weave") requires no such change.

2. Initial *ie* → *ye, ue* → *hue*

No Spanish word begins with the written letter combinations *ie*- or *ue*-, these being replaced by *ye*- and *hue*-, respectively. This accounts for the forms of words like *yegua* ("mare") and *hueso* ("bone"), rather than the "expected" forms **iegua* and **ueso*. For verbs with initial *e*- and *o*- subject to diphthong, a similar modification is required. The three verbs affected are *errar*, *oler*, and *erguir*.

	errar (to err)			*oler* (to smell)			*erguir* (to place erect)		
1s	*ierro	→	**ye**rro	*uelo	→	**hue**lo	*iergo	→	**ye**rgo
2s	*ierras	→	**ye**rras	*ueles	→	**hue**les	*iergues	→	**ye**rgues
3s	*ierra	→	**ye**rra	*uele	→	**hue**le	*iergue	→	**ye**rgue
1p			erramos			olemos			erguimos
2p			erráis			oléis			erguís
3p	*ierran	→	**ye**rran	*uelen	→	**hue**len	*ierguen	→	**ye**rguen

The same modification occurs in the other forms which have diphthongs, i.e., the present subjunctive (singulars and third person plural) and the *tú* form of the imperative.

An analogous modification occurs in the present participle of ir:

*iendo → **ye**ndo

3. Unstressed -*i* between Vowels → *y*

Whenever an *unstressed* -*i* appears between two vowels, neither of which is -*i*, it changes to -*y*.[1] This affects -*er* and -*ir* verbs whose *stem* ends in a vowel, in the following 9 conjugations:

(a) simple past (3s, 3p)
(b) imperfect subjunctive (all 6)
(c) present participle

---

[1] If an *unstressed* -*i* is either followed or preceded by another -*i*, the first -*i* disappears (see *reír* in no. 4). A *stressed* -*i* appears between vowels in the imperfect indicative for -*er* and -*ir* verbs with stem ending in a vowel: *caíamos, leíamos, oíamos, construíamos*, etc.

SIMPLE PAST				
	caer	*leer*	*construir*	*oír*
1s	caí	leí	construí	oí
2s	caíste	leíste	construiste	oíste
3s	*cayó* not *caió	*leyó*	*construyó*	*oyó*
1p	caímos	leímos	construimos	oímos
2p	caísteis	leísteis	construisteis	oísteis
3p	*cayeron* not *caieron	*leyeron*	*construyeron*	*oyeron*

For *construir* and *oír,* unlike the present tense where a *-y* is added somewhat superfluously, here the *-y* is completely "regular".[2]

When the stem ends in *-a* (*caer*), *-e* (*leer*), or *-o* (*oír*), a written accent is added to the simple past 2s/1p/2p in order to preserve the pronunciation of *-i* distinct from that of the preceding vowel. This does not occur when the stem ends in *-u* (*constru**i**r*), for reasons which will become clear at a later stage when we introduce the notion of *strong* versus *weak* vowels.

IMPERFECT SUBJUNCTIVE (I)				
1s	*cayera* not *caiera	*leyera*	*construyera*	*oyera*
2s	*cayeras*	*leyeras*	*construyeras*	*oyeras*
3s	*cayera*	*leyera*	*construyera*	*oyera*
1p	*cayéramos*	*leyéramos*	*construyéramos*	*oyéramos*
2p	*cayerais*	*leyerais*	*construyerais*	*oyerais*
3p	*cayeran*	*leyeran*	*construyeran*	*oyeran*

The identical change occurs for the second form of the imperfect subjunctive: *cayese, leyese, construyese, oyese,* etc.[3]

PRESENT PARTICIPLE				
cayendo not *caiendo	*leyendo*	*construyendo*	*oyendo*

4. *Reír: i + i → i*

Reír undergoes "normal" umlauts (*e → i*) in all of the conjugations in which the rule in number 3, above, would otherwise apply. In the simple past 3s and 3p, for example, the newly umlauted stem vowel would normally be followed directly by

---

[2] In accordance with the rule "add *-y* except before *-i*", no *-y* is added; instead, the *existing -i* is modified to *-y* since it has vowels on either side.

[3] And also for the (rarely used) future subjunctive.

a diphthong -*io* or -*ie*. As in Spanish neither of the letter combinations -*ii* or -*yi* is normally allowed,[4] an -*i* is omitted:

		reí
		reíste
*ri-ió	→	*rió*[5]
		reímos
		reísteis
*ri-ieron	→	*rieron*

As for verbs like *caer, leer,* and *oír,* written accents are added to the simple past 2s/1p/2p to mark the independent pronunciation of -*i* (see no. 6, below).

The imperfect subjunctive is formed in the normal manner using the stem *rie-* (derived from the third person plural simple past minus the final -*ron*). The present participle also sheds an -*i*:

*ri-iendo → *riendo*

Other verbs following the model of *reír* are: *desleír* ("to dissolve"), *engreír* ("to infatuate"), *freír* ("to fry"), *refreír* ("to refry"), *sofreír* ("to fry lightly"), and *sonreír* ("to smile").

5a. Verbs with -*ll* and -*ñ* Omit First Element of Following -*ie* or -*io*

The -*ie* or -*io* represents a diphthong whose first element is pronounced "Y". Since this "Y" sound is already incorporated in the immediately preceding palatal sound represented by -*ll* or -*ñ*, the *written* -*i* is eliminated. This modification affects the same conjugations as in number 3, above: (i) simple past (3s/3p); (ii) imperfect subjunctive (all 6); and (iii) present participle.

	bullir (to boil) simple past	*tañer* (to play [an instrument])
1s	bullí	tañí
2s	bulliste	tañiste
3s	*bulló* not *bullió	*tañó* not *tañió
1p	bullimos	tañimos
2p	bullisteis	tañisteis
3p	*bulleron* not *bullieron	*tañeron* not *tañieron

---

[4] Among the handful of exceptions are *antiimperialismo, antiinflamatorio, chiita* ("Shiite"), and *yiddish.*

[5] As discussed in the appendix to this chapter, a recent orthographic change instituted by the RAE now allows (in fact favors) the spelling *rio,* without written accent.

	imperfect subjunctive (I)	
1s	*bullera* not **bulliera*	*tañera* not **tañiera*
2s	*bulleras*	*tañeras*
3s	*bullera*	*tañera*
1p	*bulléramos*	*tañéramos*
2p	*bullerais*	*tañerais*
3p	*bulleran*	*tañeran*
	present participle	
	bullendo not **bulliendo*	*tañendo* not **tañiendo*

5b. *Irregular* Verbs with *-j* Omit First Element of Following *-ie*

A similar modification takes place for *irregular* verbs having a *-j* stem consonant in their simple past and (hence) imperfect subjunctive, specifically *decir, traer,* and verbs ending in *-ducir*. By contrast, *regular* verbs with stem consonant *-j* (e.g., *tejer*) do not undergo such a modification.[6]

	decir	*traer*	*producir*	but *tejer*
simple past				
3p	dijeron	trajeron	produjeron	tejieron
imperfect subjunctive (I)				
1s	dijera	trajera	produjera	tejiera
2s	dijeras	trajeras	produjeras	tejieras
3s	dijera	trajera	produjera	tejiera
1p	dijéramos	trajéramos	produjéramos	tejiéramos
2p	dijerais	trajerais	produjerais	tejierais
3p	dijeran	trajeran	produjeran	tejieran

Additional Written Accents

All of the consonant changes dealt with above are *obligatory,* in the sense that they *always* occur in the prescribed circumstances. The situation with regard to

---

[6] The *-j* in both cases was *-x* in Old Spanish. This was pronounced "SH", a palatal sound, and hence a following *-ie* or *-io* lost the *-i* (e.g., *dixeron, texeron*). When Spanish "SH" shifted to the *non-palatal* "H", regular verbs like *tejer* had the "normal" *-i* restored (*tejieron*), while the irregular verbs *decir, traer,* and *-ducir,* in conformity with Murphy's law, were able to resist these pressures. Note that no modification is required for the simple past 3s (which, like other irregular verbs, ends in *-o* rather than *-io*) or for the present participle (where *-j* does not appear).

orthographic *written accent* changes is on occasion less clear-cut—some verbs display the modifications, others do not. In all cases, knowledge of the form taken by the first person singular present is sufficient to determine the entire conjugation.

A Note on the Orthographic Treatment of Potential Diphthongs

The rules governing the treatment of two adjacent vowels are almost certainly the most complicated and frequently misunderstood element in the Spanish orthographic system. Their complete explanation falls outside the scope of the present work. For an understanding of verb conjugations, the essential elements can be summarized as follows:

(a) The vowels *a, e,* and *o* are called "strong vowels", *i* and *u* "weak vowels".

(b) Two *strong* vowels in succession are always pronounced in *hiatus*, i.e., as separate vowels in separate syllables.

(c) For the combination of a weak and strong vowel, the orthography allows no determination of the pronunciation *unless* the stress accent falls on the *weak* vowel, in which case it has a written accent mark and the two vowels are pronounced in hiatus.

pa**í**s	pa•**ís**
Mar**í**a	Ma•**rí**•a
fl**ú**or	**flú**•or
ata**ú**d	a•ta•**úd**

In all other circumstances, a weak/strong or strong/weak combination is *assumed* for the purposes of orthography to be pronounced as a diphthong, independent of its actual pronunciation. When the stress falls on the *strong* vowel in a *weak/strong* combination, there is a written accent if the syllable is not the "expected" one; however, this provides no information as to the actual pronunciation of the vowel combination. For example, *adiós* can be pronounced as either *a•**diós*** or *a•di•**ós***. The same logic applies to *strong/weak* vowel combinations where the stress falls on the strong vowel (e.g., *veintis**éis***), but in practice these *always* are pronounced as diphthongs. When the stress falls in the "expected" syllable on the strong vowel of a weak/strong or strong/weak combination, there is no written accent, e.g. *di**o**sa* (*di•**o**•sa* or *di**o**•sa*) and *s**ei**se* (*s**ei**•se*).

(d) Two *weak* vowels in succession can in principle be pronounced *either* as a diphthong or hiatus—there is no way to tell from the spelling of the word. For *purposes of orthography* they are *always* assumed to be pronounced as a diphthong, independent of their actual pronunciation. When the (assumed) diphthong *-iu* or *-ui* is stressed, a written accent is placed on the *second* element according to the normal rules, i.e., when the stress does not fall on the "expected" syllable:

written accent	no written accent
jesu**í**tico	jesu**i**ta
dru**í**dico	dru**i**da
veinti**ún**	veinti**u**no
intervi**ú**	intervi**u**var

A written accent is required for *jesuítico* (*je·**sui**·ti·co* or *je·su·**i**·ti·co*) which otherwise would be pronounced **je·sui·**ti**·co* or **je·su·**i**·ti·co*, while no such accent is required for *jesuita* (*je·su·**i**·ta* or *je·**sui**·ta*) since the stress falls on the "expected" syllable. That this written accent (or lack thereof) provides *no* information about the pronunciation of the vowel combination is clearly illustrated by the contrasting examples of *veintiún* and *veintiuno.*

6. *-er* and *-ir* Verbs with Stems Ending in *-a, -e,* or *-o*

The different treatment accorded to strong and weak vowels allows us to understand the orthographic distinction observed in Chapter 1 for the past participles of verbs whose stem ends in a vowel, which we repeat here for convenience:

Rule. If an *-er* or *-ir* verb has a stem ending in *-a, -e,* or *-o,* then the ending of the past participle has a written accent (*-ído* rather than *-ido*). For all other cases in which the stem ends in a vowel, no change is made.

The four basic cases covered by this rule are presented below:

	infinitive	past participle	
(i)	caer	caído	[AI: strong/weak, stress falls on weak]
	oír	oído	[OI: strong/weak, stress falls on weak]
(ii)	crear	creado not *creádo	[EA: strong/strong]
(iii)	criar	criado not *criádo	[IA: weak/strong, stress falls on strong]
(iv)	construir	construido not *construído	[UI: weak/weak]

In (i) the fact that the stress falls on the *weak* vowel *-i* allows it to carry a written accent, which in this case clearly distinguishes its independent pronunciation. For *-ar* verbs like *crear,* the two *strong* vowels *-e* and *-a* are automatically pronounced separately (hiatus) without the need for a written accent. For *-ar* verbs like *criar,* where the stress falls on the *strong* vowel *-a,* the *weak/strong* combination *-ia* is *assumed* for the purposes of orthography to be pronounced as a diphthong—even though the majority of speakers pronounce the two vowels separately. The same holds for the *weak/weak* combination *-ui* in *-ir* verbs like *construir.*[7]

Analogous reasoning accounts for the written accents added to the simple past (2s/1p/2p) for *-er* and *-ir* verbs whose stems end in a strong vowel (e.g., *caer, leer, oír, reír*) but not for those whose stems end in a weak vowel (e.g., *construir*).

2s	caíste	leíste	oíste	reíste	construiste
1p	caímos	leímos	oímos	reímos	construimos
2p	caísteis	leísteis	oísteis	reísteis	construisteis

The rules of Spanish orthography *always* assume that *-ui* (and *-iu*) are pronounced as diphthongs.

Such reasoning also explains the presence of (additional) written accents in the present indicative and subjunctive for *reír.*[8]

	indicative	subjunctive
1s	*río*	*ría*
2s	*ríes*	*rías*
3s	*ríe*	*ría*
1p	*reímos*	riamos
2p	reís	riáis
3p	*ríen*	*rían*

A good test of one's comprehension is to see whether one can explain why *reímos* has a written accent but *riamos* does not.[9]

7. Verbs with Two Vowels in Stem: *Reinar* versus *Reunir*

There is a fundamental contrast in the pronunciation of *reinar* ("to reign") compared to *reunir* ("to reunite"). In the first case the two vowels in the stem

---

[7] Until the RAE's orthographical "reform" of 1952, *construido* had in fact been written *construído.* The change had nothing to do with pronunciation but rather with the notion that combinations of the "weak" vowels *u* and *i* should always be assumed to be diphthongs for purposes of orthography. Needless to say, many erroneously interpreted the new spelling as requiring a diphthong *pronunciation.*

[8] As well as the 1p present indicative *oímos* of *oír.*

[9] In *reímos* the stress falls on the *weak* vowel of a strong/weak vowel combination (*re•í•mos*) and hence Spanish orthography requires a written accent. In *riamos* the stress falls on the *strong* vowel in the "expected" syllable (*ri•a•mos* or *ria•mos*), hence no written accent is required (or permitted).

(-*e* and -*i*) are pronounced as part of the same syllable—i.e., they form a diphthong. In the second case the two vowels (-*e* and -*u*) are pronounced separately, i.e., in *hiatus*. Thus, for the infinitive and first person singular present one has (with the stressed syllable in bold):

infinitive	1s present	
rei•**nar**	**rei**•no	2 syllables
re•u•**nir**	re•**ú**•no	3 syllables

One of the important characteristics of the Spanish orthographic system is that it is able to distinguish between these two types of pronunciations *only in those conjugations in which the stress accent falls on the stem*. For the present indicative, *reunir* thus has "separating" written accents on the -*u* for the three singulars and the third person plural, but not for the first or second person plural, nor for the infinitive—where the stress does not fall on the stem.

infinitive		*reinar*	*reunir*
present	1s	reino	reúno
	2s	reinas	reúnes
	3s	reina	reúne
	1p	reinamos	reunimos
	2p	reináis	reunís
	3p	reinan	reúnen

For *reunir,* the lack of written accent on the -*u* in the infinitive and 1p/2p does *not* mean that they are necessarily pronounced as diphthongs, only that the Spanish orthographic system lacks a means of clearly identifying the specific nature of their pronunciation.

> **Rule.** Verbs like *reunir* have a written accent *only* in those conjugations in which the stress accent is on the stem syllable.

A written accent is therefore also found in the present subjunctive (1s/2s/3s/3p) and the *tú* form of the imperative.

Other examples of verbs with stems having a *strong/weak* vowel combination—i.e., whose second element is -*i* or -*u*—include:

	no written accents (diphthong)		written accents in 9 conjugations	
	infinitive	1s present	infinitive	1s present
ai	arraigar	arraigo	aislar	aíslo
	bailar	bailo	enraizar	enraízo
	envainar	envaino	ahincar[10]	ahínco
au	aplaudir	aplaudo	aullar	aúllo
	causar	causo	aunar	aúno
	pausar	pauso	maullar	maúllo
	desahuciar	desahucio	ahumar	ahúmo
ei	afeitar	afeito	descafeinar	descafeíno
	peinar	peino	sobrehilar	sobrehílo
oi	coitar	coito	prohibir	prohíbo
eu	adeudar	adeudo	rehundir	rehúndo

Important Note

The above discussion applies only to cases where the first vowel is "strong" (-*a*, -*e*, or -*o*) and the second one is "weak" (-*i* or -*u*). In all other cases of two adjacent stem vowels there are no written accents: when both vowels are strong (e.g., *coercer*) the pronunciation is as hiatus, while in weak-weak (e.g., *cuidar*) or weak-strong (e.g., *amueblar*) combinations the pronunciation is generally as a diphthong.[11]

8. -*uar* and -*iar* Verbs

A situation very similar to the above occurs for verbs ending in -*uar* or -*iar*. For some of these verbs the two vowels are pronounced separately, for others jointly, and the orthography seeks to distinguish, where permitted, between the two.

---

[10] The letter -*h* has no phonetic value. When it appears in the verb stem between two vowels it is an almost certain indicator that the verb is of the hiatus type (an exception being *desahuciar*—"to give up as hopeless").

[11] *Triunfar, arruinar*, and *orientar* are examples, however, of verbs pronounced by many speakers—in some if not all conjugations—with hiatus pronunciations of the stem. The orthographic rules do not allow such pronunciations to be distinguished: for *triunfar* and *arruinar* since a weak/weak vowel combination is always *assumed* to be a diphthong, for *orientar* since even when the weak vowel -*i* is pronounced separately, the stress still falls on the strong vowel -*e*.

-uar Verbs

There are two patterns: (i) completely regular with no written accents, in which -*u* + *following vowel* is pronounced consistently as a diphthong; and (ii) written accents in certain conjugations, marking a pronunciation of -*u* and the following vowel as part of separate syllables (i.e., *hiatus*) rather than as a diphthong. The first pattern is represented by *adecuar* ("to adapt"), the second by *actuar* ("to actuate").

	present indicative		present subjunctive	
	adecuar	*actuar*	*adecuar*	*actuar*
1s	adecuo	*actúo*	adecue	*actúe*
2s	adecuas	*actúas*	adecues	*actúes*
3s	adecua	*actúa*	adecue	*actúe*
1p	adecuamos	actuamos	adecuemos	actuemos
2p	adecuáis	actuáis	adecuéis	actuéis
3p	adecuan	*actúan*	adecuen	*actúen*

For -*uar* verbs there is a very simple rule for distinguishing between those following the first pattern and those following the second.

> **Rule.** Verbs ending in -*cuar* and -*guar* follow the first pattern (no written accents); all other -*uar* verbs follow the second (written accents in selected conjugations) pattern.

There is an equally simple rule for determining precisely in which conjugations the written accents are placed.

> **Rule.** Verbs following the second pattern display the written accent *only* in those conjugations in which the stress accent is on the stem syllable.

Thus, written accents are found in precisely the same conjugations as in number 7, above: (a) present indicative and subjunctive (1s/2s/3s/3p); and (b) *tú* form of the imperative.

Other examples:

| no written accents (diphthong) | | written accents in 9 conjugations | |
infinitive	1s present	infinitive	1s present
amortiguar	amortiguo	acentuar	acentúo
apaciguar	apaciguo	continuar	continúo
atestiguar	atestiguo	efectuar	efectúo
averiguar	averiguo	evaluar	evalúo
desaguar	desaguo	fluctuar	fluctúo
evacuar	evacuo	habituar	habitúo
menguar	menguo	insinuar	insinúo
santiguar	santiguo	perpetuar	perpetúo

Pronunciation Note

We have seen that verbs like *actuar* and *acentuar* have a written accent for 9 of the 47 basic forms of the verb, indicating that in these cases the *-u* is pronounced as an independent vowel, not as an element of a diphthong, e.g.,

actuar		*adecuar*
ac•**tú**•o	as compared to	ade•**cwo**
ac•**tú**•as	as compared to	ade•**cwas**

Does this mean that in the remaining 38 forms *-u* is pronounced as part of a diphthong? Popular opinion to the contrary, the answer is not necessarily. Analogous to the situation described in number 7, above, for verbs like *reunir,* Spanish orthography simply does not allow a determination of the pronunciation of *-ua,* *-uo,* or *-ue* in a non-stressed syllable. *In general,* for verbs like *actuar* the *-u* is pronounced in hiatus throughout the verb conjugation (including the infinitive), although in less "careful" speech—and perhaps influenced by the absence of written accents—diphthongs tend to emerge for the first and second person plurals.

-iar Verbs

The situation is analogous to that of *-uar* verbs: there are two classes, one with no written accents, the other with written accents in those conjugations in which the stress falls on the stem syllable. *Cambiar* ("to change") is an example of the former, *enviar* ("to send") of the latter.

	present indicative		present subjunctive	
	cambiar	*enviar*	*cambiar*	*enviar*
1s	cambio	*envío*	cambie	*envíe*
2s	cambias	*envías*	cambies	*envíes*
3s	cambia	*envía*	cambie	*envíe*
1p	cambiamos	enviamos	cambiemos	enviemos
2p	cambiáis	enviáis	cambiéis	enviéis
3p	cambian	*envían*	cambien	*envíen*

Unlike the -*uar* verbs, however, there is no simple rule to allow one to determine from the form of the infinitive to which class the verb belongs. However, verbs which diphthong (i.e., no written accents) are more numerous—representing approximately 70 percent of the total—and *tend* to be more easily recognizable, formed from or closely linked to adjectives and nouns.

Other examples:

(a) no written accents (diphthong)

abreviar	"to shorten"	envidiar	"to envy"
aliviar	"to alleviate"	estudiar	"to study"
asociar	"to associate"	incendiar	"to set on fire"
beneficiar	"to benefit"	iniciar	"to initiate"
codiciar	"to covet"	injuriar	"to insult"
copiar	"to copy"	limpiar	"to clean"
denunciar	"to denounce"	odiar	"to hate"
diferenciar	"to differentiate"	pronunciar	"to pronounce"
distanciar	"to distance"	reconciliar	"to reconcile"
divorciar	"to divorce"	refugiar	"to shelter"
ensuciar	"to dirty"	remediar	"to remedy"

(b) written accents in 9 conjugations (hiatus)

ampliar	"to enlarge"	guiar	"to guide"
criar	"to rear"	liar	"to bind"
desviar	"to deviate"	piar	"to chirp"
enfriar	"to chill"	repatriar	"to repatriate"
espiar	"to spy"	vaciar	"to empty"
fiar	"to (en)trust"	variar	"to vary"

For the "ambiguous" pronunciations of the 38 forms of class (b) without written accent, diphthongs seem to be more prevalent than for -*uar* verbs, and sometimes affect the infinitive as well (e.g., *variar*).

9. Combinations of Changes

The verbs *avergonzar* and *traer* provide noteworthy illustrations of the possibility of combining orthographic and other predictable changes within the same verb.

As confirmed by the closely associated noun *vergüenza* ("shame") which diphthongs, *avergonzar* is an *-ar* diphthong verb (basic model *mostrar*). At the same time it offers not one but *two* separate orthographic changes:

(1) $z \rightarrow c$ (model *cazar*)
(2) $gu \rightarrow g\ddot{u}$ in those conjugations in which the diphthong changes the stem vowel from *-o* to *-ue.*

The two orthographic changes and the diphthong occur *simultaneously* in the present subjunctive (three singulars and third person plural):

present indicative	present subjunctive
avergüenzo	*avergüence*
avergüenzas	*avergüences*
avergüenza	*avergüence*
avergonzamos	*avergoncemos*
avergonzáis	*avergoncéis*
avergüenzan	*avergüencen*

Traer combines two irregularities with three regular orthographic modifications:

Irregularity	1st person singular *-go*	*traigo*
	simple past	*traje*
Orthographic	#3 unstressed *-i* between vowels $\rightarrow$ *-y*	*trayendo*
	#5b irregular verbs with *-j* omit 1st element of following *-ie*	e.g., *trajeron*
	#6 additional written accent for past participle	*traído*

Appendix
Recent Changes Affecting Verbs like *Reír, Criar,* and *Huir*

The Real Academia Española has recently implemented an orthographic change affecting a number of very short verbs. While not much attention has yet been paid to this change, over time—unless rescinded—it is likely to cause some confusion.

The change can best be explained by comparing the simple past tense conjugations, and pronunciations, of *sonreír* ("to smile") and *reír* ("to laugh"). The stressed syllable is shown in bold.

1s	sonreí	reí	son•re•**í**	re•**í**
2s	sonreíste	reíste	son•re•**ís**•te	re•**ís**•te
3s	sonrió	rió	son•ri•**ó** *or* son•**rió**	ri•**ó** *or* **rió**
1p	sonreímos	reímos	son•re•**í**•mos	re•**í**•mos
2p	sonreísteis	reísteis	son•re•**ís**•teis	re•**ís**•teis
3p	sonrieron	rieron	son•**rie**•ron	**rie**•ron

For the third person singular there is an ambiguity in the pronunciation.[12] *Most* Spanish speakers use the *hiatus* forms *son•ri•ó* and *ri•ó* . Spanish orthography, however, is incapable of distinguishing between the hiatus and diphthong pronunciations, since the written accent on the *-o* serves only to indicate that the stress falls on the final syllable, *not* whether the combination *-io* is to be pronounced as a *diphthong* or *hiatus*.

In its 1999 *Ortografía de la Lengua Española*, the RAE attempted to resolve this ambiguity by decreeing that, *for the purposes of orthography only,* such ambiguous situations are assumed to represent diphthongs *independent of the actual pronunciation of the word.* Thus for the third person singular, the "assumed" pronunciations are now *son•rió* (2 syllables) and *rió* (1 syllable). For *rió* this creates a small problem: as an (assumed) one-syllable word it no longer has the right to a written accent—whose purpose is to identify the stressed syllable in a word of two or more syllables—and it has therefore been eliminated. For *sonreír,* on the other hand, the written accent is still required to signal that the stress is on the final syllable (independent of whether that syllable is *-io* or *-o*). Thus, according to the RAE's new norms, there is now a contrast between the forms of *sonreír* and *refreír* on the one hand, *reír* and *freír* on the other:

simple past 3s	sonrió	*rio*
	refrió	*frio*

A similar contrast exists in the second person plural of the present subjunctive, where *riáis* and *friáis* have relinquished their written accent:[13]

present subjunctive 2p	sonriáis	*riais*
	refriáis	*friais*

---

[12] While there is also ambiguity for the third person plural (*ri•e•ron* or **rie**•ron), this has no effect on the orthography and will not be considered here.

[13] The logic is the following: the combination *-iai* consists of the weak vowel *-i* and the diphthong *-ai*. Since the stress falls on the diphthong and not on the weak vowel, the (orthographic) assumption is that the two elements are enunciated as a single vowel, i.e., that they form a *triphthong* and hence that *riais* has only one syllable. In the contrasting case of *roáis* (*roer*), since the *strong* vowel *-o* is assumed to be pronounced in a separate syllable from the following diphthong, a written accent is required to show that *ro•áis* is stressed on the second syllable and not the first (**ro•ais*).

Other verbs affected by this change are the simple past and present tenses for "short" -*iar* and -*uir* verbs.

SIMPLE PAST

	old forms		new forms	
	1s	3s	1s	3s
criar	crié	crió	*crie*	*crio*
fiar	fié	fió	*fie*	*fio*
guiar	guié	guió	*guie*	*guio*
liar	lié	lió	*lie*	*lio*
piar	pié	pió	*pie*	*pio*
fluir	fluí	fluyó	*flui*	*fluyó*
huir	huí	huyó	*hui*	*huyó*

PRESENT TENSE, 2P

	old forms		new forms	
	indicative	subjunctive	indicative	subjunctive
criar	criáis	criéis	*criais*	*crieis*
fiar	fiáis	fiéis	*fiais*	*fieis*
guiar	guiáis	guiéis	*guiais*	*guieis*
liar	liáis	liéis	*liais*	*lieis*
piar	piáis	piéis	*piais*	*pieis*
fluir	fluís	fluyáis	*fluis*	*fluyáis*
huir	huís	huyáis	*huis*	*huyáis*

Note that for the "short" -*uir* verbs the (multi-syllable) 3s simple past and 2p present subjunctive have not changed. Related compound verbs—*malcriar, confiar, desliar, influir, rehuir*, etc.—are not affected by the new rules.

A New Ambiguity in Place of the Old

The RAE was aware of the potential problem of public acceptance of this change and has therefore sought to satisfy both its logical instincts and public preferences by permitting, under certain circumstances, *both* the new and old spellings. Thus (italics added):

> …algunas palabras que antes de esta fecha se consideraban bisílabas pasan ahora a ser consideradas monosílabas a efectos de acentuación gráfica, por contener alguna de las secuencias vocálicas antes señaladas, y, como consecuencia de ello, deben escribirse sin tilde … No obstante, *es admisible acentuar gráficamente estas palabras, por ser agudas acabadas en -n, -s o vocal, si quien escribe articula nítidamente como*

hiatos las secuencias vocálicas que contienen y, en consecuencia, las considera bisílabas:
fié, huí, riáis, guión, truhán, etc.[14]

...some words which before this date were considered disyllabic [having two syl-
lables] are now considered to be monosyllabic for the purposes of written accentuation, on account of their containing one of the vowel sequences signaled above, and,
in consequence, they should be written without an accent.... Notwithstanding, *it is*
permitted to use a written accent with these words, on account of their being stressed
on the final syllable and ending in -n, -s, or vowel, *so long as whoever does this articu-*
lates very clearly as hiatuses the vowel sequences they contain and, in consequence, con-
siders them to be disyllabic: fié, huí, riáis, guión, truhán, etc.

Thus if you not only pronounce (inadvertently or otherwise) *rió/rio* and *fié/fie* with two
syllables but truly *consider* them to be two-syllable words, you have the right to use the old
spelling; otherwise only the new spelling is acceptable.

---

[14] From the RAE's online *Diccionario panhispánico de dudas* (<www.rae.es>, July 2004), section
1.2 (*Tilde²*). The RAE notes that the diphthong pronunciation "is predominant in wide zones of Latin
America, especially in Mexico and in Central America, while in other Latin American countries such
as Argentina, Ecuador, Colombia and Venezuela, as well as in Spain" the hiatus pronunciation is more
common.

CHAPTER 8
Vosotros/Ustedes and *Tuteo/Voseo*

As noted in the Introduction, one of the most noticeable differences between the Spanish spoken in Spain and that spoken in the Americas is the contrast in how one says "you":

	Spain		*Americas*	
	singular	plural	singular	plural
familiar	tú	***vosotros***	tú/***vos***	ustedes
formal	usted	ustedes	usted	ustedes

In the *formal* sense, the treatment is identical: *usted* for the singular, *ustedes* for the plural. However, for *familiar* (or "informal") *you*, usage *always* differs for the plural, and *often* for the singular.

Familiar Plural: *Vosotros* versus *Ustedes*

American Spanish uniformly uses *ustedes* along with its associated pronouns, while the Spanish of Spain uses *vosotros* and its associated pronouns. One thus has the following contrasts:

Spain	Latin America (All)	
Vosotros cantáis muy bien.	*Ustedes cantan* muy bien.	"You sing very well."
Os levantáis temprano.	*Ustedes se levantan* temprano.	"You get up early."
Salís temprano.	*Ustedes salen* temprano.	"You leave early."
Esto es para *vosotros*.	Esto es para *ustedes*.	"This is for you."
Vengo con *vosotros*.	Vengo con *ustedes*.	"I come with you."
Os veo.	*Los* veo (a ustedes).	"I see you."
Os doy un regalo.	*Les* doy un regalo (*a ustedes*).	"I give you a present."

Familiar Singular: *Tuteo* versus *Voseo*

Here the situation is considerably more complicated. In somewhere between one third to one half of the Americas, *vos* is used—instead of or in addition to *tú*—a practice known as *voseo* (compared to Spanish *tuteo*). Somewhat surprisingly, the object pronoun used for direct/indirect objects is *te* rather than *vos* (or *os*), while *vos* is used following prepositions. Thus one has:

Spain + Latin America (*tuteo*)	Latin America (*voseo*)	
Tú cantas muy bien.	*Vos cantás* muy bien.	"You sing very well."
Te levantas temprano.	*Te levantás* temprano.	"You get up early."
Sales temprano.	*Salís* temprano.	"You leave early."
Esto es para *tí*.	Esto es para *vos*.	"This is for you."
Vengo *contigo*.	Vengo *con vos*.	"I come with you."
Te veo.	*Te* veo.	"I see you."
Te doy un regalo.	*Te* doy un regalo.	"I give you a present."

The verb forms used with *vos* are generally those of *vosotros* but simplified by reducing the *diphthong* (-*áis* or -*éis*) to a simple vowel (-*ás*, -*és*). For -*ar* and -*er* verbs this produces the corresponding *tú* verb form of normal Spanish. However, in the three forms in which there is a different pattern of stress accentuation for the *tú* and *vosotros* forms—the present indicative, present subjunctive and imperative—*voseo* practitioners generally maintain the *vosotros* stress pattern. This is illustrated below, with the traditional Spanish (*tuteo*) forms shown in parentheses.

	cantar	*comer*	*subir*
present indicative	cantás (cantas)	comés (comes)	subís (subes)
present subjunctive	cantés (cantes)	comás (comas)	subás (subas)
imperative	cantá (canta)	comé (come)	subí (sube)

1. The *voseo* forms for the present subjunctive are utilized less widely than the other two and are often seen as less "cultured." Under pressure from some of the American academies, the Real Academia Española has given official status to the *voseo* forms for the present indicative and imperative, but not for the present subjunctive.
2. There are many variants. In some areas, the diphthong is maintained (*vos cantáis, coméis*). Some *voseo* speakers use the personal pronoun *vos* but with the normal Spanish second-person singular verbs (*cantas* rather than *cantás*). Still others use the personal pronoun *tú* but with the *voseo* verbs (e.g., *tú cantás*).

Finally, it is worth noting that in post-Franco Spain *tú* has become omnipresent, even in advertisements. This marks a dramatic reversal: English "how to learn Spanish" books in the 1950s and 1960s frequently omitted or paid scant attention to *tú* on the grounds that a foreigner would likely never have the opportunity to use it.

Appendix
Historical Background

In Latin the distinction between TU and vos was purely singular versus plural. Apart from being somewhat egotistical (it was EGO ET TU, "I and you", compared to *tú y yo* in Spanish), Romans were, at least initially, egalitarian in treating all "second" persons equally. The distinction between what can be called *formal* "you" and *familiar* "you" arose during the early Middle Ages and is characteristic of many European languages, including the Romance languages, German, and Middle English. It seems to have arisen out of the requirement to address one's superior in a more respectful manner, e.g., "Would his lordship like to have his pudding now?" The lord would of course continue to address his subjects in the familiar way, much as today a French school teacher or prison guard will use the familiar *tu* in addressing his or her wards and expect to receive the formal *vous* in return.

At an early stage Spanish usage was similar to that of modern French,[1] as the plural pronoun *vos* came to be used in the singular with a *formal* sense while maintaining its role as the unique plural (both formal and informal).

OLD SPANISH		
	singular	plural
familiar	tú	vos
formal	vos	vos

Vos then began to encroach on the one remaining form of "you" not yet conquered, the singular *familiar* form *tú*. This was probably an overreach on its part, for its increasing use in a familiar sense provided the opportunity in the fifteenth century for a new *formal* "you" to develop: *vuestra merced* (pl. *vuestras mercedes*), which can be translated into English as "your grace" or "your lordship/ladyship". Through a process of evolution, passing through various stages including *vuesa merced, vuesarced, vuced,* and *vusted,* this arrived at the modern Spanish form *usted* (pl. *ustedes*). In formal correspondence one frequently finds these terms abbreviated, either *Vd.* and *Vds.,* or *Ud.* and *Uds.* As in the formal form of address in English ("Is your ladyship happy with her meal?"), a *third-person* verb is used with both *usted* and *ustedes*—singular for the former, plural for the latter.

At the same time that *vos* was losing out to *usted* (and *ustedes*) for the formal market, its use in the familiar sense as *both* a singular (in competition with *tú*) and plural led to

---

[1] In French, *vous* is used for either a group of people—formal or familiar—or for one person in a formal setting.

the development of a new *plural* familiar form, *vosotros* (*vos* + *otros,* "you others"). At the time of Cervantes (1547–1616) the situation was thus:

"GOLDEN AGE" SPANISH

	singular	plural
familiar	tú/vos	vosotros
formal	vuestra merced	vuestras mercedes

It is interesting to note that *merced* did not initially mean "grace" or "lordship/ladyship" but rather "wages", "payment", or "reward". It was with this latter meaning, expanded metaphorically in a religious context,[2] that it passed into French as *merci* (now restricted to "thank you") and thence into English as *mercy*. The original sense has been preserved in *mercenary* (Sp. *mercenario*).

The "we" pronoun, while not facing any serious competition, analogously shifted from *nos* to *nosotros*. While *nosotros* has survived in all forms of Spanish, *vosotros* has had considerably less success: it has been replaced in much of Andalucia, in the Canary Islands, and in all of Latin America by *ustedes*.[3]

The only domain left to *vos* was the familiar singular "you", where it remained in heated competition with the original *tú*. In Spain, *tú* was victorious and today is used almost universally to refer to a singular "you" with whom one is on familiar terms. However, much of Spanish-speaking America was colonized when *vos* was still flourishing in Spain, so that a substantial portion uses *vos* (Argentina, Uruguay, most of Central America, and parts of most of the other countries). There are in addition a not insubstantial number of people who use both *tú* and *vos* as familiar singular "you", though not necessarily in the same context.

English "You"

In Old English, as in Latin, there were separate singular and plural forms for "you": *thou* and *ye* in the nominative, and *thee* and *you* for the accusative (and dative). *You* was thus initially used only as an object, not as the subject:

> *Thou* art a good man.
> I gave it to *thee.*
> *Ye* are good men.
> I gave it to *you.*

---

[2] I.e., the reward in heaven which one earns (on earth) by being kind to those who are not in a position to offer anything in return.

[3] The similarity of American Spanish with that of the Canaries and Andalucia is no coincidence, as a disproportionate share of colonists either originated from these areas or spent considerable time there en route to the Americas.

The evolution of *you* in Middle English was analogous to what occurred in both French and Spanish: the plural *ye/you* replaced the singular *thou/thee* for formal use. Subsequently, in early Modern English, *ye/you* replaced *thou/thee* for informal use as well. The distinction between nominative and accusative lasted until the seventeenth century and is found in the King James Bible:

> And Isaac said unto them, Wherefore come *ye* to me, seeing *ye* hate me, and have sent me away from *you*? (Genesis 26:27)

The evolution of "you" as described above can be summarized as follows:

	familiar		*formal*	
	singular	plural	singular	plural
Classical Latin	TU	VOS	TU	VOS
Old Spanish	tú	vos	vos	vos
"Golden Age" Spanish	tú/vos	vosotros	vuestra merced	vuestras mercedes
Modern Spanish				
Spain	tú	vosotros	usted	ustedes
Americas	tú/vos	ustedes	usted	ustedes
Modern French	tu	vous	vous	vous
Old English				
nominative	thou	ye	thou	ye
dative & accusative	thee	you	thee	you
Middle English				
nominative	thou	ye	ye	ye
dative & accusative	thee	you	you	you
Modern English	you	you	you	you

CHAPTER 9
Summary and Presentation of Verb Classes

Spanish verbs can essentially be classified as follows:

> **Basically regular verbs** are those with regular simple past tenses and include verbs that
> (a) are (perfectly) regular
> (b) are predictably regular
> (c) are irregular in the first person singular present, but otherwise (largely) predictable
> (d) have mixed patterns
> **Fundamentally irregular verbs** are those 17 with irregular simple past tenses.

Certain basic patterns facilitate considerably the learning of the individual verb forms.

Imperfect

For all but three verbs—*ser, ir, ver*—the imperfect is completely regular.

Future/Conditional

The future and conditional always share the same stem. There are 12 verbs which have truncated stems not equal to the infinitive, of which all except *salir* and *valer* are "fundamentally irregular" verbs.

Present Subjunctive

Only four verbs have "unpredictable" present subjunctives—*ser, ir, haber,* and *saber.* Predictably regular verbs (including those with irregular first person singular present indicative) have well-defined patterns for their present subjunctives, while each of the "mixed pattern" verbs follows its own particular pattern (see below).

Imperfect Subjunctive

The imperfect subjunctive stem of *all* verbs is equal to the third person plural simple past *minus* the final *-ron*.

Present Imperative

All verbs have regular imperatives for the second person plural. Nine verbs have irregular one-syllable imperatives for the second person singular.

Present Participle

All verbs have regular present participles, with the single exception of *poder* (*pudiendo*).

Past Participle

Apart from the simple past, the past participle is the least regular of the verb forms. Fourteen verbs have irregular past participles, of which 11 are from the basically regular category.

Orthographic Changes

Consonant changes are obligatory, in the sense that they always occur in the prescribed circumstances. While this is not always the case with written accent modifications, knowledge of the form of the first person singular present is always sufficient for determining the entire conjugation.

Below are presented 35 categories or classes into which all Spanish verbs can be placed. Annex A presents the complete conjugations for model verbs in each of the categories, as well as highlighting the changes for sub-classes which display orthographic modifications or have irregular past participles. Annex B provides an alphabetical index of approximately 4,800 verbs, showing for each its class and, where applicable, sub-class.

Basically Regular: Verbs Having Regular Simple Past

I. Perfectly regular

    1. cantar   2. comer   3. subir

II. Predictably regular

A. *Diphthongs* (*e* →*ie, o* →*ue*) and/or *umlauts* (*e* →*i, o* →*u*) of
stem vowel

4A. pensar	4B. mostrar	
5A. perder	5B. mover	
6A. sentir	6B. pedir	6C. dormir

B. First person singular -*zco*

7A. conocer	(most verbs ending in -*cer*)
7B. lucir	(all verbs ending in -*ucir*)[1]

C. Add -*y* **except before -***i*

8. construir

III. Irregular first person singular -*go* **but otherwise (largely) predictable**

9. caer	10. oír	11. salir	12. valer	(13. asir)[2]

IV. Mixed patterns

14. ver	15. discernir	16. jugar	17. adquirir	18. argüir

Fundamentally Irregular: Irregular Simple Past Tense

19. ser	20. estar	21. haber	22. saber	23. caber
24. ir	25. dar	26. poder	27. querer	28. decir
29. hacer	30. poner	31. tener	32. venir	33. traer
34. -ducir	35. andar			

Observations

I. Perfectly Regular

Six otherwise "perfectly regular" verbs—none of which is an -*ar* verb—have irregular past participles: *romper, abrir, cubrir, escribir, imprimir,* and *pudrir.*

II. Predictably Regular Verbs

1. Four otherwise "predictably" regular verbs have irregular past participles: *resolver, volver, freír, morir.*

---

[1] Verbs ending in -*ducir* additionally have irregular simple past tenses and hence are classified as a separate class (34).

[2] As noted in Chapter 2, for *asir* the conjugations with -*g* are generally avoided.

2. *-ar* and *-er* diphthong verbs (4A/B, 5A/B) have diphthongs in the 9 conjugations in which the stress falls on the stem syllable:

	pensar/perder	*mostrar/mover*
present indicative (1s/2s/3s/3p)	ie	ue
present subjunctive (1s/2s/3s/3p)	ie	ue
imperative (2s)	ie	ue

Such verbs can generally be identified through the existence of a closely related noun or adjective whose stressed vowel has the same diphthong (e.g. *almorzar* "to lunch" and *almuerzo* "lunch"). Where no such help is available (e.g., *descender*), knowledge of the first person singular present (*desciendo*) is sufficient to determine the entire conjugation.

3. For *-ir* verbs, the *regla milagrosa* cited in Chapter 2 allows one to determine whether a given verb with stem vowel *-e* is of the mixed diphthong/umlaut (6A) or umlaut alone (6B) types. Of the three common *-ir* verbs with stem vowel *-o*, *dormir* and *morir* are of the mixed diphthong/umlaut type (6C).[3] For all of these verbs, 20 of the 47 conjugations are affected, as follows:

REGULAR VS. "PREDICTABLY" IRREGULAR CONJUGATIONS				
	total	regular	diphthong	umlaut
sentir/dormir	47	27	9	11
pedir	47	27	0	20

An extension of *la regla milagrosa* defines the precise conjugations in which these "predictable" irregularities occur:

La regla milagrosa (extended)

A. For verbs with conjugations like *pedir* (6B), the stem vowel "umlauts" (*e* → *i*) *unless* the following vowel is *-i*.

B. For verbs with conjugations like *sentir* (6A), as well as *dormir/morir* (6C), the stem vowel:
   (i) diphthongs (*e* → *ie* or *o* → *ue*) whenever it is stressed (i.e., in exactly the same conjugations as for 4A/B, 5A/B);
   (ii) otherwise it "umlauts" (*e* → *i* or *o* → *u*) *unless* the following vowel is *-i*.

---

[3] *Oír* (10) has neither diphthongs nor umlauts.

The stem vowel contrast in unstressed syllables is perhaps best illustrated by the first person plural present indicative and subjunctive:

pedimos	*sentimos*	*dormimos*	where the following vowel is *-i*
pidamos	*sintamos*	*durmamos*	where the following vowel is *-a*

Note that a *diphthong* in the next syllable involving *-i* does *not* prevent umlaut,[4] thus providing the contrasts:

pedí	*sentí*	*dormí*	where the following vowel is *-i*
pidió	*sintió*	*durmió*	where the following vowel is the diphthong *-io*
pedido	*sentido*	*dormido*	where the following vowel is *-i*
pidiendo	*sintiendo*	*durmiendo*	where the following vowel is the diphthong *-ie*

The conjugations in which these predictable changes take place are:

	sentir	*pedir*	*dormir*
present indicative (1s/2s/3s/3p)	ie	i	ue
simple past (3s/3p)	i	i	u
present subjunctive (1s/2s/3s/3p)	ie	i	ue
present subjunctive (1p/2p)	i	i	u
imperfect subjunctive (all 6)	i	i	u
imperative (2s)	ie	i	ue
present participle	i	i	u

4. For *-ocer* and *-ucir* verbs (7A/B) with first person singular present *-zco*, the *-zc* propagates itself to all 6 forms of the present subjunctive.[5]

5. For verbs like *construir* which "add *-y* except before *-i*", *-y* is added to 11 conjugations: present indicative (singulars and 3p), present subjunctive (all 6), and *tú* imperative. In addition, a regular orthographic change (e.g., *constru[i]endo* → *construyendo*) introduces a *-y* into 9 other conjugations: simple past (3s/3p), imperfect subjunctive (all 6), and present participle.

---

[4] Since "-i" in this case has the phonetic value of the consonant "Y".
[5] This holds as well for the *-ducir* verbs (34).

III. Irregular First Person Singular *-go* but Otherwise (Largely) Predictable

The first person singular present *-go* propagates itself to all 6 forms of the present subjunctive. *Oír, salir,* and *valer* have additional irregularities:

(1) *Oír* "adds *-y* except before *-i*" (like *construir*).
(2) *Salir* and *valer* have modified future/conditional stems (*saldr-, valdr-*).
(3) *Salir* has a shortened *tú* imperative *sal.*

IV. Mixed Patterns

1. *Ver* used to be *veer* and has maintained the additional *-e* in the following conjugations: first person singular present, imperfect (all 6), and present subjunctive (all 6). *Ver* also has an irregular past participle *visto.*

2. *Discernir* used to be *discerner* and behaves throughout its conjugation as if it were an *-er* diphthong verb (model *perder*). Viewed in this sense, the only "irregularities" are the second *-i* in the infinitive, the 1p/2p present indicative, and the 2p imperative.

3. *Jugar* has 9 diphthongs *-ue* in exactly the same locations where diphthong verbs (e.g., *mostrar*) have such diphthongs. *Jugar* in fact used to be *jogar;* it subsequently changed the stem vowel *-o* to *-u* while leaving intact the diphthongs *-ue.*

4. *Adquirir* is analogous to *jugar*. Previously it was *adquerir* with 9 regular *-ie* diphthongs (model *sentir*). It subsequently changed the stem vowel *-e* (including that of the infinitive) to *-i,* while leaving intact the diphthongs *-ie.*

5. *Argüir* essentially follows the model of *construir:* add *-y* except before *-i.* The complication is that the combination *-güy,* with pronunciation "GWY", would be virtually unpronounceable, hence it is changed to *-guy.*

Summary Tables

The three tables below provide summary information for essentially all of the "unpredictable" irregularities found in Spanish verbs.

Table 9.1 highlights the basic irregularities for the 17 "fundamentally" irregular verbs which have irregular simple pasts. The present indicatives for *poder* and *querer* are shown in parentheses since they are "predictable" diphthongs. Similarly, present subjunctive forms are shown in parentheses in those cases—e.g., *(quepa)*—in which they are "regularly" based on the first person singular present indicative. The present subjunctive for *dar* is shown in brackets *[dé]* since it has an orthographic written accent in the first and third person singulars.

Table 9.2 shows irregularities for *ver* and for the 4 principal "basically regular" verbs which have irregular first person singulars ending in *-go: caer, oír, salir,* and *valer.* The present subjunctives are shown in parentheses, since they are regularly based on the first person singular present indicative.

Table 9.3 shows the remaining 10 verbs with irregular past participles.

TABLE 9.1. FUNDAMENTAL IRREGULARITIES: SEVENTEEN VERBS WITH IRREGULAR SIMPLE PASTS

infinitive	present indicative		simple past	imperfect	past participle	future stem	subjunctive	imperative
	1s	other conjugations	1s	1s			present 1s	2s
ser	soy	eres/es/somos/sois/son	fui (3s: fue)	era	—	—	sea	sé
estar	estoy	estás (etc.)	estuve	—	—	—	(esté)	—
haber	he	has/ha/hemos/—/han	hube	—	—	habr-	haya	he
saber	sé	—	supe	—	—	sabr-	sepa	—
caber	quepo	—	cupe	—	—	cabr-	(quepa)	—
ir	voy	vas (etc.)	fui (3s: fue)	iba	—	—	vaya	ve
dar	doy	—	di (3s: dio)	—	—	—	[dé]	—
poder[1]	(puedo)	—	pude	—	—	podr-	(pueda)	—
querer	(quiero)	—	quise	—	—	querr-	(quiera)	—
decir	digo	—	dije	—	dicho	dir-	(diga)	di
hacer	hago	—	hice (3s: hizo)	—	hecho	har-	(haga)	haz
poner	pongo	—	puse	—	puesto	pondr-	(ponga)	pon
tener	tengo	tienes . . . tenemos	tuve	—	—	tendr-	(tenga)	ten
venir	vengo	vienes . . . venimos	vine	—	—	vendr-	(venga)	ven
traer	traigo	—	traje	—	—	—	(traiga)	—
-ducir	-duzco	—	-duje	—	—	—	(-duzca)	—
andar	—	—	anduve	—	—	—	—	—

[1]*Poder* also has irregular present participle *pudiendo*.

TABLE 9.2. *VER* + FOUR "BASICALLY" REGULAR VERBS WITH FIRST PERSON SINGULAR PRESENT -g[1]

infinitive	present indicative		simple past	imperfect	past participle	future stem	subjunctive	imperative
	1s	other conjugations	1s	1s			present 1s	
ver	veo	—	—	veía	visto	—	(vea)	—
caer	caigo	—	—	—	—	—	(caiga)	—
oír	oigo	oyes . . . oímos . . .	—	—	—	—	(oiga)	—
salir	salgo	—	—	—	—	saldr-	(salga)	sal
valer	valgo	—	—	—	—	valdr-	(valga)	—

[1]*Caer* and *oír* in addition display several regular orthographic modifications.

TABLE 9.3. TEN OTHER VERBS WITH IRREGULAR PAST PARTICIPLE

abrir	abierto	**morir**	muerto
cubrir	cubierto	**pudrir**	podrido
escribir	escrito	**resolver**	resuelto
freír	frito, freído	**romper**	roto
imprimir	impreso, imprimido	**volver**	vuelto

PART II

USES OF VERBS

CHAPTER 10
Indicative

Present Tense

The Spanish present tense is used in virtually the same way as in English:

"True" present:

Canta la canción.	"He/she/it *sings* the song."
Comes con mucha prisa.	"You *eat* in a big hurry."
Subo las escaleras muy despacio.	"I *climb* the stairs very slowly."
El chico *lee* el libro.	"The boy *reads* the book."

To describe permanent situations or habitual actions:

Nunca *fuma* ni *bebe.*	"He/she never *drinks* nor *smokes.*"
Los caballos *comen* hierba.	"Horses *eat* grass."
En nuestra casa *comemos* a las tres.	"In our house we *eat* at three o'clock."
En invierno los días *son* muy cortos.	"In winter the days *are* very short."

To describe future activities:

Mañana *subimos* al Everest.	"Tomorrow we *climb* Everest."
¿Adónde *vas* este verano?	"Where *are you going* this summer?"
Voy a España.	"I *am going* to Spain."

To narrate activities from the past:

Y en ese momento César *toma* su decisión, *pasa* el Rubicón y *avanza* con su ejército hacia Roma.

"And in that moment Caesar *takes* his decision, *crosses* the Rubicon, and *advances* with his troops towards Rome."

Past Tense: Simple and Compound, and Past Participle

In general, the simple and compound pasts are used in very similar manners in English and Spanish.

Simple Past

Colón *descubrió* América en 1492.	"Columbus *discovered* America in 1492."
Tomé el primer avión y *llegué* a mediodía.	"I *took* the first plane and *arrived* at noon."
El año pasado *visité* Granada.	"Last year I *visited* Granada."
Franco *murió* en 1975.	"Franco *died* in 1975."

Compound Past

He visitado tres veces Granada.	"I *have visited* Granada three times."
Hemos trabajado todo el día.	"We *have worked* all day."
Juan, *¿has hecho* todos tus deberes?	"Juan, *have you done* all your homework?"
Siempre *he tenido* mucha suerte.	"I *have* always *had* a lot of luck."

In both languages, the theoretical difference governing the use of the two tenses is that the *simple past* refers to a period of time which has completely expired, while the *compound past* refers to a period which still exists at the moment of speaking.

REMOTE PAST		PRESENT
simple past	compound past →	

In practice, there is of course a large gray area where both can be used and the choice of one or the other is largely a matter of personal choice and desired nuance, e.g.,

I *have studied* all day.
I *studied* all day.
I *have* already *been* to Europe [in 1965].
I *went* to Europe last year.

There is a considerable difference between usage in Spain and that in the Americas: in Spain the compound past tense is generally used whenever there is a connection, however tenuous, with the present, while in American Spanish the more common practice is to always use the simple past unless referring to a situation very *directly* linked to the present.

Spain (generally)

He leído el periódico hoy.	"I *have read* the newspaper today."
He tenido muchas malas experiencias en mi vida.	"I *have had* a lot of unpleasant experiences in my life."
He ido al cine tres veces esta semana.	"I *have gone* to the movies three times this week."

Americas (generally)

Leí el periódico hoy.	"I *read* the newspaper today."
Tuve muchas malas experiencias en mi vida.	"I [have] *had* a lot of unpleasant experiences in my life."
Fui al cine tres veces esta semana.	"I *went* to the movies three times this week."

The usage in Spain is not dictated simply by how long ago the action took place. Thus, with *ayer* ("yesterday") the simple past is generally used, while the compound past can be used with reference to situations where the action took place many years ago (e.g., "earlier this century . . ."). Even in Spain there seems to be some movement toward greater use of the simple at the expense of the compound past, to judge by warnings in manuals of "proper" Spanish:

ABUSO DEL PRETÉRITO INDEFINIDO O PERFECTO SIMPLE
Los titulares de la prensa y las emisiones radiadas peninsulares han dado en preferir el perfecto simple para hechos recientes o inmediatos que en el uso espontáneo . . . se expresan con el perfecto compuesto: *Llegó a Madrid el equipo de la Juventus; Oyeron ustedes "Los clásicos de la canción"* . . . en este resurgimiento—arcaizante para el sentir lingüístico del español medio—parecen haberse juntado influjos del inglés estadounidense y del español americano, uno y otro apegados al perfecto simple.[1]

ABUSE OF INDEFINITE PRETERITE OR SIMPLE PAST
The headlines of the peninsular [i.e., Spanish] press and broadcast emissions have shown a preference for the simple past for recent or immediate events which in spontaneous (natural) use are expressed with the compound past: "The team of Juventus arrived in Madrid"; "You heard 'the classics of song'[?]" . . . In this resurgence—archaic sounding for the average Spanish

---

[1] Rafael Lapesa, *El español moderno y contemporáneo* (Barcelona: Crítica, 1996), quoted in Manuel Casado, *El Castellano actual: Usos y normas* (Pamplona: Ediciones Universidad de Navarra, 1997), p. 89; translation mine.

ear—there seems to be a mixture of influence of U.S. English and American Spanish, both attached to the simple past.

Past Participle as Adjective

As in English, the past participle can be used adjectivally, in which case it agrees with the noun it modifies in both gender and number.

el tesoro *robado*	"the *stolen* treasure"
con los ojos *cerrados*	"with the [his] eyes *closed*"
Aprobada la propuesta,	"The proposition *approved,* the
se levantó la sesión.	meeting adjourned."

Alternative Past Participles

During the transition from Latin to Spanish, the large majority of irregular Latin past participles were regularized. While displaced from their role as participles, a number of the original irregular forms have survived and have become ordinary Modern Spanish *adjectives.* Thus, the adjective *confuso* exists alongside the regular past participle *confundido, incluso* alongside *incluido,* etc. In some cases the meaning of the adjective has come to differ from that of the related past participle, e.g.:

adjective		past participle	
atento	"attentive"	atendido	(well/badly) "looked after"
convicto	"convicted"	convencido	"convinced"
correcto	"correct"	corregido	"corrected"
distinto	"distinct", "different"	distinguido	"distinguished"
tuerto	"one-eyed"	torcido	"twisted", "crooked"

In these cases there is no danger of confusion between the two forms which can both be used as adjectives, e.g.,

Es un esposo muy *atento.*	"He is a very *attentive* husband."
Es un esposo muy *atendido.*	"He is a very *well looked after* husband."
El libro es *correcto.*	"The book is *correct.*"
El libro está *corregido.*	"The book is *corrected*" [i.e., has previously been corrected].
Es un hombre muy *distinguido.*	"He is a very *distinguished* man."
Es un hombre muy *distinto.*	"He is a very *different* man."

El cuadro está *torcido*.	"The picture is *crooked*."
En tierra de ciegos el *tuerto* es rey.	"In the land of the blind the *one-eyed* man is king."

In other cases the meanings are virtually the same, in which case the general practice in adjectival constructions is to use the adjectival (i.e., irregular) form rather than the (regular) past participle. Common examples are:

		past participle	adjective
confundir	"to confuse"	confundido	confuso
despertar	"to wake (up)"	despertado	despierto
elegir	"to elect"	elegido	electo
fijar	"to (af)fix"	fijado	fijo
freír	"to fry"	frito/freído	frito
hartar	"to satiate"	hartado	harto
imprimir	"to print"	impreso/imprimido	impreso
juntar	"to join"	juntado	junto
soltar	"to loosen", "to let go of"	soltado	suelto
suspender	"to suspend"	suspendido	suspenso

Thus one generally says

estoy *despierto*	not *despertado*	"I am awake"
el presidente *electo*	not *elegido*	"the president-elect"
con los ojos *fijos* en ella	not *fijados*	"with his eyes fixed on her"
estoy *harto*	not *hartado*	"I'm fed up"
el libro *impreso*	not *imprimido*	"the printed book"
dar rienda *suelta*	not *soltada*	"to give free rein"

The use of double participles is an area of rapid change, generally in favor of the regular forms. For example, today one says almost equally

los animales *extinguidos*   **or**   los animales *extintos*

whereas in the past the use of *extinguido* in this context would have been seen as bad form.

Historical and Usage Note: Development of Compound Past

The Latin *perfect* tense was used to convey the meanings of both the simple ("remote") and compound ("near") pasts. During the evolution to Romance languages, the perfect came to specialize in the remote past and gave birth to the Romance simple past tense. To express the near past, the Romance languages came up with a structure analogous to that used in English, i.e., the combination of the auxiliary verb "to have" with the past participle. In fact it was a relatively short step from expressions of the form

I *have* two books already *written.*

to the formal compound past

Ya *he escrito* dos libros.   "I *have written* two books already."

Before settling on this form, Spanish experimented with a number of other auxiliary verbs conveying similar notions of something already accomplished, notably *tener* (possession) and *llevar* ("to bring"). Such constructions continue to be employed occasionally, particularly when one wants to stress the immediacy of the past action, e.g.,

Tengo los ojos *cerrados.*   "I *have* my eyes *closed.*"
(or: tengo cerrados los ojos)
Llevamos ahorrados dos mil pesos.   "We *have saved* 2,000 pesos."

Unlike the formal compound past with auxiliary *haber,* "informal" constructions with other auxiliaries require agreement between the past participle and the direct object it modifies, in terms of gender and number. With such constructions the auxiliary can be separated from the past participle, something which cannot occur with the regular compound past using *haber:*

| | *Llevo* cuatro páginas *escritas.* | "I *have* four pages *written.*" |
| but not | **He* cuatro páginas *escrito.* | |

"Immediate" Past

The construction *acabar de* + *infinitive* is frequently used in place of the simple or compound past to refer to an event which has just happened, literally one *finishes to do something:*

Ella *acaba de* llegar.   "She *has just arrived.*"

With reference to something which had just occurred at a point in the past, the analogous construction is used with the *imperfect* of *acabar:*

Fui a visitarla pero ella   "I went to see her but she *had just left.*"
acababa de salir.

Imperfect Tense

As noted in the Introduction, the imperfect does not correspond directly to any simple English verb form. It refers to a past action without conveying any information as to whether or not the action was completed. Thus the contrast:

imperfect	*Llovía* ayer.	"It *was raining* yesterday."
simple past	*Llovió* ayer.	"It *rained* yesterday."

Based on the first statement we cannot say for sure that the rain yesterday ever stopped—it is possible that it has continued until the present moment. In contrast, the second statement indicates unequivocally that the rain yesterday terminated, and if by chance it is raining at the present time then it is not the same rain shower as yesterday.

The most common uses of the imperfect are in:

(1) *Indefinite* statements about the past

En aquel tiempo *reinaba* la paz, y la gente *era* muy feliz.	"In that era peace *reigned,* and the people *were* very happy."
Cuando *era* joven *jugaba* mucho al béisbol.	"When I *was* young *I played* a lot of baseball."

(2) Statements relating to a condition existing at the moment of a specific action in the past (the latter expressed in the simple past tense)

	Lavaba la ropa cuando sonó el teléfono.	"I *was washing* the laundry when the phone rang."
or	*Estaba* lavando … [see *gerundio,* below]	
	Todavía *iba* a la escuela cuando murió Franco.	"I *was* still *going* to school when Franco died."

There is a gray area between the definite and indefinite historical past, i.e., between the use of the simple past and imperfect, where the two can be used almost interchangeably:

En el siglo XVIII *hubo* muchas revoluciones en América Latina. El el siglo XVIII *había* muchas revoluciones en América Latina.	"In the eighteenth century there *were* many revolutions in Latin America." [same as above]

In the first formulation the focus is on a large number (e.g., 22) of finite events, while the second is nuanced toward the general condition of having many revolutions.

> En el principio *creó* Dios los cielos y la tierra. Y la tierra *estaba* sin orden y vacía, y las tinieblas *cubrían* la superficie del abismo, y el Espíritu de Dios se *movía* sobre la superficie de las aguas. (Génesis 1:1–2, La Biblia de las Américas)

Creó is simple past; the other three verbs are imperfects. Thus,

> In the beginning God *created* the heaven and the earth. And the earth *was* without form, and void; and darkness *was* upon [i.e., *covered*] the face of the deep. And the Spirit of God *moved* upon the face of the waters. (King James Version)

Identity between First and Third Person Singulars

For all Spanish verbs, the imperfect for the first and third person singulars is the same. It wasn't always this way, as in Latin times the first person singular ended with *-m*, the third person with *-t*. But phonetic evolution did away with most final consonants, including *-m* and *-t*. In principle, the context should make clear whether the subject is the first or third person singular, and whenever this is not the case the subject should be specified explicitly. In practice confusion and ambiguity occasionally arise, particularly since the context is often clearer in the mind of the speaker (or writer) than in that of the listener (or reader).

Consider, for example, the following situation:

My bicycle collides with John's. My friend Mary asks me what happened. I reply:

> Desgraciadamente, no miraba por donde iba.

What did I say, or rather, *mean* to say? With no personal pronouns or names used (because I think the context is perfectly clear), this could be understood by Mary in any one of the following ways.

(1) "Unfortunately, *I* wasn't looking where *I* was going."
(2) "Unfortunately, *I* wasn't looking where *he* (John) was going."
(3) "Unfortunately, *he* (John) wasn't looking where *I* was going."
(4) "Unfortunately, *he* (John) wasn't looking where *he* (John) was going."

Past Perfect

The primary use of the past perfect is to express an action in the past which occurred prior to another past action or point in time.

Ya *había preparado* la cena cuando llegaron mis invitados.	"I *had* already *prepared* the dinner when my guests arrived."
Juan *había vivido* feliz hasta que se casó.	"Juan *had lived* happily until he married."
Estábamos contentos porque *habíamos recibido* buenas noticias.	"We were happy because we *had received* good news."
Yo creía (creí) que ya te *habías ido*.	"I thought that you *had already* left."

The verb expressing the "other" action is in the simple past or imperfect, according to the normal rules. Used with a "time" conjunction, the past perfect can also refer to a habitual action in the past, in which case the verb in the main clause is in the imperfect:

Cada día cuando *había terminado* su trabajo, *daba* un paseo por el parque.	"Each day when he *had finished* his work, he *took* a walk in the park."

Past Anterior

Like the past perfect, the past anterior refers to an action which occurred prior to another action in the past, with the nuance that the action occurred *immediately* prior.

Hube preparado la cena cuando llegaron mis invitados.	"I *had* **just** *prepared* the dinner when my guests arrived."
Cuando *hubo amanecido,* salí.	"**As soon as** *dawn broke,* I left."

The past anterior has disappeared completely from the spoken language and appears only rarely in literary works. It has been replaced by the simple past, or less frequently the past perfect:

Tan pronto como *preparé* (*había preparado*) la cena llegaron mis invitados.	"As soon as I *had prepared* the dinner my guests arrived."
Luego que *amaneció* salí.	"As soon as *dawn broke,* I left."

The immediacy formerly conveyed by the past anterior is thus expressed instead by an adverbial expression: *luego que, tan pronto como, no bien, así que, apenas, en cuanto,* etc.[2]

Present Participle (*Gerundio*)

The Spanish *gerundio* combines elements of the English present participle and gerund. Examples of its use:

Los niños salieron *corriendo.*	"The children left [e.g., the room] *running.*"
Ganó este dinero *trabajando* durante las vacaciones.	"He earned this money [by] *working* during the vacation."
Vi a su hermano *atravesando* la calle.	"I saw your brother *crossing* the street."
Atravesando la calle, vi a su hermano sentado en el café.	"[While] *crossing* the street I saw your brother seated in the café."
Estando en París, decidí visitar la Torre Eiffel.	"*Being* in Paris I decided to visit the Eiffel Tower."
No *viendo* ninguna alternativa, vendí mi carro.	"Not *seeing* any alternative, I sold my car."
Ya *habiendo* visto tres veces esta misma película, no tengo ganas de verla otra vez.	"Already *having* seen this [same] movie three times I have no desire to see it again."
Viviendo sola, a menudo se siente inquieta.	"*Living* alone, she often feels uneasy at night." (or "a woman often feels . . .")

---

[2] In its rare literary use today, the past anterior is almost always accompanied by one of these same adverbial expressions. This is somewhat redundant, since the idea of immediacy is conveyed twice: by the past anterior itself and by the accompanying adverb ("*As soon as* I had *just* prepared . . .").

Probably the most common use of the *gerundio* is in expressions identical to the English "progressive" tenses, with the verb *estar* assuming the role of the auxiliary *to be:*

Juan *está jugando* en la calle.	"Juan *is playing* in the street."
Juan *estaba jugando* en la calle.	"Juan *was playing* in the street."

This progressive sense can also be expressed with the verbs *ir, venir, seguir, continuar,* and *andar.*

Continúas *haciendo* la misma cosa.	"You continue *doing* the same thing."
Siguió *trabajando* a pesar de su enfermedad.	"He continued *working* in spite of his illness."
La situación va *empeorando.*	"The situation continues *getting worse.*"

As with the infinitive and imperative, a pronoun object is "glued" to the *gerundio:*

Acercánd*olo,* vi que no era Diego.	"Approaching *him,* I saw that it wasn't Diego."
Contánd*omelo* se sentía más seguro.	"Telling *it to me* he felt more secure."

This applies as well to reflexive verbs:

Acostánd*ome* temprano duermo mejor.	"Going to bed early I sleep better."

When the gerundio is used with *estar,* pronoun objects can either be attached to the gerundio or placed before *estar:*

	Estábamos miránd*ola* desde la ventana.	"We were looking at *her* from the window."
or	*La* estábamos mirando desde la ventana.	

When pronouns are attached to the *gerundio,* the stress accent remains on the same syllable, so that a written accent is always required:

a•cer•**can**•do	acercando	a•cer•**cán**•do•lo	acercándolo
con•**tan**•do	contando	con•**tán**•do•me•lo	contándomelo

There are a number of cases where English *-ing* constructions are *not* expressed by the Spanish *gerundio*. For example:

(1) When the action is simultaneous, the construction *al* + *infinitive* is commonly used:

Al salir del hotel tomó un taxi.	"*Leaving* the hotel he took a taxi."
Al salir yo del hotel, María estaba esperándome.	"[On] *leaving* the hotel, Maria was waiting for me."

(2) Where English allows *either* a gerund or the infinitive, Spanish generally permits only the infinitive:

Ver es *creer.*	"*Seeing* is *believing.*"
	"*To see* is *to believe.*"
Correr es bueno para el corazón.	"*Running* is good for the heart."
	"*To run* is good for the heart."
Me gusta *cocinar.*	"I like *cooking.*"
	"I like *to cook.*"

(3) While it can be used in adjectival constructions ("I saw the man *running* in the park"),[3] the Spanish *gerundio* cannot (in theory) be used as an adjective directly modifying a noun ("the *running* man"). One way to remember this: if it were used in this manner ("*Sleeping* Beauty"), the final *-o* would have to be changed to *-a* when modifying feminine nouns and this never occurs with the *gerundio*.

In many cases, there is a related *verbal adjective* ending in *-ante* or *-iente*, descended from the Latin present participle (a separate verbal form from the gerund), that can be used instead:

correct	incorrect	
mi *ardiente* deseo	*ardiendo	"my *ardent* (burning) desire"
el sol *brillante*	*brillando	"the *brilliant* sun"
el agua *corriente*	*corriendo/a	"*running* water"
la Bella *durmiente*	*durmiendo/a	"*Sleeping* Beauty"
el hombre *sonriente*	*sonriendo	"the *smiling* man"
el platillo *volante*	*volando	"*flying* saucer"

---

[3] *Vi al hombre corriendo en el parque.*

Thus one says that

el niño está durmiendo	"the child is sleeping"
el hombre está sonriendo	"the man is smiling"
el platillo está volando	"the saucer is flying"
but	
el niño durmiente	"the sleeping child"
el hombre sonriente	"the smiling man"
el platillo volante	"the flying saucer"

The large majority of Spanish verbs, however, do *not* have verbal adjectives ending in -*nte*, so that it is necessary to find a different adjective to express the English present participial adjective or to use a different structure altogether. Thus, if asked which of two children—one smiling, one crying—is yours, you could respond either:

	"el sonriente"	"the smiling one"
or	"el que llora" / "el llorón"	"he who cries" / "the tearful one"

since in the latter case there is no verbal adjective *llorante*. The prohibition against using *gerundios* as direct adjectives seems to have evaporated in the case of *boiling water*. While many sources continue to indicate that the adjectival form of "boiling" is *hirviente*, it is more common today to see *agua hirviendo*. In 1992 the Real Academia Española went so far as to remove *hirviente* from its dictionary, although it continues to be found in most others. Note that it is *agua hirviendo* not *agua hirvienda*, which it would be if *hirviendo* had become a full-fledged adjective. Other forms are likely to follow this path: e.g., one frequently sees *ardiendo* in place of *ardiente*.

In some cases an English present participle translates instead into a Spanish *past* participle:

el hombre sentado a la mesa	*not* *sentando	"the man sitting at the table"
		i.e., "the man *seated* at the table"

Future Tense

The Spanish future tense is used very similarly to that in English:

Mañana *iré* al médico.	"Tomorrow I *will go* to the doctor."
Venderemos nuestra casa el año próximo.	"We *will sell* our house next year."

The future tense is also used frequently in *if* and *when* clauses:

Si eres bueno Papá Noel te *dará* unos regalos.	"If you are good Santa Claus *will give* you some presents."
Cuando estés listo *saldremos*.	"When you are ready we *will leave*."

In the *when* clause the verb following *cuando* (*estés*) is in the present subjunctive, a use we will discuss in Chapter 12.

The future tense is also used occasionally to denote probability, e.g., in response to the question *What time is it?*, one could respond:

Serán las cinco y media.	"It *will be* [around] five thirty."

Another example:

No la he visto hoy. *Estará* enferma.	"I haven't seen her today. She *must be* ill."

Alternative Forms of Future

In English the future tense is often replaced by a more informal construction using the verb *to go*, particularly when the future being referred to is not too distant:

future:	I *will do* my homework tomorrow.
near-future:	I *am going to do* my homework tomorrow.

The same substitution also occurs in Spanish, using the verb *ir* ("to go") plus the preposition *a:*

future:	Mañana *haré* mis deberes.
	El próximo año *compraremos* un nuevo auto.
near-future:	Mañana *voy a hacer* mis deberes.
	El próximo año *vamos a comprar* un nuevo auto.

As noted earlier, the *present* tense is also used at times to replace the future, particularly with regard to the verb *ir*.

future:	Mañana *iremos* a la playa.
present:	Mañana *vamos* a la playa.
	"Tomorrow we will go [we go] to the beach."

Future Perfect

The Spanish use of the future perfect parallels that in English:

Lo *habré terminado* para el viernes.	"I *will have finished* it by Friday."
Si llegamos tarde, ya *se habrá ido*.	"If we arrive late, he *will have left* already."

Conditional Tense

The conditional tense initially developed to fulfill the role of a future in the past and only later was extended to situations in the present and future. Its major uses include:

Future in the Past

He said: *I will be there at noon.*
Dijo que *estaría* allí a mediodía.   "He said he *would be* there at noon."

Similarly,

Pensaba que *llegarías* más temprano.   "I thought that you *would arrive* earlier."

Present Conditional Meaning

Supongo que *te gustaría* comer un helado.	"I suppose that you *would like* to eat an ice cream."
Yo no lo *haría*.	"I *wouldn't do* it."

Politeness

Podrías pasarme la mantequilla?	"*Could* you pass me the butter?"
Querrías ir al cine conmigo?	"*Would* you *like* to go to the cinema with me?"

In this use the conditional is in competition with the imperfect subjunctive (Chapter 12). Note also that the conditionals for the verbs *poder* and *querer* are irregular.

If-Then Clauses

The conditional tense is used very frequently in *if-then* clauses, of the form

Si fueras mejor estudiante, *recibirías* mejores notas.	"If you were a better student, (then) you *would receive* better grades."

As the verb in the "if" clause is in the imperfect subjunctive, we will defer discussion of this type of phrase until Chapter 12.

Conditional Perfect

Me *habría gustado* estar allí. "*I would have liked* to be there."

The most common use of the conditional perfect is in *si* clauses, and will be dealt with in Chapter 12. With the verbs *deber, poder,* and *querer* an alternative form of the conditional perfect is more commonly employed when an infinitive immediately follows, using the construction *conditional + haber + past participle:*

	Debería haber hecho mis deberes.	"*I should have done* my homework."
vs	Habría debido hacer mis deberes.	
	Podría haber ido a París.	"*I could have gone* to Paris."
vs	Habría podido ir a París.	
	Querría haber ido a París.	"*I would have liked to go* to Paris."
vs	Habría querido ir a París.	

Reflexive Verbs

Many verbs used with a *reflexive* pronoun—i.e., one which refers to the subject—have become so identified with a particular meaning that the two have become permanent partners in a union known as a *reflexive* verb.[4] Some dictionaries provide separate entries for these, others include them as part of the overall definition of the verb. While often the meaning is simply that of the simple verb used reflexively, in other cases there is a substantially different nuance. A few common examples:

simple verb		reflexive	
acordar	"to agree"	acordarse	"to remember"
acostar	"to put to bed"	acostarse	"to go to bed"
casar	"to marry" (others)	casarse	"to marry" (one another)
dormir	"to sleep"	dormirse	"to fall asleep"
ir	"to go"	irse	"to go away", "to leave"

---

[4]The Spanish more accurately call these *verbos pronominales* ("pronominal verbs") because in a number of cases there is no direct reflexive action, e.g., *irse* ("to leave").

levantar	"to lift"	levantarse	"to get up" (out of bed)
llamar	"to call"	llamarse	"to be named"
restablecer	"to reestablish"	restablecerse	"to recover" (from illness)
sentar	"to seat"	sentarse	"to sit (down)"
volver	"to return"	volverse	"to become"

El sacerdote *casa* a Juan y a María.	"The priest *marries* Juan and Maria."
Juan *se casa* con María.	"Juan *marries* Maria."
Acordamos comenzar el trabajo mañana.	"We *agree(d)* to start the work tomorrow."
¿No *te acuerdas* de mí?	"Don't you *remember* me?"
La policía *restablece* el orden en la ciudad.	"The police *restore* order in the city."
Se restablece lentamente de sus heridas.	"He *recovers* slowly from his injuries."
Hoy *voy* a la piscina.	"Today I *go* to the swimming pool."
Se va sin decir nada.	"He *leaves* without saying anything."
Llamo al médico.	"I *am calling* the doctor."
Me llamo Carlos.	"*My name is* Carlos."

The following example shows that it is sometimes necessary to determine from the context whether the meaning is that of a reflexive verb or of a simple verb used with a normal direct object pronoun.

Me levanto a las seis.	"*I get up* at six (from the bed)."
Me levanto del sofá.	"*I raise myself* from the sofa."

Reflexive verb constructions often serve to eliminate the need for possessive pronouns:

Se pone *el* sombrero.	"He puts on *his* hat."
Me lavo *las* manos.	"I wash *my* hands."
Me duele *la* cabeza.	"*My* head hurts."

Reflexive verbs can also translate the idea of reciprocity:

Los dos hermanos *se* abrazan.	"The two brothers[5] embrace *each other*."

---

[5] Or "The brother and sister . . ."

Reflexive constructions can allow transitive verbs to be used intransitively:

El tren *se detuvo* en la estación.　　　　"The train *stopped* in [or at] the station."

The verb *detener* ("to stop") normally requires a direct object ("to stop *something*") which in this case is provided by the reflexive pronoun acting as a direct object ("the train stopped *itself*").

Some verbs can *only* be used reflexively, in which case they are normally shown in dictionaries with the reflexive pronoun attached at the end of the verb, e.g.,

arrepentirse　　　　"to repent"[6]

Note on Use of Haber

Sometime during the "Golden Age" of Spanish *haber* lost its primary role as the verb of possession to *tener* so that today one says

Tengo muchos amigos.　　　　"I have many friends."

rather than

*He muchos amigos.　　　　(French: *J'ai beaucoup d'amis.*)

At the same time, however, *haber* consolidated its role as the *only* auxiliary verb in Spanish (unlike French where both *avoir* and *être* "to be" are used). As we have seen in Chapter 6, *all* compound Spanish verb tenses are formed with *haber:*

verb form	=	(form of) *haber* + past participle
compound past		present
past perfect		imperfect
past anterior (rare)		simple past
future perfect		future
conditional perfect		conditional
compound past subjunctive		present subjunctive
past perfect subjunctive		imperfect subjunctive

---

[6] In general, the *smaller* a dictionary is, the more likely that for a given verb all of the definitions will involve reflexive uses, and hence the more likely it is that the verb will be shown in its reflexive form. For example, most dictionaries show *abstener* ("to abstain") and *atener* ("to keep to") in their reflexive forms (*abstenerse* and *atenerse*) while the more complete *RAE* and *Moliner* show them in their "normal" forms.

Apart from its role as an auxiliary, *haber* is used very frequently in constructions of the form "there is" or "there are". Until the Golden Age, this would have been written using the old Spanish adverb *y:*[7]

Ha **y** 40 personas en mi casa.	"There are 40 people in my house."
En Inglaterra ha **y** mucha lluvia.	"In England there is much rain."

The adverb *y* disappeared from Modern Spanish but remained fixed in expressions like this, so that one now says and writes:

Hay 40 personas en mi casa.
En Inglaterra *hay* mucha lluvia.

In other words, the *y* has become "glued" to *ha* to produce the form *hay*. This is the only context in which such agglutination with *haber* occurs, and only in the present tense: in "yesterday there were 40 people in my house" the simple past of *haber* (*hubo*) is used with no *y* either as part of the verb or elsewhere.

Ayer *hubo* 40 personas en mi casa.

Similarly,

Mañana *habrá* 40 personas en mi casa.	"Tomorrow *there will be . . .*"

Note that in all cases the third person singular is used in such expressions, so that one is literally saying *there is/was 40 persons.*

---

[7] As in modern French: "Il y a 40 personnes dans ma maison."

CHAPTER 11

Special Topic: *Ser* versus *Estar*

The Latin origins of these verbs can provide some assistance in understanding their different uses. *Ser* represents a merger of the Latin verbs "to be" (ESSE) and "to be seated" (SEDERE). ESSE is the ultimate origin of English *essence* and *essential,* SEDERE of *sedentary* and *residence. Estar* is derived from the Latin verb "to stand" (STARE), the origin of English *state* and *status* and, via Old French, the verb *to stay.*

Thus one can think of *ser* as applying to the *essence* of an object, a characteristic which is *seated* or innate, as opposed to the less permanent *state* (or *status*) of an object represented by *estar.* The basic distinction, admittedly not always clear, is thus that:

Ser expresses the fundamental essence of a thing or being, as well as its defining characteristics:
    physical or moral characteristics
    nature
    nationality, religion
    profession
    form
    color
    weight
    what it is made from
    ownership

ser o no *ser*	"*to be* or not *to be*"
un *ser* humano	"a human *being*"
es decir	"i.e.", "that *is* to say"
"La insoportable levedad del *ser*"	"The Unbearable Lightness of *Being*"
(una novela por Milan Kundera)	(a novel by Milan Kundera)
Soy francés.	"I *am* French."
Somos estudiantes.	"We *are* students."
Es médico.	"He *is* a doctor."
Eres muy alto.	"You *are* very tall."
Dos por cuatro *son* ocho.	"Two times four *is* eight."
Ya *son* las nueve.	"It *is* already nine o'clock."
El avión *es* muy grande.	"The airplane *is* very big."

La bandera *es* azul.	"The flag *is* blue."
Es más pesado que un saco de plomo.	"It *is* heavier than a lead sack."
El libro *es* mío.	"The book *is* mine."
Esta casa *es* de mi tío.	"This *is* my uncle's house."
Mi reloj *es* de oro.	"My watch *is* (made) of gold."
Soy de Filadelfia.	"I *am* from Philadelphia."

Estar expresses the **state** or **status** in which something exists:
   location, whether permanent or temporary
   state of mind or being
   situation

Los Alpes *están* en Europa.	"The Alps *are* in Europe."
Hoy *está* en casa.	"Today he/she *is* at home."
Estoy de pie.	"I *am* standing." (literally "I *am* on my feet")
Estamos sin dinero	"We *are* without money."
Estoy enfermo.	"I *am* ill."
Estás cansada.	"You (fem.) *are* tired."
Estoy bien.	"I *am* well."
Estoy mal.	"I *am* not well." ("I *am* sick.")
El que no *está* contra nosotros, *está* con nosotros.	"For he that *is* not against us *is* for us." (Mark 9:40, American Standard Version)
El café *está* muy caliente.	"The coffee *is* very hot."
El cielo *está* encapotado.	"The sky *is* overcast."
El vino *está* a un euro el litro.	"Wine *is* one euro per liter."
Estamos en verano.	"We *are* in summer."
Estamos de vacaciones.	"We *are* on vacation."
Hoy *estamos* a 28 de enero.	"Today *is* January 28." ("We *are* at January 28.")
but: Hoy **es** 28 de enero. (*ser*)	"Today *is* January 28." (fundamental quality)

Consider a piece of green (*verde*) paper which happens to be wrinkled (*arrugado*). This particular piece of paper by its very nature is green; this is an *essential* characteristic. On the other hand, the fact that it is wrinkled reflects its *status* rather than its essence. It presumably hasn't always been wrinkled and it is at least in principle possible that at some point in the future it might return to an unwrinkled *state*. Thus

El papel **es** verde.	"The paper *is* green."
but	
El papel **está** arrugado.	"The paper *is* wrinkled"

The same adjective can generally be used with *ser* and *estar,* often merely with an "essence-status" distinction:

Es una chica tranquila.	"She *is* a calm girl."	(essence)
Hoy *estás* un poco más tranquilo.	"Today you *are* a bit calmer.	(status)

Este niño *es* muy impaciente.	"This child *is* very impatient."	(essence)
Estoy muy impaciente por verlos.	"I *am* very impatient to see them."	(status)

For some adjectives, however, the meaning can be considerably changed:

El hombre *es* rico.	"The man is *rich.*"
Los tomates *están* ricos.	"The tomatoes are *delicious.*"

Other examples of adjectives whose meanings can differ:

adjective	with *ser*	with *estar*
aburrido	"boring"	"bored"
bueno	"good"	"healthy", "tasty", "in good condition"
cansado	"tiring" (e.g., journey)	"tired"
completo	"complete"	"full"
consciente	"conscious" (of something)	"conscious" (state)
divertido	"amusing"	"amused"
listo	"intelligent"	"ready"
malo	"bad"	"ill", "deteriorated"
orgulloso	"haughty"	"proud (of)"
verde	"green" (color)	"unripe"
vivo	"alive" (vivid)	"alive" (living)

La manzana *es* verde.	"The apple is green."
La manzana *está* verde.	"The apple is unripe."
Esta manzana aunque roja *está* verde.	"This apple although red is not ripe."

Eres aburrido.	"You are boring."
Estás aburrido.	"You are bored."

El ritmo de esta música *es* muy vivo.	"The rhythm of this music is very vibrant."
El fuego todavía *está* vivo.	"The fire is still burning."

One common difficulty lies with expressions relating to the location where an event takes place. While it might seem that the verb employed should be *estar,* which after all refers to the location of things, it is instead *ser* which normally is employed:

El concierto *es* en el aula principal.	"The concert is in the main hall."
La exhibición *es* en el museo.	"The exhibition is in the museum."
La Copa del Mundo *es* en Francia.	"The World Cup is in France."

compared to:

El cine *está* en el centro comercial.	"The cinema is in the shopping center."
La Mona Lisa *está* en el museo.	"The Mona Lisa is in the museum."
El estadio donde juegan la Copa del Mundo *está* en Francia.	"The stadium where they play the World Cup is in France."

The second group of examples refers to the physical location of a tangible object and hence uses the verb *estar.* The first group refers to the *realization* of an event, and there is an *implicit* verb indicating "taking place" which effectively transforms the phrase into a *passive* construction requiring the verb *ser* (see Passive and "False Passive" Constructions, below):

"The concert is [taking place] in the main hall."

There are also a number of seeming exceptions to the rules. Thus for the two similar adjectives *feliz* (as in *Feliz Navidad* "Merry Christmas") and *contento* ("happy") one typically says

Soy feliz.	"I am happy."
but	
Estoy contento.	"I am happy."

Being alive is temporary; by analogy so is being dead, whether literally or figuratively:

Está muerto.	"He is dead."
Está muerto de risa.	"He is dying of laughter."

Is one permanently or temporarily married? Most commonly *estar* is used with *casado, divorciado, separado:*

Está casada con un francés.	"She is married to a Frenchman."
Está divorciado/separado.	"He is divorced/separated."
but	
Es soltero.	"He is single."

Notes:

1. Usage of *ser* and *estar* with adjectives relating to *el estado civil* (marriage status) is far from uniform.

2. The basic reason for the distinction *casado/soltero* is that *casado* is a past participle of a verb (*casar*) and thus expresses the result of a process (that of getting married), while *soltero* is an ordinary adjective describing an inherent state. This, more than the analogy with *vivo*, is perhaps the better explanation for *estar muerto*.[1] This will be discussed in more detail below when we deal with passive constructions, one of the major areas of confusion between *ser* and *estar*.

3. In a legal or administrative sense one normally uses *ser* with *casado* and *divorciado*.

No podemos casarnos por la Iglesia porque *eres* divorciado.
"We can't get married in the Church because you are divorced."

4. *Soltero* and *virgen*, which in the past have always been associated with *ser* because they describe innate conditions, are now used increasingly with *estar*. This presumably reflects both the analogy with *casado* and *divorciado* and the recognition that as with other conditions susceptible to change, *estar* is more appropriate. The same logic would suggest that one might say *estoy estudiante,* but this is rarely if ever heard.

5. One of the relatively few things which can be said with some confidence is that *bien* and *mal* are used only with *estar*.[2]

6. There is considerable regional variation in usage, and one person's *ser* is often another's *estar*. Usage frequently is not in accord with "the law."

---

[1] *Muerto* is the irregular past participle of *morir* ("to die").

[2] In the expressions "*todo fue bien*" and "*todo me fue bien*", *fue* represents the past tense of the verb *ir* rather than that of *ser* (so that the literal meaning is "all *went* well"). In a phrase like "*el mensaje fue bien recibido*", the adverb "*bien*" modifies the past participle "*recibido*", not the past tense "*fue*".

Passive and "False Passive" Constructions

As in English, the past participle of transitive verbs can be used adjectivally in passive constructions:

active

Cervantes *escribió* "Don Quijote" en el siglo XVII.	"Cervantes *wrote* "Don Quixote" in the seventeenth century."

passive

El libro *fue escrito* en el siglo XVII.	"The book *was written* in the seventeenth century."
Este edificio *fue construido* en 1842.	"This building *was constructed* in 1842."
Las abejas *son atraídas* por las flores.	"Bees *are attracted* by flowers."

In each of these examples, the passive construction can be converted into an active one (and vice versa) *in the same tense,* e.g., "flowers *attract* bees" (present), "[somebody] *constructed* the house in 1842" (past).

There is a related type of construction, sometimes called *false passive,* which involves the *result* (status, condition) of an action completed in an earlier time period. Compare the first four sentences below which describe the *action* of shutting a door—

1. The door *is shut* by the doorkeeper.	true passive, present
2. The door *was shut* by the doorkeeper.	true passive, simple past
3. The door *has been shut* by the doorkeeper.	true passive, compound past
4. The door *had been shut* by the doorkeeper.	true passive, past perfect

with the next two sentences which describe the *status* of the door—

5. The door *is shut.*	*false* passive, present
6. When I arrived, the door *was shut.*	*false* passive, past ("imperfect")

The fifth sentence describes the *present* status of a *past* action, the sixth the *past* status of a *prior* action. In contrast to each of the first four sentences,[3] neither can be converted into an active form without changing the tense.

---

[3] The doorkeeper *shuts/shut/has shut/had shut* the door.

In English the distinction between true and false passives is of little practical importance, since both are constructed using the verb *to be*. In Spanish the difference assumes much greater significance because true passives are constructed with *ser,* while false passives use *estar.* Spanish thus avoids the inherent ambiguity in the English passive (*the door is shut, the door was shut*) but at the cost of making one choose explicitly between *ser* and *estar.* Thus,

passive (*ser*)

1. La puerta *es cerrada* por el portero. (present)	"The door *is* [being] *shut* by the doorkeeper."
2. La puerta *fue cerrada* por el portero. (simple past)	"The door *was shut* by the doorkeeper."
3. La puerta *ha sido* cerrada por el portero. (compound past)	"The door *has been shut* by the doorkeeper."
4. La puerta *había sido* cerrada por el portero. (past perfect)	"The door *had been shut* by the doorkeeper."

false passive (*estar*)

5. La puerta *está cerrada.* (present)	"The door *is shut.*"
6. Cuando llegué, la puerta *estaba cerrada.* (imperfect)	"When I arrived the door *was shut.*"

Similarly,

La casa *está construida* con ladrillos.	"The house is of brick construction [*is constructed* with bricks]."
La casa *es construida* con ladrillos [por la empresa Jiménez].	"The house *is* (being) *constructed* with bricks [by Jiménez Co.]."
El nuevo museo *fue inaugurado* la semana pasada; esta semana *está abierto* todos los días.	"The new museum *was inaugurated* last week; this week it *is open* every day."
Los actores *son aplaudidos* por todos; *están cubiertos* de sudor.	"The actors *are applauded* by everyone; they *are covered* with sweat."

A potential confusion arises if one compares:

La casa *está construida* con ladrillos   El reloj *es* de oro. ("The watch is of
                                               gold.")

Both appear to relate to an essential, embedded, nature of an object, yet the first uses *estar,* the second *ser*. The fundamental difference is that in the first case the introduction of an explicit verb (*construir*) forces one to make a choice between process (*ser*) and outcome (*estar*).

There are a number of *stative* verbs which relate essentially to a process and have no definite outcome, e.g. *love, like, hate, envy, esteem, admire, search, contemplate, listen, know*. These are (in principle at least) used only with *ser*:

El Prado *es* muy conocido.   "The Prado *is* very well known."
La reina *es* amada por todos.   "The queen *is* loved by everyone"

The following is *normally* a safe way to determine which verb to use:

If there is an explicit agent introduced with *por,* or if one can add the agent without changing the sense ("The Prado is very well known . . . *by all connoisseurs of art*"), then a true passive is involved and *ser* is used.

However, there are some verbs with a seeming agent introduced by *por* which nonetheless can be, and often have to be, used with *estar*. These include verbs whose English translation would be *occupied, surrounded, covered, composed of, formed*.

La ciudad *está rodeada por* altas   "The city *is surrounded by* high mountains."
montañas
El senado *está constituido por* un   "The Senate consists of (*is constituted by*)
diputado de cada distrito del país.   one deputy from each district of the
                                          country."
El suelo *está cubierto por* dos metros   "The ground *is covered by* (*with*) two meters
de nieve.   of snow."
El tercer piso del hotel *está ocupado*   "The third floor of the hotel *is occupied by*
por turistas ingleses.   English tourists."

In each of these examples, the noun following *por* is not really an active agent and in most cases could be replaced by another preposition (generally *de* or *con*) without changing the meaning.

Most of these verbs can also be used with *ser,* when the focus is on the process rather the result or status, something which is much easier to conceive when one is looking backward and hence uses the past tense:

En menos de dos días, la ciudad *fue rodeada por* el ejército enemigo.	"In less than two days, the city *was surrounded by* [true passive] the enemy army."
versus	
Cuando llegué la ciudad *estaba rodeada por* el ejército enemigo.	"When I arrived the city *was surrounded by* [false passive] the enemy army."

Similarly,

En 15 minutos el suelo *fue* totalmente *cubierto por* la nieve (de nieve).	"In 15 minutes the ground *was covered by* snow."
El edificio *fue ocupado por* dos mil estudiantes para protestar contra la guerra.	"The building *was occupied by* 2,000 students to protest against the war."

This distinction between the use of *ser* and *estar* in "true" and "false" passive constructions is relatively recent. Thus in *Don Quijote,* one finds the phrase

—Luego, ¿no es baptizada?—replicó Luscinda.[4]	"Then, she is not baptized?" replied Luscinda.

where the verb *ser* is used in a false passive construction (she *was* baptized in the past, she *is* presently in the state or condition of having been baptized). In Modern Spanish this would be expressed as:

—Luego, ¿no está bautizada?—replicó Luscinda.	false passive, present of *estar*
or	
—Luego, ¿no fue bautizada?—replicó Luscinda.	true passive, simple past of *ser*
or	
—Luego, ¿no ha sido bautizada?— replicó Luscinda.	true passive, compound past of *ser*

---

[4]Miguel de Cervantes Saavedra, *El Ingenioso Hidalgo Don Quijote de la Mancha* (Bogota: Panamericana, 1998), p. 365 (primera parte, capítulo 37).

Passive constructions are far less common in Spanish than English, as Spanish often replaces them with either an active or reflexive construction. Thus, the passive *I am very surprised by your visit* can be reformulated actively as:

Me sorprende mucho tu visita.   "Your visit greatly surprises me."

When no obvious subject is in sight, a reflexive or "pseudo-passive" construction is frequently employed using the reflexive pronoun *se.*

	literal meaning	practical meaning
Aquí se habla inglés.	"Here English speaks itself."	"English is spoken here."
Aquí se construye una casa.	"Here a house builds itself."	"Here a house is being built."
Se prohibe entrar.	"To enter prohibits itself."	"It is prohibited to enter."
¿Cómo se hace esto?	"How does this do itself?"	"How does one do this?"

Note that with this type of construction the verb is always in the singular: *se hablan (en) inglés* would mean "they speak English among themselves." *Hablan inglés,* without the pronoun, would be an acceptable substitute: "they speak English" (in general, not only among themselves).

The popularity of this "pseudo-passive" has led to its expansion to areas of active meaning:

Se me ocurre una idea.   "An idea occurs to me."
Se le olvidó hacer sus deberes.   "He forgot to do his homework."
Se nos robó el carro.   "They robbed us of our car."

The literal translations of these phrases are "an idea occurs itself to me", "to do his homework forgot itself to him", and "the car robbed itself to us".

CHAPTER 12

Subjunctive

Only traces of the subjunctive remain in Modern English:

(a) the third person singular, where the present indicative ending -s contrasts with the "null" subjunctive ending (*he does* versus *he do*);
(b) the verb *to be*, whose present subjunctive for all six conjugations is "be" (*if I be, if you be,* etc.); and
(c) the use of *were* rather than *was* in statements of the form *if I were, if he were, were he to* (past subjunctive of *to be*).

Consider, for example, the following phrase pairs:

indicative	subjunctive
He *is* here; he *was* here.	I wish that he *were* here.
He *does* it.	It is essential that he *do* it.
He *is* punished.	I demand that he *be* punished.
He *leaves.*	It is my desire that he *leave* at once.
He *is* elected.	God forbid that he *be* elected.
The king *lives.*	Long *live* the king.
It *is* so; it *was* so.	If only it *were* so!
He *understands.*	In order that he *understand* . . .
I *am* wicked.	"If I *be* wicked, woe unto me . . ." (Job 10:15)
It *pleases* the court.	"If it *please* the court . . ."

If John *was* at the meeting last night he certainly maintained a very low profile.
versus
If John *were* at the meeting, it would make a big difference.

Some General Comments on the Use of the Subjunctive

The subjunctive is often explained as representing the expression of an opinion or state of mind of the speaker, in the form of a wish, order, sentiment, or judgment. Its use in Spanish (as well as its traces in English) generally obeys these precepts. The difficulty for the student of Spanish, and the advanced practitioner as well, is that in its finer detail the use of subjunctive does not represent a fully consistent system. This can perhaps best be illustrated by contrasting the use of subjunctives in Spanish, French, and Italian, each of which derived both the form and use of its subjunctives from a common source. Consider the following sentences:

1. When I *am* rich I will buy a house.
2. I think that you *are* right.
3. He is the richest man that I *know.*
4. I will call you when I *arrive.*
5. Take an umbrella, in case it *rains.*
6. If I *were* rich, I would buy a castle.
7. I wonder if this *is* true.
8. Although it *is raining,* I will go for a walk.
9. Even if it *rains,* I will go for a walk.

Translated into the three languages, these phrases would typically employ the following moods for the italicized verb:

Spanish	French	Italian
1. **subjunctive**	indicative (future)	indicative (future)
2. indicative	indicative	**subjunctive**
3. indicative	**subjunctive**	**subjunctive**
4. **subjunctive**	indicative (future)	indicative (future)
5. **subjunctive**	indicative (conditional)	**subjunctive**
6. **subjunctive** (imperfect)	indicative (imperfect)	**subjunctive** (imperfect)
7. indicative	indicative	**subjunctive**
8. indicative	**subjunctive**	**subjunctive**
9. **subjunctive**	indicative	**subjunctive**

In each case, the Spanish usage differs from one or both of the others; nor is there uniformity between the French and Italian forms. Any "logical" explanation of why the subjunctive is used as it is in one of these languages is unlikely to convince practitioners of the other two.

The uses of the subjunctive in Spanish fall into two general categories, depending upon whether such use is *obligatory* or *optional.* Contrary to what might be one's initial thought, its correct use is more important in the second case than in the first. That is, an error with an obligatory subjunctive does not impede the accurate conveyance of what the person is trying to say, whereas in an optional one it is likely to do so.

Thus in English if one incorrectly says

*I wish that he *leaves.*   rather than   I wish that he *leave.*

this will not prevent anyone understanding what the speaker is trying to say. Converse examples (i.e., of optional subjunctives) are rather hard to come up with in English, but consider the following pair of sentences:

subjunctive   Though I *be* sick I will go to school tomorrow
                (i.e., I am not sick at the moment but even if I am sick tomorrow
                I will still go to school).
indicative   Though I *am* sick I will go to school tomorrow
                (i.e., I am sick at the moment but still intend to go to school
                tomorrow).

While archaic, the first phrase is grammatically correct (native English speakers would almost certainly say "Even if I am sick" . . .). The incorrect use of one of these forms in place of the other would convey inaccurate information as to the current health of the speaker.

Numerous books have been written on the Spanish subjunctive[1] (as well as the French, Italian, etc.) to attempt to come up with a coherent theory for its use. The following is a somewhat typical explanation:[2]

> . . . podemos decir que el indicativo presupone la afirmación o negación
> de un hecho, esto es, el hablante se compromete con la verdad de lo que
> dice, en tanto que el subjuntivo carece de semejante presuposición, el
> hablante adopta una postura neutra acerca de la verdad de lo dicho;
> esto es particularmente claro, por ejemplo, en la alternancia
>
> *Aunque no sabe nada, aprobará/Aunque no sepa nada, aprobará,*
>
> donde la carencia de conocimientos tan solo se constata en el primer caso.

which can be translated as:

> . . . we can say that the indicative presupposes the affirmation or negation of
> a fact, i.e., the speaker commits himself to the truth of what he says, while
> the subjunctive lacks a similar presumption, the speaker adopting a neutral

---

[1] The reader is recommended at an appropriate stage to refer to one of the Spanish-language texts on the subjunctive having exercises and answers, e.g., Borrego, Asencio, and Prieto (1992) or Porto Dapena (1991), both of which also contain extensive bibliographies.

[2] Porto Dapena, pp. 33–34.

posture with regard to the truth of what is said; this is particularly clear, for example, in the alternation

> *Although I know nothing I will approve (it) / Although I might not know anything, I will approve (it),*

where the lack of knowledge is evident [and hence the indicative is used] only in the first case.

Imperfect Subjunctive I versus Imperfect Subjunctive II

So why are there two different forms for the imperfect subjunctive, and how, if at all, does their usage differ? The easiest way to answer these questions is to look at the historical origins of the two forms:

Spanish form	Latin origin
imperfect subjunctive I (*-ra* form)	*indicative* past perfect
imperfect subjunctive II (*-se* form)	subjunctive past perfect

The imperfect subjunctive I thus started off life as an *indicative* form and has undergone the following metamorphoses:

indicative past perfect → indicative conditional → imperfect subjunctive

While passing through these stages, it maintained, at least in part, its previous meanings, so that in Modern Spanish, apart from its principal use as an imperfect subjunctive, the *-ra* form continues to have residual uses both as a conditional and as an indicative past perfect. The *-se* form cannot be used in either of these two manners; in all other (i.e., subjunctive) uses the *-se* and *-ra* forms can be used interchangeably.

-ra Form Used with Conditional Meaning

In the past, the *-ra* forms of *all* verbs could be used with conditional meaning. This usage has now largely been restricted to the auxiliary verb *haber* and the "modal" verbs *querer, poder,* and (more rarely) *deber.* Thus,

often	instead of	
hubiera hecho	habría hecho	"I (he) would have done"
Quisiera vino.	Querría vino.	"I (he) would like wine."
Pudiera haberlo hecho.	Podría haberlo hecho.	"I (he) could have done it."
	Habría podido hacerlo.	

less often

Debiera hacerlo.   Debería hacerlo.   "I (he) should do it."

Many students become confused with this conditional use of the *-ra* form and make the mistake of employing the *-se* form, e.g.,

*Quisiese un vino tinto, por favor.   "I would like a red wine, please."

To avoid this problem, one can either constantly remind oneself of the fundamental rule that

> **the -se form can *never* be used in situations where its value is not subjunctive**

or one can avoid all confusion by using *only* the *-ra* form. This is certainly the recommended strategy for the new student, particularly since outside of Spain the large majority of Spanish speakers seem to use this form exclusively. Within Spain there are many who continue to use the *-se* form and it is not unusual to find authors, particularly those affecting a literary style, using both forms, sometimes even in the same sentence.

-ra Form Used with Meaning of Indicative Past Perfect

Unlike the use of *-ra* forms with conditional meanings, this use is relatively rare and is generally discouraged by grammarians, e.g.,

> Se utiliza *cantaras* como arcaísmo o dialectismo en lugar de la forma compuesta *habías cantado,* con valor modal de indicativo e indicando anterioridad a un punto del pretérito.[3]

> *Cantaras* is used as an archaism or dialectalism in place of the compound form [i.e., indicative past perfect] *habías cantado,* with the "value" of the indicative mode and indicating [action] prior to a point in the past.

---

[3] Alarcos Llorach (p. 199).

Nonetheless, one occasionally finds examples in literary and journalistic works, e.g.,

Confirmó las noticias que ya *diera* el ministro hace unos días.
instead of
Confirmó las noticias que ya *había dado* el ministro hace unos días.
"He confirmed the news which the minister *had given* several days earlier."

Correspondence of Tenses

We have seen that Spanish has five simple *tenses* in the indicative: present, simple past, imperfect, future, and conditional. As there are only two tenses for the subjunctive, it is clear that these have double (or treble) duty. In general, indicative tenses correspond to subjunctive ones in the following manner:

indicative		subjunctive
present future	→	present
imperfect simple past conditional	→	imperfect (I or II)

These correspondences extend to compound tenses as well:

	indicative		subjunctive
compound past *future perfect*	he notado habré notado	→	*haya* notado
past perfect *conditional perfect*	había notado habría notado	→	*hubiera/hubiese* notado

Uses of the Subjunctive

The major uses of the subjunctive can be broadly divided among the following categories:

1. desire, fear, order
2. sentiment or judgment

3. possibility, probability, doubt
4. *"if…then"* and other conditional clauses
5. Excluding phrases: *unless, instead of,* etc.
6. adjectival clauses: *indefinite or negative*
7. adverbial clauses (*purpose, temporal, although, as if, if only*)

1. Desire, Fear, Order

The unifying idea in this group is that of contrasting the actual situation with a hypothetical version: a desired one, a feared one, etc. Examples using the present and compound past subjunctive:

(a) Wish/Desire/Fear

Quiero que *salga* de aquí inmediatamente.	"I wish that he *leave* immediately."
Desea que nosotros *hagamos* todo el trabajo.	"He wishes that we *do* all the work."
Espero que España *gane* la Copa del Mundo.	"I hope Spain *wins* the World Cup."
Temo que España no *gane* la Copa del Mundo este año.	"I fear that Spain *will* not *win* the World Cup this year."
Espero que ya *hayas leído* este libro.	"I hope that you *have* already *read* this book."
Espero que *hayas leído* este libro dentro de una semana.	"I hope that in a week you *will have read* this book."

(b) Command/Request/Permission

Nos manda que *salgamos* de aquí.	"He orders that we *leave.*"
Te aconsejo que *hagas* tus deberes hoy.	"I advise that you *do* your homework today."
Te pido que me *des* tu dinero.	"I request that you *give* me your money."
Me mandan que yo *asista* en su lugar.	"They order that I *take* his place."

Note that because of the double duty of the present subjunctive, there can be ambiguity as to the precise meaning, e.g., *hayas leído,* which can refer either to the past (*you have read*) or the future (*you will have read*).

As with English, in many cases an infinitive construction can be used in place of the subjunctive. This is *obligatory* in the case of *wish/desire* verbs when the two clauses have the same subject:

	Quiero *salir* de aquí inmediatamente.	"I want *to leave* from here immediately."
not	*Quiero que (yo) *salga* de aquí.	
	Espero *ganar* una medalla de oro.	"I hope *to win* a gold medal."
not	*Espero que (yo) *gane* una medalla de oro.	

Command/request/permission verbs in principle do not normally permit the subjects of the two clauses to be the same (*I order that I do it*) and hence are not subject to the above rule. Nevertheless, with these verbs an infinitive construction is almost always possible and frequently preferred, although it is not wrong to use the subjunctive.

Nos manda *salir* de aquí.	"He orders us *to leave.*"
Te aconsejo *hacer* tus deberes hoy.	"I advise you *to do* your homework today."
Te pido *darme* tu dinero.	"I request you *to give* me your money."
Me mandan *asistir* en su lugar.	"They order me *to take* his place."

Some examples using the imperfect and past perfect subjunctive:

Esperaba que España *ganara* la Copa del Mundo.	"I was hoping that Spain *would win* the the World Cup."
Esperaba que *llegaran* a tiempo.	"I was hoping that they *arrived/would arrive* on time."
Me mandaron que *yo asistiera* en su lugar.	"They ordered that I *take* his place."
(*or* Me mandaron asistir en su lugar.)	
Esperaba que ya *hubieras acabado* con tus deberes antes de llegar.	"I was hoping that you *had already finished* your homework before arriving."
Esperaba que *hubieras acabado* con tus deberes antes del próximo fin de semana.	"I was hoping that you *would have finished* your homework before the coming weekend."

The last pair of examples illustrate that the subjunctive past perfect (*hubieras acabado*) can correspond to either an indicative past perfect (*habías acabado*) or to an indicative conditional perfect (*habrías acabado*).

It is also worth noting that *esperar* is one of the more semantically charged verbs in Spanish: apart from "to hope" it can also mean "to expect" or "to wait for." Thus the first phrase above could also be translated as "I was expecting that Spain would win the World Cup."

2. Sentiment or Judgment

(a) Sentiment

Me alegra que te *encuentres* mejor.	"I am glad that you are (*find* yourself) better."
Me molesta que lo *hagas.*	"It bothers me that you *do* it."
Me molestaba que lo *hicieras.*	"It bothered me that you *were doing* it / *did* it."
Me extraña que María *esté* ausente.	"I am surprised that Maria *is* absent."

Note again the potential ambiguities: in the last phrase for example, I may have just been informed that Maria will not be at the meeting tomorrow, in which case the English translation would be "I am surprised that Maria *will be* absent."

(b) Judgment or Valuation

These are frequently of the form "it is . . ."

Es normal que *llueva* en el verano.	"It's normal that it *rain(s)* in the summer."
Es preciso que *terminemos* hoy.	"It's necessary that we *finish* today."
Fue necesario que *termináramos* ayer.	"It was necessary that we *finish* yesterday."
Hace falta que *compres* leche.	"It is necessary that you *buy* milk."
Parece injusto que *seamos* tan pobres.	"It seems unjust that we *are* so poor."
Parecía injusto que *fuéramos* tan pobres.	"It seemed unjust that we *were* so poor."
Lo mejor es que nos lo *digas.*	"The best thing is that you *tell* us."
Es horrible que todavía no lo *hayan hecho.*	"It's horrible that they still *have* not *done* it."

We shall see below that *parecer* ("to appear, seem") is most commonly used with the indicative; here the subjunctive is used because the expression *parece injusto* expresses a judgment or evaluation and is essentially equivalent to *es injusto*.

As with the first group, when the subjects of the two clauses are the same, an infinitive construction is preferred, if not required. This is also the case for impersonal constructions ("it is necessary", etc.)

Me molesta no *poder* ir al cine.	"It bothers me not *to be able* to go to the cinema."
Te hace falta *comprar* leche.	"You have *to buy* milk."
Es necesario *terminar* antes de las ocho.	"It is necessary *to finish* by eight o'clock."
Lo mejor es no *decir*les nada.	"The best thing is *to tell* them nothing."

3. Possibility, Probability, Doubt

Consider the following hierarchy of likelihood:

impossible → improbable → possible → probable → certain

Spanish *generally* uses the subjunctive with all except the last.

Era imposible que *viniera*.	"It was impossible that he *come*."
Es posible que *vengamos*.	"It's possible that we *will come*."
Puede ser que *venga* mañana.	"It's possible that he *will come* tomorrow."
Es probable que *vaya* al parque.	"It's likely that I *will go* to the park."
Yo dudo que lo *haya hecho*.	"I doubt that he *has done/will have done* it."
Dudaba que ella *llegara* a tiempo.	"I doubted that she *would arrive* on time."
but	
Estoy *seguro* que ella *llegará* mañana.	"I am *certain* that she *will arrive* tomorrow."

Note:

(i) The use of *llegara* (imperfect subjunctive) and *llegará* (future) in the last two examples is differentiated only by a written accent.[4]

(ii) In several of the expressions there is ambiguity as to whether the verb refers to third person singular or first person singular.

There are a number of adverbs which mean "perhaps" or "possibly":

quizás (or *quizá*), literally "who knows" (from Old Spanish *qui sabe*)
tal vez
posiblemente
acaso
a lo mejor

---

[4] Orally, the two forms are of course distinguished by differing stress accent: on the final syllable for *llegará*, on the penultimate for *llegara*.

All except *a lo mejor* generally take the subjunctive when they are used *before* the verb:

Quizás no *fueran* minutos sino segundos.	"Perhaps it *was* not minutes but seconds."
Tal vez lo *hagamos* mañana.	"Perhaps we *will do* it tomorrow."
Posiblemente *sea* la mejor novela del año.	"It *is* possibly the best novel of the year."
Acaso *estemos* todos equivocados.	"Perhaps we *are* all wrong."

They are *always* used with the indicative when they *follow* the verb.

¿No *entiendes,* acaso, lo que te decimos?	"Perhaps you don't *understand* what we are saying to you?"
Esta solución *es* quizás la mejor.	"This solution *is* perhaps the best."

A lo mejor always takes the indicative, regardless of position.

A lo mejor *vendrá* mañana.	"Perhaps he *will come* tomorrow."

When one "thinks" something, the process apparently involves fewer doubts in Spanish than in Italian, and the indicative rather than the subjunctive is thus (almost always) used:

Creo que *vendrá* mañana.	"I think he *will come* tomorrow."

Similarly, the indicative is used in expressions of the form *parece que* ("it appears that") when this refers to likelihood and not to appearance.

Parece que *lloverá* mañana.	"It looks like it *will rain* tomorrow."
Parece que *han descubierto* un nuevo planeta.	"It seems that they *have discovered* a new planet."

When constructions in the "certainty" range are put in negative form, they move into the uncertainty range and are generally used with the subjunctive:

No creo que *venga* mañana.	"I don't think he *will come* tomorrow."
No creía que Dios *existiera.*	"He didn't believe God *existed.*"
No estoy seguro que *venga* mañana.	"I am not sure that he *will come* tomorrow."
No me parece que *sea* verdad.	"It doesn't seem (likely) to me that it *is* true."

When some expressions of the "doubtful" type are put in the negative, they become expressions of (near) certainty and hence are used with the indicative. Thus,

Dudo que *venga* mañana.	"I doubt that he *will come* tomorrow."
but	
No dudo que *vendrá* mañana.	"I do not doubt that he *will come* tomorrow."

4. "If … then" and Other Conditional Clauses

In Spanish, as in English, there are essentially three types of conditional phrases, two in the present (possible and purely hypothetical) and one in the past (hypothetical only); the latter can in turn be subdivided into two categories, depending upon whether the main (resultant) clause refers to the past or present.

	possible	hypothetical
ENGLISH		
present	If I *win* the lottery I *will buy* a new house.	If I *were* rich I *would buy* a new house.
past	—	(a) If I *had won* the lottery, I *would have bought* a new house.
		(b) If I *had won* the lottery, today I *would be* a very rich man.
SPANISH		
present	Si *gano* la loto *compraré* una nueva casa.	Si *fuera* rico *compraría* una nueva casa.
past	—	(a) Si *hubiera ganado* la loto, *habría comprado* una nueva casa.
		(b) Si *hubiera ganado* la loto, hoy *sería* un hombre muy rico.

The use of Spanish verb tenses in such phrases, which to a certain extent parallels the English usage, is as follows:

	if	then
present possible	present indicative	future (less commonly present or imperative)
present hypothetical	imperfect subjunctive	conditional
past hypothetical	past perfect subjunctive	(a) conditional perfect
		(b) conditional

Since

past perfect subjunctive	=	imperfect subjunctive of *haber* +	past participle
conditional perfect	=	conditional of *haber* +	past participle

the use of verb tenses can be summarized as:

	if	then
possible	present indicative	future
hypothetical	imperfect subjunctive	conditional

It is essential to keep in mind that the indicative future or conditional can **never** be used in the *if* clause, although they are often used in the corresponding English phrases:

Si me *ayudas* mañana, te *daré* 50 pesos. "If you **will help** me tomorrow,
  I *will give* you 50 pesos."

(not *ayudarás)

Si *estudiaras* más, *recibirías* mejores notas. "If you **would study** more, you
  would get better grades."

(not *estudiarías)

We remarked previously that the -*ra* form of the subjunctive is often used in place of the conditional for several verbs, including *haber*. Thus in place of the perfect conditional (*habría comprado*) one frequently finds the past perfect subjunctive (*hubiera comprado*):

Si hubiera ganado la loto, *hubiera* "If I had won the lottery, I *would*
comprado una nueva casa. *have bought* a new house."

One of the obvious advantages of this alternative is that the identical verb form is then used in both the *if* and *then* clauses.
    Other examples:

Si *llueve* mañana no *iré* al parque. "If it *rains* tomorrow I *will* not *go* to
  the park."
Será un desastre si *llueve* mañana. "It *will be* a disaster if it *rains*
  tomorrow."
Sería un desastre si *lloviera* mañana. "It *would be* a disaster if it *were to rain*
  tomorrow."

Si *has leído* todos estos libros, el
examen *será* fácil para ti.

"If you *have read* all these books the test
will be easy for you."

Habría (hubiera) sido un desastre
si ese hombre *hubiera ganado*
las elecciones.

"It *would have been* a disaster if that
man *had won* the elections."

Si *hubieras estudiado* más cuando
joven, ahora *serías* médico.

"If you *had studied* more when young,
today you *would be* a doctor."

Conditional Phrases with Conjunctions Other than "If"

As in English, conditional phrases can also be expressed with conjunctions other
than *if,* e.g.,

en (el) caso de que	"in case that", "if"
a condición de que	"on condition that"
siempre y cuando, siempre que[5]	"provided that"
con tal (de) que	"provided that"

The rules are the same as for conditional clauses with *si,* with the exception
that in a present "possible" conditional the present *subjunctive* is used in the
conditional part of the phrase rather than the present indicative. Thus the correspondences are:

	if	then
present possible	*present subjunctive*	future
present hypothetical	imperfect subjunctive	conditional
past hypothetical	past perfect subjunctive	(a) conditional perfect
		(b) conditional

En caso de que *llueva* esta noche,
no *iré* al parque mañana.

"In the event that it *rains* tonight I *will*
not *go* to the park tomorrow."

En caso de que *haya llovido* anoche,
no *iré* al parque hoy.

"In the event that it *rained* last night
[it may have, but I haven't looked outside
yet] I *will* not *go* to the park today."

En el caso de que ese hombre
ganara las elecciones, *sería* un
desastre para el país.

"In the event that that man *were to win* the
elections it *would be* a disaster for the
country."

---

[5] *Siempre que* can also be used in temporal clauses ("whenever"), in which case the verb can be
either subjunctive or indicative; see number 7(b).

En el caso de que ese hombre *hubiera ganado* las elecciones, *habría (hubiera) sido* un gran desastre para el país.

"In the event that that man *had won* the elections it *would have been* a great disaster for the country."

Compraré los tiquetes a condición de que (con tal de que, siempre y cuando, etc.) me *des* el dinero suficiente.

"I *will buy* the tickets provided that you *give* me sufficient money."

5. Excluding Phrases

There are a range of "excluding" conjunctions governing phrases which express a condition or something contrary to reality, in both cases calling for the use of the subjunctive:

a menos que	"unless"
a no ser que	"unless"
sin que	"without"
lejos de que	"far from"
en lugar de que	"instead of"
en vez de que	"instead of"

A no ser que uno se *convierta* en perro, nunca entenderá lo que ellos piensan.

"Unless one *converts* oneself into a dog, one will never understand what they think."

Argentina no pagará la deuda a menos que *haya* un acuerdo con el FMI.

"Argentina will not pay (its) debt unless there *is* an agreement with the IMF."

En este país no se pueden comprar ciertos artículos a no ser que se *sea* extranjero o se *obtenga* autorización del gobierno.

"In this country one can't buy certain articles unless one *is* a foreigner or *obtains* authorization from the government."

Se fue sin que nadie lo *supiera.*

"He left without anyone *noticing* it."

There are several excluding conjunctions which are used with the subjunctive when they have a conditional or counter-reality sense, but with the indicative when referring to a real situation:

excepto que	"except", "unless"
salvo que	"unless", "save that"

subjunctive

No quiero nada, salvo que *salgas* de aquí inmediatamente.	"I don't want anything, except that you *leave* immediately."
O'Neal descarta jugar en Atenas '04 salvo que el técnico *sea* Phil Jackson.	"O'Neal rules out playing in Athens '04 unless the coach *is* Phil Jackson."

indicative

Ningún problema, salvo que *he perdido* mi pasaporte y todo mi dinero.	"No problem, except that I *have lost* my passport and all my money."

6. Adjective Clauses: Indefinite or Negative

An adjective clause is typically introduced by *que* or *quien* (pl. *quienes*). When it is specific and non-negative the *indicative* is used:

Tengo un secretario que *habla* inglés.	"I have a secretary who *speaks* English."

But when the reference is either nonspecific or negative the subjunctive is generally used:

Busco un secretario que *hable* inglés.	"I am looking for a secretary who *speaks* (*would speak*) English."
No conozco ningún secretario que *hable* inglés.	"I don't know any secretary who *speaks* (*would speak*) English."

Similarly,

Quiero una habitación que *tenga* balcón.	"I want a room which *has* a balcony."
Quise una habitación que *tuviera* balcón	"I wanted a room which *had* a balcony."
¿Le dieron una habitación que *tenga* balcón?	"Did they gave him a room which *has* a balcony?"

The subjunctive is required in the last phrase because the person who is asking the question presumably is not referring to a specific room. In either of the cases below the indicative would be used:

Le dieron una habitación que *tenía* balcón.	"They gave him a room which *had* a balcony."
¿Le dieron la habitación que *tiene* balcón?	"Did they give him *the* room which *has* a balcony?"

In the first case the reference is to a historical fact (he was given a room with balcony) while in the second the question refers to a *specific* room, i.e., the (only) one with a balcony.

Other examples with the subjunctive:

Cualquier cosa que *haga* este hombre es mal hecha.	"Whatever (thing) this man *makes* (or *does*) is poorly made (done)."
Quería ir de vacaciones a un lugar donde *hubiera* sol.	"I wanted to go for vacation to a place where there *was* sun."
En este país no hay ningún político en quien uno *pueda* tener confianza.	"In this country there isn't any politician in whom one *can* have confidence."

7. Adverbial Clauses

These are generally of the form:

Main Clause + Conjunction + Adverbial Clause

where the adverbial clause provides information relating to the *how, why, when* of the main clause. Adverbial clauses can be a bit tricky, because some conjunctions govern the subjunctive, others the indicative and yet others (the largest number) can be used with either depending on the meaning they are meant to convey.

(a) Purpose versus Consequence

Consider the following two sentences:

Consequence: Mary spoke in such a manner that all were able to understand.
Purpose: Mary spoke in such a manner so that John could understand.

The first sentence says nothing about *why* Mary spoke the way she did; perhaps it is her natural speaking style. The fact that others were able to understand her is a *consequence* of her speaking style but we cannot say with certainty that this was its *purpose.* The situation is entirely different with the second sentence. Here Mary has made a concerted effort to speak in a manner in which John would understand her, and in fact we can make this even clearer in the form:

Mary spoke in such a manner so that John *would be able* to understand.

Spanish similarly distinguishes between these two types of phrases, using the indicative for the first (consequence) and the subjunctive for the second (purpose).

Conjunctions of Purpose Always Followed by Subjunctive:

para que
a fin de que, con el fin de que
con el objeto de que, con el propósito de que, con la finalidad de que

María hizo un esfuerzo especial para que Juan *pudiera* comprender.	"Mary made a special effort so that John *could* understand."
Saldremos muy temprano a fin de que *lleguemos* a la hora.	"We will leave very early in order that we *will arrive* on time."

Conjunctions of Consequence Generally Followed by Indicative

así que	"so that"
conque	"so then", "now then"
luego	"therefore"
por consiguiente, en consecuencia	"consequently", "accordingly"
por eso	"for that reason"
por lo tanto	"therefore"
pues	"since", "therefore"
de manera que	"in a manner that"
de modo que	"
de forma que	"

Pienso, luego *existo*.	"I think, therefore I *am*." (Descartes)
María habló de manera que todos *pudieron* comprender.	"Mary spoke in a manner that everyone *was able* to understand."

The last three conjunctions, particularly when accompanied by the adverb *tal* ("such"), can also refer to the purpose of an action in which case they require a verb in the subjunctive:

de tal manera que	"in such a manner that"
de tal modo que	"
de tal forma que	"

María habló de tal manera que todos *pudieran* comprender.	"Mary spoke in such a manner that everyone *was (would be) able to* understand."

This would perhaps be a good point to note that *causal* conjunctions, like those of consequence, are normally used with the *indicative*.

porque	"because"
puesto que	"since"
ya que	"since", "as"
como	"since", "as"

Juan comprende lo que dice María porque *habla* lentamente.	"John understands what Mary says because she *speaks* slowly."
Ya que *llueve* no iré al parque.	"Since it *is raining*, I won't go to the park."
Como *era* muy tarde no te llamé.	"As it *was* very late I didn't call you."

Como can be used in a number of other senses as well, some requiring the subjunctive, e.g.,

Puedes hacerlo como *quieras*.	"You can do it however you (*might*) *like*."

In negative expressions in which the cause is called into doubt, *porque* can be used with the subjunctive:

María está ausente hoy, no porque *esté* enferma, sino porque *está* cansada.	"Maria is absent today, not because she *is* ill, but because she *is* tired."

The second verb (*esté*) is in the subjunctive because the speaker is not committing himself as to the state of Maria's health. The third verb is in the indicative: the speaker not only affirms that Maria is tired but that this is the reason for her absence.

(b) Temporal

When the action governed by the conjunction is situated at a *future* point, with respect to either the present or a fixed point of reference, the subjunctive is used. In all other cases the indicative is used. The basic distinction is thus between something that has not yet occurred and hence is uncertain, and an event which is either occurring contemporaneously or has already taken place.

cuando	"when", "whenever"
antes de que	"before"
apenas	"as soon as" ("scarcely")
después de que	"after"
en cuanto	"as soon as"

hasta que	"until"
mientras	"while", "so long as"
siempre que	"whenever"
tan pronto como	"as soon as"

With Subjunctive:

Vendré cuando *termine* mis deberes.	"I will come when I *have finished* my homework."
Cuando *sea* grande, me haré futbolista.	"When I grow up (*will be* older), I will be a soccer player."
Te llamaré en cuanto *llegue.*	"I will call you as soon as I *arrive.*"
Te llamaré en cuanto *haya llegado.*	"I will call you as soon as I *will have arrived.*"
Deberías salir, antes de que *sospechen* de ti.	"You should leave, before they *suspect* you."
Esperemos hasta que *lleguen.*	"We (will) wait until they *arrive.*"
Mientras *estemos* en París, visitaremos el Arco de Triunfo.	"While we *are* in Paris we will visit the Arc of Triumph."
Siempre que *puedas,* ven a verme.	"Whenever you *are able,* come see me."
Dijo que vendría en cuanto *terminara* sus deberes.	"He said that he would come as soon as he *finished* his homework."
Salí antes de que *llegaran* mis amigos.	"I left before my friends *(had) arrived.*"

Antes de que refers to a future event (with reference to the main clause) and hence, at least in theory, always requires the subjunctive. The other conjunctions can at times be used with the indicative, particularly in recounting events which already have occurred or which are habitual.

Salí después de que *llegaron* mis amigos.	"I left after my friends *arrived.*"
Esperé hasta que *llegaron.*	"I waited until they *arrived.*"
Salimos cuando *terminó* sus deberes.	"We left when he *finished* his homework."
Me saludaba siempre que me *veía.*	"He greeted me whenever he *saw* me."
Me saluda siempre que me *ve.*	"He greets me whenever he *sees* me."
Tan pronto como lo *hice,* supe que fue un gran error.	"As soon as I *did* it, I knew it was a big mistake."
Cuando *hay* sol no hay lluvia.	"When there *is* sun there is no rain."
Siempre cuando no *hago* mis deberes el profesor hace un examen.	"Always when I do not *do* my homework the teacher gives an exam."

Used in a future sense *después de que* normally takes the subjunctive:

Limpiaré la casa después de que todos se *hayan* ido.	"I will clean the house after everyone leaves (will have left)."

In the past tense the indicative should theoretically be required since in this case *después de que* refers to a *prior* action with regard to the fixed point of reference. Nonetheless, probably through confusion with *antes de que,* which always takes the subjunctive, it is not uncommon to find the subjunctive:

Limpié la casa después de que todos se *fueron*/se *fueran*.	"I cleaned the house after everyone *left.*"

(c) *Although*

"Although" clauses take the form:

Although [*condition*], [action]

The most important of the various conjunctions denoting "although" is *aunque*. The general rule is that if the condition specified by *aunque* (or equivalent) is *real* rather than *hypothetical* the indicative is used; if the condition is counter to fact (or the speaker is not vouching for its veracity) the subjunctive is used. Several conjunctions are used only with real conditions and hence always require the indicative.

"Although" clauses thus distinguish between conditions which exist, and are hence *obstacles,* and those which do not exist. The latter are differentiated in turn according to whether they are *possible* or *unlikely/impossible.* The tense used in the "although" clause is shown below: it depends on both the nature of the "although" and whether the "action" in the main clause takes place in the present/future or past.

main clause	tense used in *although* clause		
	real (obstacle) *indicative*	possible *subjunctive*	unlikely/impossible *subjunctive*
present/future	present/future	present	imperfect
past	imperfect/simple past/ compound past/ past perfect	—	past perfect

When the imperfect or past perfect subjunctive is used in the *although* clause, the verb in the *main* clause is usually in one of the forms of the conditional (present or perfect).

Conjunctions Used with Either Subjunctive or Indicative

aunque	"although"
aun cuando	"even though"
a pesar de que	"in spite of"
por + [adverb, adjective] + que	"for all the . . ."

real obstacle, hence indicative

Aunque *eres* mi hijo no te daré ningún dinero.	"Although you *are* my son, I will not give you any money."
Aunque *llueve* iré al parque.	"Although it *is raining* I will go to the park."
Aunque ayer *llovía* (*llovió*) fui al parque.	"Although yesterday it *was raining* (*rained*) I went to the park."
Aunque hoy *he trabajado* mucho, no he logrado terminar.	"Although I *have worked* a lot today, I have not managed to finish."
Aunque *estará* muy decepcionado no iré a la playa con él mañana.	"Although he *will be* very disappointed I will not go to the beach with him tomorrow."
A pesar de que *estaba (estuve)* enfermo seguí trabajando.	"Despite the fact that I *was* sick I continued working."
A pesar de que *había estado* muy enfermo en mayo, en junio fui al polo norte.	"Despite the fact that I *had been* very sick in May, in June I went to the North Pole."
Por más que *trabaja* nunca tiene el dinero suficiente.	"For all that he *works* he never has enough money."

possible, hence present subjunctive

Aunque *llueva* voy (iré) al parque hoy.	"Even if it *rains (should rain)* I will go to the park today."
La reconocerás aunque no la *hayas visto* en muchos años.	"You will recognize her even if you *have* not *seen* (will not have seen) her for many years."
Por mucho que *trabaje* nunca será rico.	"For all that he *may work (will work)* he will never be rich."

unlikely or impossible, hence imperfect or past subjunctive

Aunque *fueras* mi hijo no te daría ningún dinero.	"Even if you *were* my son I wouldn't give you any money."
Aunque ayer *hubiera llovido,* habría (hubiera) ido al parque.	"Even if yesterday it *had rained* I would have gone to the park."
Aunque *hubiera estado* enfermo, habría (hubiera) terminado con el proyecto.	"Even if I *had been* sick I would have finished the project."

Conjunctions Used Only with Indicative

si bien	"while", "though"
y eso que	"even though"
(aun) a sabiendas de que	"knowingly", "consciously"

These conjunctions refer to real conditions, hence their use with the indicative.

Si bien no *es* todo lo que esperaba, estoy muy contento.	"Even if it *is* not everything I was hoping for, I am very happy."
Voy al partido a sabiendas de que *van* a perder otra vez.	"I am going to the match even though I know they *are going* to lose again."

(d) As If

You look *as if* you had just been hit by a train.

By their very nature *as if* clauses present things which are counterfactual and hence are presented in the subjunctive. The principal conjunction used with this meaning is *como si;* others include *cual si, lo mismo que si,* and *igual que si.* The use of tenses is similar to the "unlikely/impossible" *although* clauses, i.e.

setting	subjunctive form
present or future	imperfect
past	past perfect (or imperfect)
Me mira (miró) como si *estuviera* loco.	"He looks (looked) at me as if I *were* crazy." (or as if *he* were crazy)
Mañana trabajaré lo mismo que si no *fuera* un día festivo.	"Tomorrow I will work just the same as if it *were* not a holiday."
Estaba tan pálido como si *hubiera visto* un fantasma.	"He was as pale as if he *had seen* a ghost."

With expressions of the form "it seems that", the situation is a bit different. As noted earlier, *parece que* is used with the indicative when it is conveys information, albeit in an attenuated fashion.

Parece que *está* durmiendo.   "It seems he's finally sleeping."

But when the verb is used not to convey information but rather the state of mind of the speaker about what the situation *appears to be* or *seems to be like,* the subjunctive can be employed—present in present situations, imperfect with the past.

Parece que *esté* durmiendo.	"It (almost) appears as if he *were* asleep."
Por fin llegamos a la cumbre	"At last we arrived at the summit of the
de la montaña; era preciosa,	mountain; it was beautiful, it seemed
parecía que *estuviéramos* en un	like we *were* in a giant bowl."
vaso gigante.	

In such (relatively rare) use *parece que* has a similar meaning to *como si,* but with the difference that while *como si* always requires an imperfect subjunctive, with *parece que* the present subjunctive is also possible.

(e) *Hopefully* and *If Only*

Ojalá is a very commonly used expression to convey a wish that something happen, or a regret that something didn't happen as one would have wished. The use of subjunctive tenses is parallel to that of *although* clauses: present for the possible, imperfect for the unlikely/impossible, and past perfect for past regrets.

¡Ojalá todavía *estén* esperando!	"Hopefully, they *are* still waiting."
	(or "they *will* still *be* waiting")
¡Ojalá no *haya* lluvia!	"Hopefully it did not rain (*will* not
	have rained)."
¡Ojalá *llueva* mañana!	"Hopefully it *will rain* tomorrow."
¡Ojalá *sea* verdad!	"Hopefully it *is* true."
¡Ojalá *fuera* verdad!	"If only it *were* true!"
¡Ojalá *hubiera sido* verdad!	"If only it *had been* true!"
¡Ojalá *ganara* la loto esta semana!	"If only I *would win* the lottery this week!"
¡Ojalá *hubiera terminado* mis	"If only I *had finished* my homework
deberes ayer!	yesterday!"

In "popular" language, *que* or *y* is often inserted:

¡Ojalá *que* no llueva!	"Hopefully, it won't rain."
¡Ojalá *y* no llueva!	"

Appendix
Future Subjunctive

In conditional clauses, using *si* or other conjunctions, there is at times ambiguity with regard to the meaning of a verb in the present tense (indicative or subjunctive), reflecting its use to represent both present and future possibilities:

indicative	Si no *cumples* esta ley, irás inmediatamente a la cárcel.
subjunctive	En caso de que no *cumplas* esta ley, irás inmediatamente a la cárcel.

These can mean *either*

(a) "If you *are* (at this moment) not in compliance with this law, then you will (now) go immediately to jail."
(b) "If (at some future moment) you *will not be* in compliance with this law, then you will (then) go immediately to jail."

This ambiguity did not always exist, as until the eighteenth century Spanish commonly employed a *future* subjunctive which allowed it to distinguish between these two meanings:

Si no *cumplieres* esta ley . . .	If (at some future time) you do not *comply* with this law . . .
En caso de que no *cumplieres* . . .	

Many texts on Spanish either make no mention of the future subjunctive or simply indicate that it is now obsolete. While this is essentially correct for the spoken language, one not infrequently encounters the future subjunctive in both legal and administrative texts, as well as in a wide range of fixed expressions of the form:

Sea lo que *fuere.*	"What will be will be."
Fuera lo que *fuere.*	"
Venga lo que *viniere.*	"
Pase lo que *pasare.*	"
Venga de donde *viniere.*	"Let it come from wherever."
siempre que *fuere* necesario	"whenever it will be necessary"

Consider, for example, the part of *La Constitución Española* (1978)[6] which deals with the possibilities of a *future* king being either a child or incapacitated:

> Cuando el Rey *fuere* menor de edad, el padre o la madre del Rey y, en su defecto, el pariente mayor de edad más próximo a suceder en la Corona, según el orden establecido en la Constitución, entrará a ejercer inmediatamente la Regencia y la ejercerá durante el tiempo de la minoría de edad del Rey.
>
> Si el Rey se *inhabilitare* para el ejercicio de su autoridad y la imposibilidad *fuere* reconocida por las Cortes Generales, entrará a ejercer inmediatamente la Regencia el Príncipe heredero de la Corona, si *fuere* mayor de edad. Si no lo *fuere,* se procederá de la manera prevista en el apartado anterior, hasta que el Príncipe heredero alcance la mayoría de edad.

An official translation reads:

> In the event of the King being under age [i.e., *If the King will be under age*], the King's father or mother or, in default thereof, the oldest relative of legal age who is nearest in succession to the Crown, according to the order established in the Constitution, shall immediately assume the office of Regent, which [he] shall exercise during the King's minority.
>
> If the King becomes [*will become*] unfit for the exercise of his authority, and this incapacity is [*will be*] recognized by the Cortes Generales, the Crown Prince shall immediately assume the Regency, if he is [*will be*] of age. If he is not [*will not be*], the procedure outlined in the foregoing paragraph shall apply until the coming of age of the Crown Prince.

In *modern* Spanish, the future subjunctives would all have to be replaced by present subjunctives or indicatives, leading to potentially ambiguous statements (as in English) such as:

	which could mean
Cuando el Rey *sea* menor	"When the [current?] king *is* under age"
Si el Rey se *inhabilita*	"If the [current?] king *is* unfit"

A text which suggests that an *existing* king (as opposed to a hypothetical future king) is unfit was not considered acceptable. The problem of course with legal texts is that they uniformly seek to avoid conditional tenses, saying what *will* happen rather than what *would* happen. In this case there is no alternative to the use of the "archaic" future subjunctive.

---

[6] Artículo 59. The Spanish Constitution (and English translation) can be found on the Constitution's "official" website: <www.constitucion.es>.

Similarly, if one compares a "classical" with a "modern" version of the Bible, one will find that the elimination of the future subjunctive has led to a loss in precision in meaning in certain passages, such as the following:

REINA VALERA VERSION:

E hizo Jacob voto, diciendo: Si *fuere* Dios conmigo, y me *guardare* en este viaje que voy, y me *diere* pan para comer y vestido para vestir ... (Génesis 28: 20–22)

Then Jacob made a vow, saying, "If God *will be* with me and *will keep* me in this way that I go, and *will give* me bread to eat and clothing to put on ..." (English Standard Version)

TYPICAL MODERN TRANSLATION:

... Si Dios *está* [7] conmigo ... me *guarda* ... me *da* alimento... (La Biblia de las Américas)

... If God *is* with me ... *keeps* me ... *gives* me food... (author's translation of La Biblia de las Américas)

The Real Academia Española has tried on various occasions to revive the future subjunctive, but without success. It remains alive and well, however, in neighboring Portuguese.

---

[7] While there might appear to be a contradiction between the newer *está* (*estar*) and previous *fuere*, *fuere* was likely being used as the future subjunctive of *ir* rather than *ser*, so that a literal translation would be "if God *will go* with me . . ."

PART III

ANNEXES

Models of Verb Classes and Sub-classes[1]

Perfectly Regular

1. cantar	1-1	tocar	1-2	pagar	1-3	averiguar
	1-4	cazar	1-5	aislar	1-6	aullar
	1-7	descafeinar	1-8	rehusar	1-9	amohinar
	1-10	ahincar	1-11	cabrahigar	1-12	enraizar
	1-13	europeizar	1-14	actuar	1-15	enviar
2. comer	2-1	vencer	2-2	coger	2-3	leer
	2-4	empeller	2-5	tañer	2-6	*romper*
3. subir	3-1	fruncir	3-2	dirigir	3-3	distinguir
	3-4	delinquir	3-5	bullir	3-6	bruñir
	3-7	reunir	3-8	prohibir	3-9	*abrir*
	3-10	*cubrir*	3-11	*escribir*	3-12	*imprimir*
	3-13	*pudrir*	3-14	abolir (*defective*)		

Diphthongs (e → ie, o → ue)

4A. pensar	4A-1	negar	4A-2	empezar	4A-3	errar
4B. mostrar	4B-1	trocar	4B-2	colgar	4B-3	forzar
	4B-4	agorar	4B-5	desosar	4B-6	avergonzar
5A. perder						
5B. mover	5B-1	cocer	5B-2	oler	5B-3	*resolver*
	5B-4	*volver*				

Diphthongs (e → ie, o → ue) and/or Umlauts (e → i, o → u)

6A. sentir	6A-1	erguir				
6B. pedir	6B-1	elegir	6B-2	seguir	6B-3	ceñir
	6B-4	reír				
6C. dormir	6C-1	*morir*				

---

[1] Italicized sub-classes (e.g., 2.6 *romper*) are identical to their class model (*comer* for *romper*) apart from their irregular past participle. *Freír* has an irregular past participle but is not listed as a separate sub-class of *reír* (6B-4).

1st Person Singular -zco

7A. **conocer**   7A-1   yacer   7A-2   placer
7B. **lucir**

"Add -y except before -i"

8. **construir**

Irregular 1st Singular -go (Otherwise Largely Predictable)

9. **caer**   9-1   raer   9-2   roer
10. **oír**
11. **salir**
12. **valer**
13. **asir**

Mixed Patterns

14. **ver**   14-1   prever
15. **discernir**
16. **jugar**
17. **adquirir**
18. **argüir**

Fundamentally Irregular

19. **ser**
20. **estar**
21. **haber**
22. **saber**
23. **caber**
24. **ir**
25. **dar**
26. **poder**
27. **querer**
28. **decir**   28-1   predecir   28-2   bendecir
29. **hacer**   29-1   rehacer   29-2   satisfacer
30. **poner**   30-1   suponer
31. **tener**   31-1   obtener
32. **venir**   32-1   convenir

33. **traer**
34. **-ducir**
35. **andar**

On the following pages the complete conjugations for all of the above verb classes are presented. For the sub-classes, in general only tenses where one or more conjugations differ from the class model are shown; for 2-3 (*leer*), 3-14 (*abolir*), 6A-1 (*erguir*), 6B-1 (*elegir*), 6B-2 (*seguir*), 6B-3 (*ceñir*), 6B-4 (*reír*) and 14-1 (*prever*) the full conjugations are shown.

For all verbs apart from *ser, haber*, and *ir*, the relevant irregularities and/or orthographic modifications are presented in summary form at the top of the page. Note that:

(i) For a number of verbs, changes occur in conjugations in which the stress accent falls on the stem (root) syllable: present indicative (1s/2s/3s/3p), present subjunctive (1s/2s/3s/3p), and imperative (2s).
(ii) An irregular first person singular present indicative always implies an irregular present subjunctive.
(iii) An irregular simple past implies a (precisely) corresponding irregular imperfect subjunctive.

| 1 | | CANTAR | TO SING | |

INDICATIVE

Present	Simple Past	Imperfect	Future	Conditional
canto	canté	cantaba	cantaré	cantaría
cantas	cantaste	cantabas	cantarás	cantarías
canta	cantó	cantaba	cantará	cantaría
cantamos	cantamos	cantábamos	cantaremos	cantaríamos
cantáis	cantasteis	cantabais	cantaréis	cantaríais
cantan	cantaron	cantaban	cantarán	cantarían

SUBJUNCTIVE

Present	Imperfect (I)	Imperfect (II)
cante	cantara	cantase
cantes	cantaras	cantases
cante	cantara	cantase
cantemos	cantáramos	cantásemos
cantéis	cantarais	cantaseis
canten	cantaran	cantasen

IMPERATIVE	canta	cantad
PAST PARTICIPLE	cantado	
PRESENT PARTICIPLE	cantando	

1-1	C → QU	TOCAR	TO TOUCH
INDICATIVE Present	SUBJUNCTIVE Present	SIMPLE PAST	IMPERATIVE
	toque	*toqué*	
	toques	tocaste	
	toque	tocó	
	toquemos	tocamos	
	toquéis	tocasteis	
	toquen	tocaron	

1-2	G → GU	PAGAR	TO PAY
INDICATIVE Present	SUBJUNCTIVE Present	SIMPLE PAST	IMPERATIVE
	pague	*pagué*	
	pagues	pagaste	
	pague	pagó	
	paguemos	pagamos	
	paguéis	pagasteis	
	paguen	pagaron	

1-3	GU → GÜ	AVERIGUAR	TO ASCERTAIN
INDICATIVE Present	SUBJUNCTIVE Present	SIMPLE PAST	IMPERATIVE
	averigüe	*averigüé*	
	averigües	averiguaste	
	averigüe	averiguó	
	averigüemos	averiguamos	
	averigüéis	averiguasteis	
	averigüen	averiguaron	

1-4	Z → C	CAZAR	TO HUNT, CHASE
INDICATIVE Present	SUBJUNCTIVE Present	SIMPLE PAST	IMPERATIVE
	cace	*cacé*	
	caces	cazaste	
	cace	cazó	
	cacemos	cazamos	
	cacéis	cazasteis	
	cacen	cazaron	

1-5	AI → AÍ[1]	AISLAR	TO ISOLATE, INSULATE
INDICATIVE Present	SUBJUNCTIVE Present	SIMPLE PAST	IMPERATIVE
aíslo	*aísle*		
aíslas	*aísles*		*aísla*
aísla	*aísle*		
aislamos	aislemos		
aisláis	aisléis		aislad
aíslan	*aíslen*		

[1] Written accents in conjugations stressed on stem syllable. There are no other verbs in 1-5.

1-6	AU → AÚ[1]	AULLAR	TO HOWL
INDICATIVE Present	SUBJUNCTIVE Present	SIMPLE PAST	IMPERATIVE
aúllo	*aúlle*		
aúllas	*aúlles*		*aúlla*
aúlla	*aúlle*		
aullamos	aullemos		
aulláis	aulléis		aullad
aúllan	*aúllen*		

[1] Written accents in conjugations stressed on stem syllable. Other verbs in 1-6: *ahumar, aunar, aupar, maullar.*

1-7	EI → EÍ[1]	DESCAFEINAR	TO DECAFFEINATE
INDICATIVE Present	SUBJUNCTIVE Present	SIMPLE PAST	IMPERATIVE
descafeíno	*descafeíne*		
descafeínas	*descafeínes*		*descafeína*
descafeína	*descafeíne*		
descafeinamos	descafeinemos		
descafeináis	descafeinéis		descafeinad
descafeínan	*descafeínen*		

[1] Written accents in conjugations stressed on stem syllable. The only other verb in 1-7 is *sobrehilar.*

1-8	E(H)U → E(H)Ú[1]	REHUSAR	TO REFUSE
INDICATIVE Present	**SUBJUNCTIVE** Present	**SIMPLE PAST**	**IMPERATIVE**
rehúso	*rehúse*		
rehúsas	*rehúses*		*rehúsa*
rehúsa	*rehúse*		
rehusamos	rehusemos		
rehusáis	rehuséis		rehusad
rehúsan	*rehúsen*		

[1] Written accents in conjugations stressed on stem syllable. There are no other verbs in 1-8.

1-9	O(H)I → O(H)Í[1]	AMOHINAR	TO ANNOY
INDICATIVE Present	**SUBJUNCTIVE** Present	**SIMPLE PAST**	**IMPERATIVE**
amohíno	*amohíne*		
amohínas	*amohínes*		*amohína*
amohína	*amohíne*		
amohinamos	amohinemos		
amohináis	amohinéis		amohinad
amohínan	*amohínen*		

[1] Written accents in conjugations stressed on stem syllable. There are no other verbs in 1-9.

1-10	C → QU A(H)I → A(H)Í[1]	AHINCAR	TO URGE
INDICATIVE Present	**SUBJUNCTIVE** Present	**SIMPLE PAST**	**IMPERATIVE**
ahínco	*ahínQUe*	ahinQUé	
ahíncas	*ahínQUes*	ahincaste	*ahínca*
ahínca	*ahínQUe*	ahincó	
ahincamos	ahinQUemos	ahincamos	
ahincáis	ahinQUéis	ahincasteis	ahincad
ahíncan	*ahínQUen*	ahincaron	

[1] Written accents in conjugations stressed on stem syllable. There are no other verbs in 1-10.

1-11	G → GU A(H)I → A(H)Í[1]	CABRAHIGAR	TO CAPRIFICATE
INDICATIVE Present	SUBJUNCTIVE Present	SIMPLE PAST	IMPERATIVE
cabrahígo	*cabrahíGUe*	cabrahiGUé	
cabrahígas	*cabrahíGUes*	cabrahigaste	*cabrahíga*
cabrahíga	*cabrahíGUe*	cabrahigó	
cabrahigamos	cabrahiGUemos	cabrahigamos	
cabrahigáis	cabrahiGUéis	cabrahigasteis	cabrahigad
cabrahígan	*cabrahíGUen*	cabrahigaron	

[1] Written accents in conjugations stressed on stem syllable. There are no other verbs in 1-11.

1-12	Z → C AI → AÍ[1]	ENRAIZAR	TO TAKE ROOT
INDICATIVE Present	SUBJUNCTIVE Present	SIMPLE PAST	IMPERATIVE
enraízo	*enraíCe*	enraiCé	
enraízas	*enraíCes*	enraizaste	*enraíza*
enraíza	*enraíCe*	enraizó	
enraizamos	enraiCemos	enraizamos	
enraizáis	enraiCéis	enraizasteis	enraizad
enraízan	*enraíCen*	enraizaron	

[1] Written accents in conjugations stressed on stem syllable. Other verbs in 1-12: *desenraizar, hebraizar, judaizar*

1-13	Z → C EI → EÍ[1]	EUROPEIZAR	TO EUROPEANIZE
INDICATIVE Present	SUBJUNCTIVE Present	SIMPLE PAST	IMPERATIVE
europeízo	*europeíCe*	europeiCé	
europeízas	*europeíCes*	europeizaste	*europeíza*
europeíza	*europeíCe*	europeizó	
europeizamos	europeiCemos	europeizamos	
europeizáis	europeiCéis	europeizasteis	europeizad
europeízan	*europeíCen*	europeizaron	

[1] Written accents in conjugations stressed on stem syllable. There are no other verbs in 1-13.

1-14	U → Ú[1]	ACTUAR	TO ACT, ACTUATE
INDICATIVE Present	SUBJUNCTIVE Present	SIMPLE PAST	IMPERATIVE
actúo	*actúe*		
actúas	*actúes*		*actúa*
actúa	*actúe*		
actuamos	actuemos		
actuáis	actuéis		actuad
actúan	*actúen*		

[1] Written accents in conjugations stressed on stem syllable. All *-uar* verbs not ending in *-cuar* or *-guar* are in 1-14.

1-15	I → Í[1]	ENVIAR	TO SEND
INDICATIVE Present	SUBJUNCTIVE Present	SIMPLE PAST	IMPERATIVE
envío	*envíe*		
envías	*envíes*		*envía*
envía	*envíe*		
enviamos	enviemos		
enviáis	enviéis		enviad
envían	*envíen*		

[1] Written accents in conjugations stressed on stem syllable. About 30% of verbs ending in *-iar* are in 1-15, the rest (e.g., *cambiar*) are conjugated like *cantar* (1).

2		COMER	TO EAT	
INDICATIVE Present	Simple Past	Imperfect	Future	Conditional
como	comí	comía	comeré	comería
comes	comiste	comías	comerás	comerías
come	comió	comía	comerá	comería
comemos	comimos	comíamos	comeremos	comeríamos
coméis	comisteis	comíais	comeréis	comeríais
comen	comieron	comían	comerán	comerían

SUBJUNCTIVE

Present	Imperfect (I)	Imperfect (II)
coma	comiera	comiese
comas	comieras	comieses
coma	comiera	comiese
comamos	comiéramos	comiésemos
comáis	comierais	comieseis
coman	comieran	comiesen

IMPERATIVE (2s/2p)	come	comed
PAST PARTICIPLE	comido	
PRESENT PARTICIPLE	comiendo	

2-1	C → Z	VENCER	TO VANQUISH

INDICATIVE Present	SUBJUNCTIVE Present	SIMPLE PAST	IMPERATIVE
venzo	*venza*		
vences	*venzas*		
vence	*venza*		
vencemos	*venzamos*		
vencéis	*venzáis*		
vencen	*venzan*		

2-2	G → J	COGER	TO GRASP, CATCH

INDICATIVE Present	SUBJUNCTIVE Present	SIMPLE PAST	IMPERATIVE
cojo	*coja*		
coges	*cojas*		
coge	*coja*		
cogemos	*cojamos*		
cogéis	*cojáis*		
cogen	*cojan*		

2-3	UNSTRESSED -*I* BETWEEN VOWELS → -*Y*	LEER	TO READ
	ADDITIONAL WRITTEN ACCENT +		

INDICATIVE

Present	Simple Past	Imperfect	Future	Conditional
leo	leí	leía	leeré	leería
lees	leíste +	leías	leerás	leerías
lee	*leyó*	leía	leerá	leería
leemos	leímos +	leíamos	leeremos	leeríamos
leéis	leísteis +	leíais	leeréis	leeríais
leen	*leyeron*	leían	leerán	leerían

SUBJUNCTIVE

Present	Imperfect (I)	Imperfect (II)
lea	*leyera*	*leyese*
leas	*leyeras*	*leyeses*
lea	*leyera*	*leyese*
leamos	*leyéramos*	*leyésemos*
leáis	*leyerais*	*leyeseis*
lean	*leyeran*	*leyesen*

IMPERATIVE (2s/2p)	lee	leed
PAST PARTICIPLE	leído +	
PRESENT PARTICIPLE	*leyendo*	

2-4	LL + IE → LLE LL + IO → LLO	EMPELLER	TO PUSH, SHOVE

SIMPLE PAST	SUBJUNCTIVE	
	Imperfect (1)	Imperfect (2)
empellí	*empellera*	*empellese*
empelliste	*empelleras*	*empelleses*
empelló (not *empellio)	*empellera*	*empellese*
empellimos	*empelléramos*	*empellésemos*
empellisteis	*empellerais*	*empelleseis*
empelleron (not *empellieron)	*empelleran*	*empellesen*

PRESENT PARTICIPLE   *empellendo* (not *empelliendo)

2-5	Ñ +IE → ÑE Ñ +IO → ÑO	TAÑER	TO PLAY (A MUSICAL INSTRUMENT)

SIMPLE PAST	SUBJUNCTIVE	
	Imperfect (1)	Imperfect (2)
tañí	*tañera*	*tañese*
tañiste	*tañeras*	*tañeses*
tañó (not *tañio)	*tañera*	*tañese*
tañimos	*tañéramos*	*tañésemos*
tañisteis	*tañerais*	*tañeseis*
tañeron (not *tañieron)	*tañeran*	*tañesen*

PRESENT PARTICIPLE   *tañendo* (not *tañiendo)

2-6	ROMPER	TO BREAK	PAST PARTICIPLE:	*ROTO*

| 3 | SUBIR | | TO RAISE, TO CLIMB | |

INDICATIVE

Present	Simple Past	Imperfect	Future	Conditional
subo	subí	subía	subiré	subiría
subes	subiste	subías	subirás	subirías
sube	subió	subía	subirá	subiría
subimos	subimos	subíamos	subiremos	subiríamos
subís	subisteis	subíais	subiréis	subiríais
suben	subieron	subían	subirán	subirían

SUBJUNCTIVE

Present	Imperfect (I)	Imperfect (II)
suba	subiera	subiese
subas	subieras	subieses
suba	subiera	subiese
subamos	subiéramos	subiésemos
subáis	subierais	subieseis
suban	subieran	subiesen

IMPERATIVE (2s/2p)	sube	subid	
PAST PARTICIPLE	subido		
PRESENT PARTICIPLE	subiendo		

| 3-1 | C → Z | FRUNCIR | TO WRINKLE (BROW, NOSE) |

INDICATIVE Present	SUBJUNCTIVE Present	SIMPLE PAST	IMPERATIVE
frunzo	*frunza*		
frunces	*frunzas*		
frunce	*frunza*		
fruncimos	*frunzamos*		
fruncís	*frunzáis*		
fruncen	*frunzan*		

| 3-2 | G → J | DIRIGIR | TO DIRECT |

INDICATIVE Present	SUBJUNCTIVE Present	SIMPLE PAST	IMPERATIVE
dirijo	*dirija*		
diriges	*dirijas*		
dirige	*dirija*		
dirigimos	*dirijamos*		
dirigís	*dirijáis*		
dirigen	*dirijan*		

3-3	GU → G	DISTINGUIR	TO DISTINGUISH
INDICATIVE Present	SUBJUNCTIVE Present	SIMPLE PAST	IMPERATIVE

INDICATIVE Present	SUBJUNCTIVE Present
distingo	*distinga*
distingues	*distingas*
distingue	*distinga*
distinguimos	*distingamos*
distinguís	*distingáis*
distinguen	*distingan*

3-4	QU → C	DELINQUIR	TO TRANSGRESS
INDICATIVE Present	SUBJUNCTIVE Present	SIMPLE PAST	IMPERATIVE

INDICATIVE Present	SUBJUNCTIVE Present
delinco	*delinca*
delinques	*delincas*
delinque	*delinca*
delinquimos	*delincamos*
delinquís	*delincáis*
delinquen	*delincan*

3-5	LL + IE → LLE LL + IO → LLO	BULLIR	TO BOIL, BUBBLE

SIMPLE PAST	SUBJUNCTIVE Imperfect (1)	Imperfect (2)
bullí	*bullera*	*bullese*
bulliste	*bulleras*	*bulleses*
bulló (not *bullio)	*bullera*	*bullese*
bullimos	*bulléramos*	*bullésemos*
bullisteis	*bullerais*	*bulleseis*
bulleron (not *bullieron)	*bulleran*	*bullesen*
PRESENT PARTICIPLE	*bullendo* (not *bulliendo)	

3-6	Ñ + IE → ÑE Ñ + IO → ÑO	BRUÑIR	TO BURNISH

SIMPLE PAST	SUBJUNCTIVE Imperfect (1)	Imperfect (2)
bruñí	*bruñera*	*bruñese*
bruñiste	*bruñeras*	*bruñeses*
bruñó (not *bruñio)	*bruñera*	*bruñese*
bruñimos	*bruñéramos*	*bruñésemos*
bruñisteis	*bruñerais*	*bruñeseis*
bruñeron (not *bruñieron)	*bruñeran*	*bruñesen*
PRESENT PARTICIPLE	*bruñendo* (not *bruñiendo)	

3-7	EU → EÚ[1]	REUNIR	TO REUNITE
INDICATIVE Present	SUBJUNCTIVE Present	SIMPLE PAST	IMPERATIVE
reúno	*reúna*		
reúnes	*reúnas*		*reúne*
reúne	*reúna*		
reunimos	reunamos		
reunís	reunáis		reunid
reúnen	*reúnan*		

[1] Written accents in conjugations stressed on stem syllable. The only other verb in 3-7 is *rehu*ndir.

3-8	O(H)I → O(H)Í[1]	PROHIBIR	TO PROHIBIT
INDICATIVE Present	SUBJUNCTIVE Present	SIMPLE PAST	IMPERATIVE
prohíbo	*prohíba*		
prohíbes	*prohíbas*		*prohíbe*
prohíbe	*prohíba*		
prohibimos	prohibamos		
prohibís	prohibáis		prohibid
prohíben	*prohíban*		

[1] Written accents in conjugations stressed on stem syllable. The only other verb in 3-8 is *cohi*bir.

3-9	**ABRIR**	TO OPEN	PAST PARTICIPLE: *ABIERTO*
3-10	**CUBRIR**	TO CLOSE	PAST PARTICIPLE: *CUBIERTO*
3-11	**ESCRIBIR**	TO WRITE	PAST PARTICIPLE: *ESCRITO*[1]
3-12	**IMPRIMIR**	TO PRINT	PAST PARTICIPLE: *IMPRESO/IMPRIMIDO*
3-13	**PUDRIR**	TO PUTREFY	PAST PARTICIPLE: *PODRIDO*

[1] The RAE also accepts the "old" forms ending in -*scripto* for all -*scribir* verbs apart from *escribir*, *rescribir*, *reescribir* and *manuscribir*: *inscripto*, *suscripto*, *transcripto*, etc.

3-14	*DEFECTIVE*	ABOLIR	TO ABOLISH	
INDICATIVE Present	Simple Past	Imperfect	Future	Conditional
—	abolí	abolía	aboliré	aboliría
—	aboliste	abolías	abolirás	abolirías
—	abolió	abolía	abolirá	aboliría
abolimos	abolimos	abolíamos	aboliremos	aboliríamos
abolís	abolisteis	abolíais	aboliréis	aboliríais
—	abolieron	abolían	abolirán	abolirían

SUBJUNCTIVE

Present	Imperfect (I)	Imperfect (II)
—	aboliera	aboliese
—	abolieras	abolieses
—	aboliera	aboliese
—	aboliéramos	aboliésemos
—	abolierais	abolieseis
—	abolieran	aboliesen

IMPERATIVE (2s/2p)	—	abolid
PAST PARTICIPLE	abolido	
PRESENT PARTICIPLE	aboliendo	

Note: All conjugations are regular, but only those where the post-stem vowel is -*i* (or diphthong -*ie*/-*io*) are used.

4A	DIPHTHONG E → IE[1]	PENSAR	TO THINK

INDICATIVE

Present	Simple Past	Imperfect	Future	Conditional
pienso	pensé	pensaba	pensaré	pensaría
piensas	pensaste	pensabas	pensarás	pensarías
piensa	pensó	pensaba	pensará	pensaría
pensamos	pensamos	pensábamos	pensaremos	pensaríamos
pensáis	pensasteis	pensabais	pensaréis	pensaríais
piensan	pensaron	pensaban	pensarán	pensarían

SUBJUNCTIVE

Present	Imperfect (I)	Imperfect (II)
piense	pensara	pensase
pienses	pensaras	pensases
piense	pensara	pensase
pensemos	pensáramos	pensásemos
penséis	pensarais	pensaseis
piensen	pensaran	pensasen

IMPERATIVE (2s/2p)	*piensa*	pensad
PAST PARTICIPLE	pensado	
PRESENT PARTICIPLE	pensando	

[1] In conjugations stressed on stem syllable.

4A-1	DIPHTHONG E → IE G → GU	NEGAR	TO DENY

INDICATIVE Present	SUBJUNCTIVE Present	SIMPLE PAST	IMPERATIVE
niego	*nieGUe*	neGUé	
niegas	*nieGUes*	negaste	*niega*
niega	*nieGUe*	negó	
negamos	neGUemos	negamos	
negáis	neGUéis	negasteis	negad
niegan	*nieGUen*	negaron	

4A-2	DIPHTHONG E → IE Z → C	EMPEZAR	TO BEGIN

INDICATIVE Present	SUBJUNCTIVE Present	SIMPLE PAST	IMPERATIVE
empiezo	*empieCe*	empeCé	
empiezas	*empieCes*	empezaste	*empieza*
empieza	*empieCe*	empezó	
empezamos	empeCemos	empezamos	
empezáis	empeCéis	empezasteis	empezad
empiezan	*empieCen*	empezaron	

4A-3	DIPHTHONG E → YE	ERRAR	TO ERR, TO WANDER

INDICATIVE Present	SUBJUNCTIVE Present	SIMPLE PAST	IMPERATIVE
yerro	*yerre*		
yerras	*yerres*		*yerra*
yerra	*yerre*		
erramos	erremos		
erráis	erréis		errad
yerran	*yerren*		

4B	DIPHTHONG O → UE[1]	MOSTRAR	TO SHOW

INDICATIVE Present	Simple Past	Imperfect	Future	Conditional
muestro	mostré	mostraba	mostraré	mostraría
muestras	mostraste	mostrabas	mostrarás	mostrarías
muestra	mostró	mostraba	mostrará	mostraría
mostramos	mostramos	mostrábamos	mostraremos	mostraríamos
mostráis	mostrasteis	mostrabais	mostraréis	mostraríais
muestran	mostraron	mostraban	mostrarán	mostrarían

SUBJUNCTIVE

Present	Imperfect (I)	Imperfect (II)
muestre	mostrara	mostrase
muestres	mostraras	mostrases
muestre	mostrara	mostrase
mostremos	mostráramos	mostrásemos
mostréis	mostrarais	mostraseis
muestren	mostraran	mostrasen

IMPERATIVE (2s/2p)	*muestra*	mostrad
PAST PARTICIPLE	mostrado	
PRESENT PARTICIPLE	mostrando	

[1] In conjugations stressed on stem syllable.

4B-1	DIPHTHONG O → UE C → QU	TROCAR	TO EXCHANGE

INDICATIVE Present	SUBJUNCTIVE Present	SIMPLE PAST	IMPERATIVE
trueco	*trueQUe*	troQUé	
truecas	*trueQUes*	trocaste	*trueca*
trueca	*trueQUe*	trocó	
trocamos	troQUemos	trocamos	
trocáis	troQUéis	trocasteis	trocad
truecan	*trueQUen*	trocaron	

4B-2	DIPHTHONG O → UE G → GU	COLGAR	TO HANG

INDICATIVE Present	SUBJUNCTIVE Present	SIMPLE PAST	IMPERATIVE
cuelgo	*cuelGUe*	colGUé	
cuelgas	*cuelGUes*	colgaste	*cuelga*
cuelga	*cuelGUe*	colgó	
colgamos	colGUemos	colgamos	
colgáis	colGUéis	colgasteis	colgad
cuelgan	*cuelGUen*	colgaron	

4B-3	DIPHTHONG O → UE Z → C	FORZAR	TO FORCE

INDICATIVE Present	SUBJUNCTIVE Present	SIMPLE PAST	IMPERATIVE
fuerzo	fuerCe	forCé	
fuerzas	fuerCes	forzaste	fuerza
fuerza	fuerCe	forzó	
forzamos	forCemos	forzamos	
forzáis	forCéis	forzasteis	forzad
fuerzan	fuerCen	forzaron	

4B-4	DIPHTHONG GO → GÜE	AGORAR	TO PREDICT (SUPERSTITIOUSLY)

INDICATIVE Present	SUBJUNCTIVE Present	SIMPLE PAST	IMPERATIVE
agüero	agüere		
agüeras	agüeres		agüera
agüera	agüere		
agoramos	agoremos		
agoráis	agoréis		agorad
agüeran	agüeren		

4B-5	DIPHTHONG O → HUE	DESOSAR[1]	TO BONE

INDICATIVE Present	SUBJUNCTIVE Present	SIMPLE PAST	IMPERATIVE
deshueso	deshuese		
deshuesas	deshueses		deshuesa
deshuesa	deshuese		
desosamos	desosemos		
desosáis	desoséis		desosad
deshuesan	deshuesen		

[1] Desosar is the "old" form of deshuesar by which it has largely been supplanted.

4B-6	DIPHTHONG GO → GÜE Z → C	AVERGONZAR	TO SHAME

INDICATIVE Present	SUBJUNCTIVE Present	SIMPLE PAST	IMPERATIVE
avergüenzo	avergüenCe	avergonCé	
avergüenzas	avergüenCes	avergonzaste	avergüenza
avergüenza	avergüenCe	avergonzó	
avergonzamos	avergonCemos	avergonzamos	
avergonzáis	avergonCéis	avergonzasteis	avergonzad
avergüenzan	avergüenCen	avergonzaron	

5A	DIPHTHONG E → IE[1]		PERDER	TO LOSE

INDICATIVE

Present	Simple Past	Imperfect	Future	Conditional
pierdo	perdí	perdía	perderé	perdería
pierdes	perdiste	perdías	perderás	perderías
pierde	perdió	perdía	perderá	perdería
perdemos	perdimos	perdíamos	perderemos	perderíamos
perdéis	perdisteis	perdíais	perderéis	perderíais
pierden	perdieron	perdían	perderán	perderían

SUBJUNCTIVE

Present	Imperfect (I)	Imperfect (II)
pierda	perdiera	perdiese
pierdas	perdieras	perdieses
pierda	perdiera	perdiese
perdamos	perdiéramos	perdiésemos
perdáis	perdierais	perdieseis
pierdan	perdieran	perdiesen

IMPERATIVE (2s/2p)	*pierde*	perded
PAST PARTICIPLE	perdido	
PRESENT PARTICIPLE	perdiendo	

[1] In conjugations stressed on stem syllable.

5B	DIPHTHONG O → UE[1]		MOVER	TO MOVE

INDICATIVE

Present	Simple Past	Imperfect	Future	Conditional
muevo	moví	movía	moveré	movería
mueves	moviste	movías	moverás	moverías
mueve	movió	movía	moverá	movería
movemos	movimos	movíamos	moveremos	moveríamos
movéis	movisteis	movíais	moveréis	moveríais
mueven	movieron	movían	moverán	moverían

SUBJUNCTIVE

Present	Imperfect (I)	Imperfect (II)
mueva	moviera	moviese
muevas	movieras	movieses
mueva	moviera	moviese
movamos	moviéramos	moviésemos
mováis	movierais	movieseis
muevan	movieran	moviesen

IMPERATIVE (2s/2p)	*mueve*	moved
PAST PARTICIPLE	movido	
PRESENT PARTICIPLE	moviendo	

[1] In conjugations stressed on stem syllable.

5B-1	*DIPHTHONG O → UE*	COCER	TO COOK
	C → Z		

INDICATIVE Present	SUBJUNCTIVE Present	SIMPLE PAST	IMPERATIVE
cueZo	*cueZa*		
cueces	*cueZas*		*cuece*
cuece	*cueZa*		
cocemos	coZamos		
cocéis	coZáis		coced
cuecen	*cueZan*		

5B-2	*DIPHTHONG O → HUE*	OLER	TO SMELL

INDICATIVE Present	SUBJUNCTIVE Present	SIMPLE PAST	IMPERATIVE
huelo	*huela*		
hueles	*huelas*		*huele*
huele	*huela*		
olemos	olamos		
oléis	oláis		oled
huelen	*huelan*		

5B-3	**RESOLVER**	TO RESOLVE, SOLVE	PAST PARTICIPLE:	*RESUELTO*

5B-4	**VOLVER**	TO TURN	PAST PARTICIPLE:	*VUELTO*

6A	*DIPHTHONG* E → IE[1] SENTIR TO FEEL
	UMLAUT E → I[2]

INDICATIVE

Present	Simple Past	Imperfect	Future	Conditional
siento	sentí	sentía	sentiré	sentiría
sientes	sentiste	sentías	sentirás	sentirías
siente	**sintió**	sentía	sentirá	sentiría
sentimos	sentimos	sentíamos	sentiremos	sentiríamos
sentís	sentisteis	sentíais	sentiréis	sentiríais
sienten	**sintieron**	sentían	sentirán	sentirían

SUBJUNCTIVE

Present	Imperfect (I)	Imperfect (II)
sienta	**sintiera**	**sintiese**
sientas	**sintieras**	**sintieses**
sienta	**sintiera**	**sintiese**
sintamos	**sintiéramos**	**sintiésemos**
sintáis	**sintierais**	**sintieseis**
sientan	**sintieran**	**sintiesen**

IMPERATIVE (2s/2p)	*siente*	sentid
PAST PARTICIPLE	sentido	
PRESENT PARTICIPLE	**sintiendo**	

[1]In conjugations stressed on stem syllable.
[2]In conjugations not stressed on stem syllable, when next vowel is *not* (simple) -*i*.

6A-1	LIKE *SENTIR* OR *PEDIR*[1] ERGUIR TO RAISE, LIFT UP
	GU → G

INDICATIVE

Present			Simple Past	Imperfect	Future	Conditional
yerGo	**or**	*irGo*	erguí	erguía	erguiré	erguiría
yergues	**or**	*irgues*	erguiste	erguías	erguirás	erguirías
yergue	**or**	*irgue*	*irguió*	erguía	erguirá	erguiría
erguimos			erguimos	erguíamos	erguiremos	erguiríamos
erguís			erguisteis	erguíais	erguiréis	erguiríais
yerguen	**or**	*irguen*	*irguieron*	erguían	erguirán	erguirían

SUBJUNCTIVE

Present			Imperfect (I)	Imperfect (II)
yerGa	**or**	*irGa*	*irguiera*	*irguiese*
yerGas	**or**	*irGas*	*irguieras*	*irguieses*
yerGa	**or**	*irGa*	*irguiera*	*irguiese*
yerGamos[2]	**or**	*irGamos*	*irguiéramos*	*irguiésemos*
yerGáis[2]	**or**	*irGáis*	*irguierais*	*irguieseis*
yerGan	**or**	*irGan*	*irguieran*	*irguiesen*

IMPERATIVE (2s/2p)	*yergue* **or** *irgue*	erguid
PAST PARTICIPLE	erguido	
PRESENT PARTICIPLE	*irguiendo*	

[1] *Sentir* model more common; diphthongs are written "ye", as for *errar* (4A-3).

[2] The forms *yergamos* and *yergáis* are irregular, since a diphthong does not normally occur in an unstressed syllable. They are not recognized by the RAE but appear elsewhere (e.g., Moliner).

6B	UMLAUT E → I[1]	PEDIR	TO REQUEST

INDICATIVE

Present	Simple Past	Imperfect	Future	Conditional
pido	pedí	pedía	pediré	pediría
pides	pediste	pedías	pedirás	pedirías
pide	**pidió**	pedía	pedirá	pediría
pedimos	pedimos	pedíamos	pediremos	pediríamos
pedís	pedisteis	pedíais	pediréis	pediríais
piden	**pidieron**	pedían	pedirán	pedirían

SUBJUNCTIVE

Present	Imperfect (I)	Imperfect (II)
pida	**pidiera**	**pidiese**
pidas	**pidieras**	**pidieses**
pida	**pidiera**	**pidiese**
pidamos	**pidiéramos**	**pidiésemos**
pidáis	**pidierais**	**pidieseis**
pidan	**pidieran**	**pidiesen**

IMPERATIVE (2s/2p)	**pide**	pedid
PAST PARTICIPLE	pedido	
PRESENT PARTICIPLE	**pidiendo**	

[1] In conjugations in which next vowel is *not* (simple) -*i*.

6B-1	UMLAUT E → I	ELEGIR	TO ELECT
	G → J		

INDICATIVE

Present	Simple Past	Imperfect	Future	Conditional
eliJo	elegí	elegía	elegiré	elegiría
eliges	elegiste	elegías	elegirás	elegirías
elige	*eligió*	elegía	elegirá	elegiría
elegimos	elegimos	elegíamos	elegiremos	elegiríamos
elegís	elegisteis	elegíais	elegiréis	elegiríais
eligen	*eligieron*	elegían	elegirán	elegirían

SUBJUNCTIVE

Present	Imperfect (I)	Imperfect (II)
eliJa	*eligiera*	*eligiese*
eliJas	*eligieras*	*eligieses*
eliJa	*eligiera*	*eligiese*
eliJamos	*eligiéramos*	*eligiésemos*
eliJáis	*eligierais*	*eligieseis*
eliJan	*eligieran*	*eligiesen*

IMPERATIVE (2s/2p)	*elige*	elegid
PAST PARTICIPLE	elegido	
PRESENT PARTICIPLE	*eligiendo*	

6B-2	UMLAUT E → I	SEGUIR	TO FOLLOW
	GU → G		

INDICATIVE

Present	Simple Past	Imperfect	Future	Conditional
siGo	seguí	seguía	seguiré	seguiría
sigues	seguiste	seguías	seguirás	seguirías
sigue	*siguió*	seguía	seguirá	seguiría
seguimos	seguimos	seguíamos	seguiremos	seguiríamos
seguís	seguisteis	seguíais	seguiréis	seguiríais
siguen	*siguieron*	seguían	seguirán	seguirían

SUBJUNCTIVE

Present	Imperfect (I)	Imperfect (II)
siGa	*siguiera*	*siguiese*
siGas	*siguieras*	*siguieses*
siGa	*siguiera*	*siguiese*
siGamos	*siguiéramos*	*siguiésemos*
siGáis	*siguierais*	*siguieseis*
siGan	*siguieran*	*siguiesen*

IMPERATIVE (2s/2p)	*sigue*	seguid
PAST PARTICIPLE	seguido	
PRESENT PARTICIPLE	*siguiendo*	

6B-3	UMLAUT E → I Ñ +IE → ÑE, Ñ +IO → ÑO *	CEÑIR	TO GIRD

INDICATIVE

Present	Simple Past		Imperfect	Future	Conditional
ciño	ceñí		ceñía	ceñiré	ceñiría
ciñes	ceñiste		ceñías	ceñirás	ceñirías
ciñe	*ciñó*	*	ceñía	ceñirá	ceñiría
ceñimos	ceñimos		ceñíamos	ceñiremos	ceñiríamos
ceñís	ceñisteis		ceñíais	ceñiréis	ceñiríais
ciñen	*ciñeron*	*	ceñían	ceñirán	ceñirían

SUBJUNCTIVE

Present	Imperfect (I)		Imperfect (II)	
ciña	*ciñera*	*	*ciñese*	*
ciñas	*ciñeras*	*	*ciñeses*	*
ciña	*ciñera*	*	*ciñese*	*
ciñamos	*ciñéramos*	*	*ciñésemos*	*
ciñáis	*ciñerais*	*	*ciñeseis*	*
ciñan	*ciñeran*	*	*ciñesen*	*

IMPERATIVE (2s/2p)	*ciñe*	ceñid
PAST PARTICIPLE	ceñido	
PRESENT PARTICIPLE	*ciñendo* *	

6B-4	UMLAUT E → I		REÍR	TO LAUGH
	II → I *			
	ADDITIONAL WRITTEN ACCENT +			

INDICATIVE

Present		Simple Past		Imperfect	Future	Conditional
río	+	reí		reía	reiré	reiría
ríes	+	reíste	+	reías	reirás	reirías
ríe	+	*rió*	*	reía	reirá	reiría
reímos	+	reímos	+	reíamos	reiremos	reiríamos
reís		reísteis	+	reíais	reiréis	reiríais
ríen	+	*rieron*	*	reían	reirán	reirían

Under new orthographic rules, *rió* can be written *rio*. Similarly for *freír: frió* can be written *frio*. For multi-syllable verbs a written accent is always required (*sonrió, refrió, sofrió, deslió, engrió*).

SUBJUNCTIVE

Present		Imperfect (I)		Imperfect (II)	
ría	+	*riera*	*	*riese*	*
rías	+	*rieras*	*	*rieses*	*
ría	+	*riera*	*	*riese*	*
riamos		*riéramos*	*	*riésemos*	*
riáis		*rierais*	*	*rieseis*	*
rían	+	*rieran*	*	*riesen*	*

Under new orthographic rules, *riáis* can be written *riais*. Similarly for *freír: friáis* can be written *friais*. For multi-syllable verbs a written accent is always required (*sonriáis*, etc.).

IMPERATIVE (2s/2p)	*ríe*	+	reíd	+
PAST PARTICIPLE[1]	reído	+		
PRESENT PARTICIPLE	*riendo*	*		

[1] *Freír* (to fry) has an irregular past participle *frito* beside the (rarer) regular form *freído*. The compound verbs *refreír* and *sofreír* similarly have dual past participles.

6C	*DIPHTHONG* O → UE[1]	DORMIR	TO SLEEP
	UMLAUT O → U[2]		

INDICATIVE

Present	Simple Past	Imperfect	Future	Conditional
duermo	dormí	dormía	dormiré	dormiría
duermes	dormiste	dormías	dormirás	dormirías
duerme	*durmió*	dormía	dormirá	dormiría
dormimos	dormimos	dormíamos	dormiremos	dormiríamos
dormís	dormisteis	dormíais	dormiréis	dormiríais
duermen	*durmieron*	dormían	dormirán	dormirían

SUBJUNCTIVE

Present	Imperfect (I)	Imperfect (II)
duerma	durmiera	durmiese
duermas	durmieras	durmieses
duerma	durmiera	durmiese
durmamos	durmiéramos	durmiésemos
durmáis	durmierais	durmieseis
duerman	durmieran	durmiesen

IMPERATIVE (2s/2p)	*duerme*	dormid
PAST PARTICIPLE	dormido	
PRESENT PARTICIPLE	**durmiendo**	

[1] In conjugations stressed on stem syllable.
[2] In conjugations not stressed on stem syllable, when next vowel is *not* (simple) -*i*.

6C-1	MORIR	TO DIE	PAST PARTICIPLE: *MUERTO*

7A	C → ZC	CONOCER	TO KNOW, BECOME ACQUAINTED WITH

INDICATIVE

Present	Simple Past	Imperfect	Future	Conditional
conozco	conocí	conocía	conoceré	conocería
conoces	conociste	conocías	conocerás	conocerías
conoce	conoció	conocía	conocerá	conocería
conocemos	conocimos	conocíamos	conoceremos	conoceríamos
conocéis	conocisteis	conocíais	conoceréis	conoceríais
conocen	conocieron	conocían	conocerán	conocerían

SUBJUNCTIVE

Present	Imperfect (I)	Imperfect (II)
conozca	conociera	conociese
conozcas	conocieras	conocieses
conozca	conociera	conociese
conozcamos	conociéramos	conociésemos
conozcáis	conocierais	conocieseis
conozcan	conocieran	conociesen

IMPERATIVE (2s/2p)	conoce	conoced
PAST PARTICIPLE	conocido	
PRESENT PARTICIPLE	conociendo	

7A-1	ALTERNATE FORMS	YACER	TO LIE (AT REST)

INDICATIVE
Present

SUBJUNCTIVE
Present

yazco **or** *yazgo* **or** *yago*	*yazca*	**or**	*yazga*	**or**	*yaga*
yaces	yazcas	**or**	yazgas	**or**	yagas
yace	yazca	**or**	yazga	**or**	yaga
yacemos	yazcamos	**or**	yazgamos	**or**	yagamos
yacéis	yazcáis	**or**	yazgáis	**or**	yagáis
yacen	yazcan	**or**	yazgan	**or**	yagan

IMPERATIVE (2s/2p)   yace **or** *yaz*   yaced

7A-2	ALTERNATE FORMS	PLACER	TO PLEASE

INDICATIVE
Present

SIMPLE PAST
Present

plazco	plací
places	placiste
place	plació **or** *plugo*
placemos	placimos
placéis	placisteis
placen	placieron **or** *pluguieron*[1]

SUBJUNCTIVE

Present	Imperfect (I)	Imperfect (II)
plazca	placiera	placiese
plazcas	placieras	placieses
plazca **or** *plegue* **or** *plega*[1]	placiera **or** *pluguiera*	placiese **or** *pluguiese*
plazcamos	placiéramos	placiésemos
plazcáis	placierais	placieseis
plazcan	placieran	placiesen

[1] The old forms *pluguieron, plegue,* and *plega* are not recognized by the RAE, nor are any of the alternate forms for *complacer.* They nonetheless can be found in various other sources.

7B	C → ZC	LUCIR	TO SHINE

INDICATIVE

Present	Simple Past	Imperfect	Future	Conditional
luzco	lucí	lucía	luciré	luciría
luces	luciste	lucías	lucirás	lucirías
luce	lució	lucía	lucirá	luciría
lucimos	lucimos	lucíamos	luciremos	luciríamos
lucís	lucisteis	lucíais	luciréis	luciríais
lucen	lucieron	lucían	lucirán	lucirían

SUBJUNCTIVE

Present	Imperfect (I)	Imperfect (II)
luzca	luciera	luciese
luzcas	lucieras	lucieses
luzca	luciera	luciese
luzcamos	luciéramos	luciésemos
luzcáis	lucierais	lucieseis
luzcan	lucieran	luciesen

IMPERATIVE (2s/2p)	luce	lucid
PAST PARTICIPLE	lucido	
PRESENT PARTICIPLE	luciendo	

Note: Verbs ending in *-ducir* have in addition an irregular simple past tense (and hence imperfect subjunctive) and are treated as a separate class (no. 34).

8	*ADD -Y EXCEPT BEFORE -I*	CONSTRUIR	TO CONSTRUCT
	UNSTRESSED -*I* BETWEEN VOWELS → -*Y*		

INDICATIVE

Present	Simple Past	Imperfect	Future	Conditional
construyo	construí	construía	construiré	construiría
construyes	construiste	construías	construirás	construirías
construye	**construyó**	construía	construirá	construiría
construimos	construimos	construíamos	construiremos	construiríamos
construís	construisteis	construíais	construiréis	construiríais
construyen	**construyeron**	construían	construirán	construirían

SUBJUNCTIVE

Present	Imperfect (I)	Imperfect (II)
construya	**construyera**	**construyese**
construyas	**construyeras**	**construyeses**
construya	**construyera**	**construyese**
construyamos	**construyéramos**	**construyésemos**
construyáis	**construyerais**	**construyeseis**
construyan	**construyeran**	**construyesen**

IMPERATIVE (2s/2p)	*construye*	construid
PAST PARTICIPLE	construido	
PRESENT PARTICIPLE	**construyendo**	

Note: For *huir* and *fluir*, the new orthographic rules allow the 1s simple past and 2p present indicative to be written without accents: e.g., *hui, huis* instead of *huí, huís*.

9	*-GO*			CAER	TO FALL

UNSTRESSED *-I* BETWEEN VOWELS → *-Y*
ADDITIONAL WRITTEN ACCENT +

INDICATIVE

Present	Simple Past		Imperfect	Future	Conditional
caigo	caí		caía	caeré	caería
caes	caíste	+	caías	caerás	caerías
cae	**cayó**		caía	caerá	caería
caemos	caímos	+	caíamos	caeremos	caeríamos
caéis	caísteis	+	caíais	caeréis	caeríais
caen	**cayeron**		caían	caerán	caerían

SUBJUNCTIVE

Present	Imperfect (I)	Imperfect (II)
caiga	**cayera**	**cayese**
caigas	**cayeras**	**cayeses**
caiga	**cayera**	**cayese**
caigamos	**cayéramos**	**cayésemos**
caigáis	**cayerais**	**cayeseis**
caigan	**cayeran**	**cayesen**

IMPERATIVE (2s/2p)	cae		caed
PAST PARTICIPLE	caído	+	
PRESENT PARTICIPLE	**cayendo**		

9-1	*ALTERNATE FORMS*	RAER	TO WEAR AWAY

INDICATIVE	SUBJUNCTIVE		
Present	Present		
raigo **or** *rayo*[1]	*raiga*	**or**	*raya*
raes	*raigas*	**or**	*rayas*
rae	*raiga*	**or**	*raya*
raemos	*raigamos*	**or**	*rayamos*
raéis	*raigáis*	**or**	*rayáis*
raen	*raigan*	**or**	*rayan*

[1] The regular form *rao* is sometimes found as well.

9-2	*ALTERNATE FORMS*	ROER	TO GNAW

INDICATIVE	SUBJUNCTIVE
Present	Present

roo **or** *roigo* **or** *royo*	roa	**or**	*roiga*	**or**	*roya*
roes	roas	**or**	*roigas*	**or**	*royas*
roe	roa	**or**	*roiga*	**or**	*roya*
roemos	roamos	**or**	*roigamos*	**or**	*royamos*
roéis	roáis	**or**	*roigáis*	**or**	*royáis*
roen	roan	**or**	*roigan*	**or**	*royan*

10	*-GO*	OÍR	TO HEAR

ADD *-Y* EXCEPT BEFORE *-I*
UNSTRESSED *-I* BETWEEN VOWELS → *-Y*
ADDITIONAL WRITTEN ACCENT +

INDICATIVE

Present	Simple Past		Imperfect	Future	Conditional
oigo	oí		oía	oiré	oiría
OYES	oíste	+	oías	oirás	oirías
OYE	**oyó**		oía	oirá	oiría
oímos	+	oímos	+	oíamos	oiremos	oiríamos
oís	oísteis	+	oíais	oiréis	oiríais
OYEN	**oyeron**		oían	oirán	oirían

SUBJUNCTIVE

Present	Imperfect (I)	Imperfect (II)
oiga	**oyera**	**oyese**
oigas	**oyeras**	**oyeses**
oiga	**oyera**	**oyese**
oigamos	**oyéramos**	**oyésemos**
oigáis	**oyerais**	**oyeseis**
oigan	**oyeran**	**oyesen**

IMPERATIVE (2s/2p)	**OYE**	oíd	+
PAST PARTICIPLE	oído	+	
PRESENT PARTICIPLE	**oyendo**		

11	-GO		SALIR	TO EXIT
	FUTURE STEM: SALDR-			
	IMPERATIVE: SAL			

INDICATIVE

Present	Simple Past	Imperfect	Future	Conditional
salgo	salí	salía	**saldré**	**saldría**
sales	saliste	salías	**saldrás**	**saldrías**
sale	salió	salía	**saldrá**	**saldría**
salimos	salimos	salíamos	**saldremos**	**saldríamos**
salís	salisteis	salíais	**saldréis**	**saldríais**
salen	salieron	salían	**saldrán**	**saldrían**

SUBJUNCTIVE

Present	Imperfect (I)	Imperfect (II)
salga	saliera	saliese
salgas	salieras	salieses
salga	saliera	saliese
salgamos	saliéramos	saliésemos
salgáis	salierais	salieseis
salgan	salieran	saliesen

IMPERATIVE (2s/2p)	**sal**	salid
PAST PARTICIPLE	salido	
PRESENT PARTICIPLE	saliendo	

12	-GO	VALER	TO BE WORTH
	FUTURE STEM: VALDR-		

INDICATIVE

Present	Simple Past	Imperfect	Future	Conditional
valgo	valí	valía	**valdré**	**valdría**
vales	valiste	valías	**valdrás**	**valdrías**
vale	valió	valía	**valdrá**	**valdría**
valemos	valimos	valíamos	**valdremos**	**valdríamos**
valéis	valisteis	valíais	**valdréis**	**valdríais**
valen	valieron	valían	**valdrán**	**valdrían**

SUBJUNCTIVE

Present	Imperfect (I)	Imperfect (II)
valga	valiera	valiese
valgas	valieras	valieses
valga	valiera	valiese
valgamos	valiéramos	valiésemos
valgáis	valierais	valieseis
valgan	valieran	valiesen

IMPERATIVE (2s/2p)	vale	valed
PAST PARTICIPLE	valido	
PRESENT PARTICIPLE	valiendo	

13	-GO	ASIR		TO GRASP

INDICATIVE

Present	Simple Past	Imperfect	Future	Conditional
asgo	así	asía	asiré	asiría
ases	asiste	asías	asirás	asirías
ase	asió	asía	asirá	asiría
asimos	asimos	asíamos	asiremos	asiríamos
asís	asisteis	asíais	asiréis	asiríais
asen	asieron	asían	asirán	asirían

SUBJUNCTIVE

Present	Imperfect (I)	Imperfect (II)
asga	asiera	asiese
asgas	asieras	asieses
asga	asiera	asiese
asgamos	asiéramos	asiésemos
asgáis	asierais	asieseis
asgan	asieran	asiesen

IMPERATIVE (2s/2p)	ase	asid
PAST PARTICIPLE	asido	
PRESENT PARTICIPLE	asiendo	

Note: Forms with -g are generally avoided.

14			VER	TO SEE
	VEO			
	IMPERFECT			
	PAST PARTICIPLE: *VISTO*			

INDICATIVE

Present	Simple Past	Imperfect	Future	Conditional
veo	vi	*veía*	veré	vería
ves	viste	*veías*	verás	verías
ve	vio	*veía*	verá	vería
vemos	vimos	*veíamos*	veremos	veríamos
veis	visteis	*veíais*	veréis	veríais
ven	vieron	*veían*	verán	verían

Note: veis, vi, vio have no written accent since they have only one syllable.

SUBJUNCTIVE

Present	Imperfect (I)	Imperfect (II)
vea	viera	viese
veas	vieras	vieses
vea	viera	viese
veamos	viéramos	viésemos
veáis	vierais	vieseis
vean	vieran	viesen

IMPERATIVE (2s/2p)	ve	ved
PAST PARTICIPLE	**visto**	
PRESENT PARTICIPLE	viendo	

14-1	ADDITIONAL WRITTEN ACCENT +		PREVER	TO FORESEE

INDICATIVE

Present		Simple Past		Imperfect	Future	Conditional
preveo		preví	+	*preveía*	preveré	prevería
prevés	+	previste		*preveías*	preverás	preverías
prevé	+	previó	+	*preveía*	preverá	prevería
prevemos		previmos		*preveíamos*	preveremos	preveríamos
prevéis	+	previsteis		*preveíais*	preveréis	preveríais
prevén	+	previeron		*preveían*	preverán	preverían

SUBJUNCTIVE

Present	Imperfect (I)	Imperfect (II)
prevea	previera	previese
preveas	previeras	previeses
prevea	previera	previese
preveamos	previéramos	previésemos
preveáis	previerais	previeseis
prevean	previeran	previesen

IMPERATIVE (2s/2p)	*prevé*	+	preved	
PAST PARTICIPLE	**previsto**			
PRESENT PARTICIPLE	previendo			

Note: Written accents are required on forms which have only one syllable in *ver* and end in *-n, -s,* or a vowel; e.g., **preves* (without written accent) would be pronounced **pre·ves** rather than *pre·vés*

15	DIPHTHONG E → IE[1]	DISCERNIR	TO DISCERN

INDICATIVE

Present	Simple Past	Imperfect	Future	Conditional
discierno	discerní	discernía	discerniré	discerniría
disciernes	discerniste	discernías	discernirás	discernirías
discierne	discernió	discernía	discernirá	discerniría
discernimos	discernimos	discerníamos	discerniremos	discerniríamos
discernís	discernisteis	discerníais	discerniréis	discerniríais
disciernen	discernieron	discernían	discernirán	discernirían

SUBJUNCTIVE

Present	Imperfect (I)	Imperfect (II)
discierna	discerniera	discerniese
disciernas	discernieras	discernieses
discierna	discerniera	discerniese
discernamos	discerniéramos	discerniésemos
discernáis	discernierais	discernieseis
disciernan	discernieran	discerniesen

IMPERATIVE (2s/2p)	*discierne*	discernid
PAST PARTICIPLE	discernido	
PRESENT PARTICIPLE	discerniendo	

[1] In conjugations stressed on stem syllable. *Discernir* is thus conjugated like *perder* (5A) apart from 4 forms: infinitive; present indicative (1p/2p); imperative (2p)

16	DIPHTHONG U → UE[1] G→GU		JUGAR	TO PLAY

INDICATIVE

Present	Simple Past	Imperfect	Future	Conditional
juego	**juGUé**	jugaba	jugaré	jugaría
juegas	jugaste	jugabas	jugarás	jugarías
juega	jugó	jugaba	jugará	jugaría
jugamos	jugamos	jugábamos	jugaremos	jugaríamos
jugáis	jugasteis	jugabais	jugaréis	jugaríais
juegan	jugaron	jugaban	jugarán	jugarían

SUBJUNCTIVE

Present	Imperfect (I)	Imperfect (II)
jueGUe	jugara	jugase
jueGUes	jugaras	jugases
jueGUe	jugara	jugase
juGUemos	jugáramos	jugásemos
juGUéis	jugarais	jugaseis
jueGUen	jugaran	jugasen

IMPERATIVE (2s/2p)	*juega*	jugad
PAST PARTICIPLE	jugado	
PRESENT PARTICIPLE	jugando	

[1] In conjugations stressed on stem syllable.

17	DIPHTHONG I → IE[1]	ADQUIRIR	TO ACQUIRE

INDICATIVE

Present	Simple Past	Imperfect	Future	Conditional
adquiero	adquirí	adquiría	adquiriré	adquiriría
adquieres	adquiriste	adquirías	adquirirás	adquirirías
adquiere	adquirió	adquiría	adquirirá	adquiriría
adquirimos	adquirimos	adquiríamos	adquiriremos	adquiriríamos
adquirís	adquiristeis	adquiríais	adquiriréis	adquiriríais
adquieren	adquirieron	adquirían	adquirirán	adquirirían

SUBJUNCTIVE

Present	Imperfect (I)	Imperfect (II)
adquiera	adquiriera	adquiriese
adquieras	adquirieras	adquirieses
adquiera	adquiriera	adquiriese
adquiramos	adquiriéramos	adquiriésemos
adquiráis	adquirierais	adquirieseis
adquieran	adquirieran	adquiriesen

IMPERATIVE (2s/2p)	*adquiere*	adquirid
PAST PARTICIPLE	adquirido	
PRESENT PARTICIPLE	adquiriendo	

[1] In conjugations stressed on stem syllable.

18	LIKE CONSTRUIR (8) EXCEPT *GÜY → GUY*	ARGÜIR	TO ARGUE

INDICATIVE

Present	Simple Past	Imperfect	Future	Conditional
arguyo	argüí	argüía	argüiré	argüiría
arguyes	argüiste	argüías	argüirás	argüirías
arguye	**arguyó**	argüía	argüirá	argüiría
argüimos	argüimos	argüíamos	argüiremos	argüiríamos
argüís	argüisteis	argüíais	argüiréis	argüiríais
arguyen	**arguyeron**	argüían	argüirán	argüirían

SUBJUNCTIVE

Present	Imperfect (I)	Imperfect (II)
arguya	**arguyera**	**arguyese**
arguyas	**arguyeras**	**arguyeses**
arguya	**arguyera**	**arguyese**
arguyamos	**arguyéramos**	**arguyésemos**
arguyáis	**arguyerais**	**arguyeseis**
arguyan	**arguyeran**	**arguyesen**

IMPERATIVE (2s/2p)	*arguye*	argüid
PAST PARTICIPLE	argüido	
PRESENT PARTICIPLE	**arguyendo**	

19	SER		TO BE	

INDICATIVE

Present	Simple Past	Imperfect	Future	Conditional
soy	*fui*	*era*	seré	sería
eres	*fuiste*	*eras*	serás	serías
es	*fue*	*era*	será	sería
somos	*fuimos*	*éramos*	seremos	seríamos
sois	*fuisteis*	*erais*	seréis	seríais
son	*fueron*	*eran*	serán	serían

SUBJUNCTIVE

Present	Imperfect (I)	Imperfect (II)
sea	*fuera*	*fuese*
seas	*fueras*	*fueses*
sea	*fuera*	*fuese*
seamos	*fuéramos*	*fuésemos*
seáis	*fuerais*	*fueseis*
sean	*fueran*	*fuesen*

IMPERATIVE (2s/2p)	*sé*	sed
PAST PARTICIPLE	sido	
PRESENT PARTICIPLE	siendo	

20		ESTAR	TO BE
	ESTOY		
	STRESS SHIFT *		
	IRREGULAR SIMPLE PAST		

INDICATIVE

Present		Simple Past	Imperfect	Future	Conditional
ESTOY		*estuve*	estaba	estaré	estaría
estás	*	*estuviste*	estabas	estarás	estarías
está	*	*estuvo*	estaba	estará	estaría
estamos		*estuvimos*	estábamos	estaremos	estaríamos
estáis		*estuvisteis*	estabais	estaréis	estaríais
están	*	*estuvieron*	estaban	estarán	estarían

SUBJUNCTIVE

Present		Imperfect (I)	Imperfect (II)
esté	*	*estuviera*	*estuviese*
estés	*	*estuvieras*	*estuvieses*
esté	*	*estuviera*	*estuviese*
estemos		*estuviéramos*	*estuviésemos*
estéis		*estuvierais*	*estuvieseis*
estén	*	*estuvieran*	*estuviesen*

IMPERATIVE	**está**	*	estad
PAST PARTICIPLE	estado		
PRESENT PARTICIPLE	estando		

21	HABER	TO HAVE

INDICATIVE

Present	Simple Past	Imperfect	Future	Conditional
he	*hube*	había	*habré*	*habría*
has	*hubiste*	habías	*habrás*	*habrías*
ha	*hubo*	había	*habrá*	*habría*
hemos	*hubimos*	habíamos	*habremos*	*habríamos*
habéis	*hubisteis*	habíais	*habréis*	*habríais*
han	*hubieron*	habían	*habrán*	*habrían*

SUBJUNCTIVE

Present	Imperfect (I)	Imperfect (II)
haya	*hubiera*	*hubiese*
hayas	*hubieras*	*hubieses*
haya	*hubiera*	*hubiese*
hayamos	*hubiéramos*	*hubiésemos*
hayáis	*hubierais*	*hubieseis*
hayan	*hubieran*	*hubiesen*

IMPERATIVE	*he*	habed
PAST PARTICIPLE	habido	
PRESENT PARTICIPLE	habiendo	

22			SABER	TO KNOW

SÉ
IRREGULAR SIMPLE PAST
FUTURE STEM: *SABR-*
SUBJUNCTIVE STEM: *SEP-*

INDICATIVE

Present	Simple Past	Imperfect	Future	Conditional
sé	*supe*	sabía	*sabré*	*sabría*
sabes	*supiste*	sabías	*sabrás*	*sabrías*
sabe	*supo*	sabía	*sabrá*	*sabría*
sabemos	*supimos*	sabíamos	*sabremos*	*sabríamos*
sabéis	*supisteis*	sabíais	*sabréis*	*sabríais*
saben	*supieron*	sabían	*sabrán*	*sabrían*

SUBJUNCTIVE

Present	Imperfect (I)	Imperfect (II)
sepa	*supiera*	*supiese*
sepas	*supieras*	*supieses*
sepa	*supiera*	*supiese*
sepamos	*supiéramos*	*supiésemos*
sepáis	*supierais*	*supieseis*
sepan	*supieran*	*supiesen*

IMPERATIVE	sabe	sabed
PAST PARTICIPLE	sabido	
PRESENT PARTICIPLE	sabiendo	

23			CABER	TO FIT

QUEPO
IRREGULAR SIMPLE PAST
FUTURE STEM: *CABR-*

INDICATIVE

Present	Simple Past	Imperfect	Future	Conditional
quepo	*cupe*	cabía	*cabré*	*cabría*
cabes	*cupiste*	cabías	*cabrás*	*cabrías*
cabe	*cupo*	cabía	*cabrá*	*cabría*
cabemos	*cupimos*	cabíamos	*cabremos*	*cabríamos*
cabéis	*cupisteis*	cabíais	*cabréis*	*cabríais*
caben	*cupieron*	cabían	*cabrán*	*cabrían*

SUBJUNCTIVE

Present	Imperfect (I)	Imperfect (II)
quepa	*cupiera*	*cupiese*
quepas	*cupieras*	*cupieses*
quepa	*cupiera*	*cupiese*
quepamos	*cupiéramos*	*cupiésemos*
quepáis	*cupierais*	*cupieseis*
quepan	*cupieran*	*cupiesen*

IMPERATIVE	cabe	cabed
PAST PARTICIPLE	cabido	
PRESENT PARTICIPLE	cabiendo	

24	IR	TO GO

INDICATIVE

Present	Simple Past	Imperfect	Future	Conditional
voy	*fui*	*iba*	iré	iría
vas	*fuiste*	*ibas*	irás	irías
va	*fue*	*iba*	irá	iría
vamos	*fuimos*	*íbamos*	iremos	iríamos
vais	*fuisteis*	*ibais*	iréis	iríais
van	*fueron*	*iban*	irán	irían

SUBJUNCTIVE

Present	Imperfect (I)	Imperfect (II)
vaya	*fuera*	*fuese*
vayas	*fueras*	*fueses*
vaya	*fuera*	*fuese*
vayamos	*fuéramos*	*fuésemos*
vayáis	*fuerais*	*fueseis*
vayan	*fueran*	*fuesen*

IMPERATIVE (2s/2p)	*ve*	id
PAST PARTICIPLE	ido	
PRESENT PARTICIPLE	*yendo*	[regular orthographic change: *initial* ie → ye]

25			DAR	TO GIVE
DOY				
IRREGULAR SIMPLE PAST				
WRITTEN ACCENTS IN SUBJUNCTIVE +				

INDICATIVE

Present	Simple Past	Imperfect	Future	Conditional
doy	*di*	daba	daré	daría
das	*diste*	dabas	darás	darías
da	*dio*	daba	dará	daría
damos	*dimos*	dábamos	daremos	daríamos
dais	*disteis*	dabais	daréis	daríais
dan	*dieron*	daban	darán	darían

SUBJUNCTIVE

Present		Imperfect (I)	Imperfect (II)
dé	+	*diera*	*diese*
des		*dieras*	*dieses*
dé	+	*diera*	*diese*
demos		*diéramos*	*diésemos*
deis		*dierais*	*dieseis*
den		*dieran*	*diesen*

IMPERATIVE (2s/2p)	da	dad
PAST PARTICIPLE	dado	
PRESENT PARTICIPLE	dando	

Note: *dais, deis, di, dio* have no written accent since they have only one syllable.

26			PODER	CAN
DIPHTHONG O → UE[1]				
IRREGULAR SIMPLE PAST				
FUTURE STEM: *PODR-*				
PRESENT PARTICIPLE: *PUDIENDO*				

INDICATIVE

Present	Simple Past	Imperfect	Future	Conditional
puedo	*pude*	podía	*podré*	*podría*
puedes	*pudiste*	podías	*podrás*	*podrías*
puede	*pudo*	podía	*podrá*	*podría*
podemos	*pudimos*	podíamos	*podremos*	*podríamos*
podéis	*pudisteis*	podíais	*podréis*	*podríais*
pueden	*pudieron*	podían	*podrán*	*podrían*

SUBJUNCTIVE

Present	Imperfect (I)	Imperfect (II)
pueda	*pudiera*	*pudiese*
puedas	*pudieras*	*pudieses*
pueda	*pudiera*	*pudiese*
podamos	*pudiéramos*	*pudiésemos*
podáis	*pudierais*	*pudieseis*
puedan	*pudieran*	*pudiesen*

IMPERATIVE (2s/2p)	*puede*	poded
PAST PARTICIPLE	podido	
PRESENT PARTICIPLE	*pudiendo*	

[1] In conjugations stressed on stem syllable.

27		QUERER	TO WANT

DIPHTHONG E → IE[1]
IRREGULAR SIMPLE PAST
FUTURE STEM: *QUERR-*

INDICATIVE

Present	Simple Past	Imperfect	Future	Conditional
quiero	*quise*	quería	*querré*	*querría*
quieres	*quisiste*	querías	*querrás*	*querrías*
quiere	*quiso*	quería	*querrá*	*querría*
queremos	*quisimos*	queríamos	*querremos*	*querríamos*
queréis	*quisisteis*	queríais	*querréis*	*querríais*
quieren	*quisieron*	querían	*querrán*	*querrían*

SUBJUNCTIVE

Present	Imperfect (I)	Imperfect (II)
quiera	*quisiera*	*quisiese*
quieras	*quisieras*	*quisieses*
quiera	*quisiera*	*quisiese*
queramos	*quisiéramos*	*quisiésemos*
queráis	*quisierais*	*quisieseis*
quieran	*quisieran*	*quisiesen*

IMPERATIVE (2s/2p)	*quiere*	quered
PAST PARTICIPLE	querido	
PRESENT PARTICIPLE	queriendo	

[1] In conjugations stressed on stem syllable.

28			DECIR	TO SAY

DIGO
UMLAUT E → I *
IRREGULAR SIMPLE PAST
FUTURE STEM: *DIR-*
PAST PARTICIPLE: *DICHO*
IMPERATIVE: *DI*
J + IE → JE †

INDICATIVE

Present		Simple Past		Imperfect	Future	Conditional
digo		*dije*		decía	*diré*	*diría*
dices	*	*dijiste*		decías	*dirás*	*dirías*
dice	*	*dijo*		decía	*dirá*	*diría*
decimos		*dijimos*		decíamos	*diremos*	*diríamos*
decís		*dijisteis*		decíais	*diréis*	*diríais*
dicen	*	*dijeron*	†	decían	*dirán*	*dirían*

SUBJUNCTIVE

Present	Imperfect (I)		Imperfect (II)	
diga	*dijera*	†	*dijese*	†
digas	*dijeras*	†	*dijeses*	†
diga	*dijera*	†	*dijese*	†
digamos	*dijéramos*	†	*dijésemos*	†
digáis	*dijerais*	†	*dijeseis*	†
digan	*dijeran*	†	*dijesen*	†

IMPERATIVE (2s/2p)	*di*	decid
PAST PARTICIPLE	*dicho*	
PRESENT PARTICIPLE	*diciendo*	*

28-1	PREDECIR	TO PREDICT

In imperative 2s, *predecir* is regular where *decir* is not. Otherwise conjugations are identical.[1]

	decir		*predecir*	
IMPERATIVE (2s/2p)	*di*	decid	predice	predecid

[1] Conjugation according to RAE. Other references (e.g., Moliner, VOX) show regular future (*prediciré*, etc.) and conditional (*prediciría*).

28-2	BENDECIR	TO BLESS

In future, conditional, imperative 2s and past participle, *bendecir* is regular where *decir* is not.

INDICATIVE

decir		*bendecir*	
Future	Conditional	Future	Conditional
diré	diría	bendeciré	bendeciría
dirás	dirías	bendecirás	bendecirías
dirá	diría	bendecirá	bendeciría
diremos	diríamos	bendeciremos	bendeciríamos
diréis	diríais	bendeciréis	bendeciríais
dirán	dirían	bendecirán	bendecirían

	decir		*bendecir*	
IMPERATIVE (2s/2p)	di	decid	bendice	bendecid
PAST PARTICIPLE	dicho		bendecido	

29	HACER	TO DO, MAKE

HAGO
IRREGULAR SIMPLE PAST
FUTURE STEM: *HAR-*
PAST PARTICIPLE: *HECHO*
IMPERATIVE: *HAZ*
C → Z *

INDICATIVE

Present	Simple Past		Imperfect	Future	Conditional
hago	hice		hacía	haré	haría
haces	hiciste		hacías	harás	harías
hace	hiZo	*	hacía	hará	haría
hacemos	hicimos		hacíamos	haremos	haríamos
hacéis	hicisteis		hacíais	haréis	haríais
hacen	hicieron		hacían	harán	harían

SUBJUNCTIVE

Present	Imperfect (I)	Imperfect (II)
haga	hiciera	hiciese
hagas	hicieras	hicieses
haga	hiciera	hiciese
hagamos	hiciéramos	hiciésemos
hagáis	hicierais	hicieseis
hagan	hicieran	hiciesen

IMPERATIVE (2s/2p)	haZ	*	haced
PAST PARTICIPLE	hecho		
PRESENT PARTICIPLE	haciendo		

29-1	E(H)I → E(H)Í[1]	REHACER	TO REDO

INDICATIVE	SUBJUNCTIVE	SIMPLE PAST	IMPERATIVE
Present	Present		
		rehíce	
		rehiciste	
		rehízo	
		rehicimos	
		rehicisteis	
		rehicieron	

[1] In the two simple past conjugations in which the stem syllable is stressed.

29-2	SATISFACER	TO SATISFY

Conjugated identically to *hacer* (satisfago, satisfaces, etc.) except for imperative:

IMPERATIVE (2s/2p) **satisfaz** *or* satisface   satisfaced

30			PONER	TO PUT

PONGO
IRREGULAR SIMPLE PAST
FUTURE STEM: *PONDR-*
PAST PARTICIPLE: *PUESTO*
IMPERATIVE: *PON*

INDICATIVE

Present	Simple Past	Imperfect	Future	Conditional
pongo	*puse*	ponía	*pondré*	*pondría*
pones	*pusiste*	ponías	*pondrás*	*pondrías*
pone	*puso*	ponía	*pondrá*	*pondría*
ponemos	*pusimos*	poníamos	*pondremos*	*pondríamos*
ponéis	*pusisteis*	poníais	*pondréis*	*pondríais*
ponen	*pusieron*	ponían	*pondrán*	*pondrían*

SUBJUNCTIVE

Present	Imperfect (I)	Imperfect (II)
ponga	*pusiera*	*pusiese*
pongas	*pusieras*	*pusieses*
ponga	*pusiera*	*pusiese*
pongamos	*pusiéramos*	*pusiésemos*
pongáis	*pusierais*	*pusieseis*
pongan	*pusieran*	*pusiesen*

IMPERATIVE (2s/2p)	*pon*	poned
PAST PARTICIPLE	*puesto*	
PRESENT PARTICIPLE	poniendo	

30-1	SUPONER	TO SUPPOSE

For imperative 2s *suponer* has a written accent where *poner* does not.

	poner		suponer	
IMPERATIVE (2s/2p)	*pon*	poned	*supón*	suponed

31			TENER	TO HAVE
	TENGO			
	DIPHTHONG E → IE *			
	IRREGULAR SIMPLE PAST			
	FUTURE STEM: *TENDR-*			
	IMPERATIVE: *TEN*			

INDICATIVE

Present		Simple Past	Imperfect	Future	Conditional
tengo		*tuve*	tenía	*tendré*	*tendría*
tienes	*	*tuviste*	tenías	*tendrás*	*tendrías*
tiene	*	*tuvo*	tenía	*tendrá*	*tendría*
tenemos		*tuvimos*	teníamos	*tendremos*	*tendríamos*
tenéis		*tuvisteis*	teníais	*tendréis*	*tendríais*
tienen	*	*tuvieron*	tenían	*tendrán*	*tendrían*

SUBJUNCTIVE

Present	Imperfect (I)	Imperfect (II)
tenga	*tuviera*	*tuviese*
tengas	*tuvieras*	*tuvieses*
tenga	*tuviera*	*tuviese*
tengamos	*tuviéramos*	*tuviésemos*
tengáis	*tuvierais*	*tuvieseis*
tengan	*tuvieran*	*tuviesen*

IMPERATIVE (2s/2p)	*ten*	tened
PAST PARTICIPLE	tenido	
PRESENT PARTICIPLE	teniendo	

31-1	OBTENER	TO OBTAIN

For imperative 2s *obtener* has a written accent where *tener* does not.

	tener		obtener	
IMPERATIVE (2s/2p)	*ten*	tened	*obtén*	obtened

32			VENIR	TO COME

VENGO
DIPHTHONG E → IE *
UMLAUT E → I: PRESENT PARTICIPLE
IRREGULAR SIMPLE PAST
FUTURE STEM: *VENDR-*
IMPERATIVE: *VEN*

INDICATIVE

Present		Simple Past	Imperfect	Future	Conditional
vengo		*vine*	venía	*vendré*	*vendría*
vienes	*	*viniste*	venías	*vendrás*	*vendrías*
viene	*	*vino*	venía	*vendrá*	*vendría*
venimos		*vinimos*	veníamos	*vendremos*	*vendríamos*
venís		*vinisteis*	veníais	*vendréis*	*vendríais*
vienen	*	*vinieron*	venían	*vendrán*	*vendrían*

SUBJUNCTIVE

Present	Imperfect (I)	Imperfect (II)
venga	*viniera*	*viniese*
vengas	*vinieras*	*vinieses*
venga	*viniera*	*viniese*
vengamos	*viniéramos*	*viniésemos*
vengáis	*vinierais*	*vinieseis*
vengan	*vinieran*	*viniesen*

IMPERATIVE (2s/2p)	*ven*	venid
PAST PARTICIPLE	venido	
PRESENT PARTICIPLE	*viniendo*	

32-1	CONVENIR	TO CONVENE, AGREE, BE SUITABLE

For imperative 2s *convenir* has a written accent where *venir* does not.

	venir		convenir	
IMPERATIVE (2s/2p)	*ven*	venid	*convén*	convenid

33			TRAER	TO BRING, CARRY

-GO
IRREGULAR SIMPLE PAST
UNSTRESSED *-I* BETWEEN VOWELS → *-Y* *
ADDITIONAL WRITTEN ACCENT +
J + IE → JE †

INDICATIVE

Present	Simple Past		Imperfect	Future	Conditional
traigo	**traje**		traía	traeré	traería
traes	**trajiste**		traías	traerás	traerías
trae	**trajo**		traía	traerá	traería
traemos	**trajimos**		traíamos	traeremos	traeríamos
traéis	**trajisteis**		traíais	traeréis	traeríais
traen	**trajeron**	†	traían	traerán	traerían

SUBJUNCTIVE

Present	Imperfect (I)		Imperfect (II)	
traiga	**trajera**	†	**trajese**	†
traigas	**trajeras**	†	**trajeses**	†
traiga	**trajera**	†	**trajese**	†
traigamos	**trajéramos**	†	**trajésemos**	†
traigáis	**trajerais**	†	**trajeseis**	†
traigan	**trajeran**	†	**trajesen**	†

IMPERATIVE (2s/2p)	trae	traed
PAST PARTICIPLE	traído +	
PRESENT PARTICIPLE	**traYendo** *	

34	C → ZC	-DUCIR	(E.G., *CONDUCIR*)

IRREGULAR SIMPLE PAST
J + IE → JE *

INDICATIVE

Present	Simple Past		Imperfect	Future	Conditional
conduzco	**conduje**		conducía	conduciré	conduciría
conduces	**condujiste**		conducías	conducirás	conducirías
conduce	**condujo**		conducía	conducirá	conduciría
conducimos	**condujimos**		conducíamos	conduciremos	conduciríamos
conducís	**condujisteis**		conducíais	conduciréis	conduciríais
conducen	**condujeron**	*	conducían	conducirán	conducirían

SUBJUNCTIVE

Present	Imperfect (I)		Imperfect (II)	
conduzca	*condujera*	*	*condujese*	*
conduzcas	*condujeras*	*	*condujeses*	*
conduzca	*condujera*	*	*condujese*	*
conduzcamos	*condujéramos*	*	*condujésemos*	*
conduzcáis	*condujerais*	*	*condujeseis*	*
conduzcan	*condujeran*	*	*condujesen*	*

IMPERATIVE (2s/2p)	conduce	conducid
PAST PARTICIPLE	conducido	
PRESENT PARTICIPLE	conduciendo	

35	*IRREGULAR SIMPLE PAST*	ANDAR	TO WALK

INDICATIVE

Present	Simple Past	Imperfect	Future	Conditional
ando	*anduve*	andaba	andaré	andaría
andas	*anduviste*	andabas	andarás	andarías
anda	*anduvo*	andaba	andará	andaría
andamos	*anduvimos*	andábamos	andaremos	andaríamos
andáis	*anduvisteis*	andabais	andaréis	andaríais
andan	*anduvieron*	andaban	andarán	andarían

SUBJUNCTIVE

Present	Imperfect (I)	Imperfect (II)
ande	*anduviera*	*anduviese*
andes	*anduvieras*	*anduvieses*
ande	*anduviera*	*anduviese*
andemos	*anduviéramos*	*anduviésemos*
andéis	*anduvierais*	*anduvieseis*
anden	*anduvieran*	*anduviesen*

IMPERATIVE	anda	andad
PAST PARTICIPLE	andado	
PRESENT PARTICIPLE	andando	

Index by Class and Sub-class for 4,818 Verbs

Verbs are listed according to the post-1994 rules under which *ch* and *ll* are now treated, for purposes of alphabetization, as simple letter combinations *c* + *h*, *l* + *l* (previously *ch* had been treated as a separate letter immediately following *c* in the alphabet, and likewise *ll* a separate letter following *l*). The *ñ* continues to be treated as a separate letter, following *n*.

"DEF" (*defective*) indicates a verb which is used only in certain conjugations—generally the infinitive, participles, and third person (singular and plural) forms. A number of *weather* verbs (including *llover* "to rain", *nevar* "to snow", *tronar* "to thunder") are frequently treated as defective, as they tend to be conjugated only impersonally (i.e., in the third person). They nonetheless have complete conjugations, since they also have rarer "personal" uses (*I thundered at the unwanted intruder.*)

Verbs which can only be used reflexively are shown with the reflexive pronoun *se* in parentheses, e.g., *arrepentir(se)*.

Verb	Class (Sub-class)	#	Verb	Class (Sub-class)	#
abajar	cantar	1	abocar	cantar (tocar)	1-1
abalanzar	cantar (cazar)	1-4	abocetar	cantar	1
abalar	cantar	1	abochornar	cantar	1
abalizar	cantar (cazar)	1-4	abocinar	cantar	1
aballar	cantar	1	abofetear	cantar	1
abanar	cantar	1	abogar	cantar (pagar)	1-2
abanderar	cantar	1	abolir	subir (abolir)	3-14
abandonar	cantar	1	abollar	cantar	1
abanicar	cantar (tocar)	1-1	abombar	cantar	1
abaratar	cantar	1	abominar	cantar	1
abarcar	cantar (tocar)	1-1	abonar	cantar	1
abarquillar	cantar	1	abordar	cantar	1
abarrotar	cantar	1	aborrecer	conocer	7A
abastecer	conocer	7A	aborregar(se)	cantar (pagar)	1-2
abatir	subir	3	abortar	cantar	1
abdicar	cantar (tocar)	1-1	abotargar(se)	cantar (pagar)	1-2
abetunar	cantar	1	abotonar	cantar	1
abigarrar	cantar	1	abovedar	cantar	1
abismar	cantar	1	abrasar	cantar	1
abjurar	cantar	1	abrazar	cantar (cazar)	1-4
ablandar	cantar	1	abrevar	cantar	1
abnegar	pensar (negar)	4A-1	abreviar	cantar	1
abobar	cantar	1	abrigar	cantar (pagar)	1-2

Verb	Class (Sub-class)	#	Verb	Class (Sub-class)	#
abrir	subir (abrir)	3-9	achacar	cantar (tocar)	1-1
abrochar	cantar	1	achantar	cantar	1
abrogar	cantar (pagar)	1-2	achaparrar(se)	cantar	1
abrumar	cantar	1	acharolar	cantar	1
absolver	mover (resolver)	5B-3	achatar	cantar	1
absorber	comer	2	achicar	cantar (tocar)	1-1
abstener(se)	tener (obtener)	31-1	achicharrar	cantar	1
abstraer	traer	33	achinar	cantar	1
abuchear	cantar	1	achispar	cantar	1
abultar	cantar	1	achuchar	cantar	1
abundar	cantar	1	acicalar	cantar	1
aburguesar	cantar	1	acidificar	cantar (tocar)	1-1
aburrir	subir	3	acidular	cantar	1
abusar	cantar	1	aclamar	cantar	1
acabar	cantar	1	aclarar	cantar	1
acaecer (DEF)	conocer	7A	aclimatar	cantar	1
acallar	cantar	1	acobardar	cantar	1
acalorar	cantar	1	acodar	cantar	1
acampar	cantar	1	acoger	comer (coger)	2-2
acanalar	cantar	1	acogotar	cantar	1
acantonar	cantar	1	acolchar	cantar	1
acaparar	cantar	1	acometer	comer	2
acaramelar	cantar	1	acomodar	cantar	1
acariciar	cantar	1	acompañar	cantar	1
acarrear	cantar	1	acompasar	cantar	1
acartonar(se)	cantar	1	acomplejar	cantar	1
acatar	cantar	1	acondicionar	cantar	1
acatarrar	cantar	1	aconsejar	cantar	1
acaudalar	cantar	1	acontecer (DEF)	conocer	7A
acaudillar	cantar	1	acoplar	cantar	1
acceder	comer	2	acoquinar	cantar	1
accidentar(se)	cantar	1	acorazar	cantar (cazar)	1-4
accionar	cantar	1	acorchar	cantar	1
acechar	cantar	1	acordar	mostrar	4B
aceitar	cantar	1	acordonar	cantar	1
acelerar	cantar	1	acorralar	cantar	1
acendrar	cantar	1	acortar	cantar	1
acentuar	cantar (actuar)	1-14	acosar	cantar	1
aceptar	cantar	1	acostar	mostrar	4B
acerar	cantar	1	acostumbrar	cantar	1
acercar	cantar (tocar)	1-1	acotar	cantar	1
acertar	pensar	4A	acrecentar	pensar	4A
achabacanar	cantar	1	acreditar	cantar	1

Verb	Class (Sub-class)	#	Verb	Class (Sub-class)	#
acribillar	cantar	1	adormilar(se)	cantar	1
acrisolar	cantar	1	adornar	cantar	1
acristalar	cantar	1	adosar	cantar	1
activar	cantar	1	adquirir	adquirir	17
actualizar	cantar (cazar)	1-4	adscribir	subir (escribir)	3-11
actuar	cantar (actuar)	1-14	aducir	conducir	34
acuartelar	cantar	1	adueñar(se)	cantar	1
acuchillar	cantar	1	adular	cantar	1
acuciar	cantar	1	adulterar	cantar	1
acuclillar(se)	cantar	1	adverbializar	cantar (cazar)	1-4
acudir	subir	3	advertir	sentir	6A
acumular	cantar	1	aerotransportar	cantar	1
acunar	cantar	1	afanar	cantar	1
acuñar	cantar	1	afear	cantar	1
acurrucar(se)	cantar (tocar)	1-1	afectar	cantar	1
acusar	cantar	1	afeitar	cantar	1
adaptar	cantar	1	afelpar	cantar	1
adecentar	cantar	1	afeminar	cantar	1
adecuar	cantar	1	aferrar	cantar	1
adelantar	cantar	1	afianzar	cantar (cazar)	1-4
adelgazar	cantar (cazar)	1-4	aficionar	cantar	1
adentrar(se)	cantar	1	afilar	cantar	1
aderezar	cantar (cazar)	1-4	afiliar	cantar	1
adeudar	cantar	1	afinar	cantar	1
adherir	sentir	6A	afincar	cantar (tocar)	1-1
adicionar	cantar	1	afirmar	cantar	1
adiestrar	cantar	1	aflautar	cantar	1
adinerar	cantar	1	afligir	subir (dirigir)	3-2
adivinar	cantar	1	aflojar	cantar	1
adjetivar	cantar	1	afluir	construir	8
adjudicar	cantar (tocar)	1-1	afofar(se)	cantar	1
adjuntar	cantar	1	afrancesar	cantar	1
administrar	cantar	1	afrentar	cantar	1
admirar	cantar	1	africanizar	cantar (cazar)	1-4
admitir	subir	3	afrontar	cantar	1
adobar	cantar	1	agachar	cantar	1
adocenar	cantar	1	agarrar	cantar	1
adoctrinar	cantar	1	agarrotar	cantar	1
adolecer	conocer	7A	agasajar	cantar	1
adoptar	cantar	1	agavillar	cantar	1
adoquinar	cantar	1	agazapar(se)	cantar	1
adorar	cantar	1	agenciar	cantar	1
adormecer	conocer	7A	agigantar	cantar	1

Verb	Class (Sub-class)	#	Verb	Class (Sub-class)	#
agilizar	cantar (cazar)	1-4	ahuevar	cantar	1
agitanar	cantar	1	ahumar	cantar (aullar)	1-6
agitar	cantar	1	ahuyentar	cantar	1
aglomerar	cantar	1	aindiar(se)	cantar	1
aglutinar	cantar	1	airear	cantar	1
agobiar	cantar	1	aislar	cantar (aislar)	1-5
agolpar	cantar	1	ajamonar(se)	cantar	1
agonizar	cantar (cazar)	1-4	ajar	cantar	1
agorar	mostrar (agorar)	4B-4	ajardinar	cantar	1
agostar	cantar	1	ajetrear	cantar	1
agotar	cantar	1	ajuntar	cantar	1
agraciar	cantar	1	ajustar	cantar	1
agradar	cantar	1	ajusticiar	cantar	1
agradecer	conocer	7A	alabar	cantar	1
agrandar	cantar	1	alabear	cantar	1
agravar	cantar	1	alambicar	cantar (tocar)	1-1
agraviar	cantar	1	alambrar	cantar	1
agredir	subir (abolir)	3-14	alardear	cantar	1
agregar	cantar (pagar)	1-2	alargar	cantar (pagar)	1-2
agremiar	cantar	1	alarmar	cantar	1
agriar[1]	cantar (enviar)	1-15	albardar	cantar	1
agrietar	cantar	1	albergar	cantar (pagar)	1-2
agrisar	cantar	1	alborear	cantar	1
agrupar	cantar	1	alborotar	cantar	1
aguantar	cantar	1	alborozar	cantar (cazar)	1-4
aguar	cantar (averiguar)	1-3	alcahuetear	cantar	1
aguardar	cantar	1	alcalinizar	cantar (cazar)	1-4
agudizar	cantar (cazar)	1-4	alcantarillar	cantar	1
aguijonear	cantar	1	alcanzar	cantar (cazar)	1-4
agujerear	cantar	1	alcoholizar	cantar (cazar)	1-4
agusanar(se)	cantar	1	aleccionar	cantar	1
aguzar	cantar (cazar)	1-4	alegar	cantar (pagar)	1-2
aherrojar	cantar	1	alegrar	cantar	1
ahincar	cantar (ahincar)	1-10	alejar	cantar	1
ahogar	cantar (pagar)	1-2	alentar	pensar	4A
ahondar	cantar	1	alertar	cantar	1
ahorcar	cantar (tocar)	1-1	aletargar	cantar (pagar)	1-2
ahornar	cantar	1	aletear	cantar	1
ahorrar	cantar	1	alfabetizar	cantar (cazar)	1-4
ahuecar	cantar (tocar)	1-1	alfombrar	cantar	1

[1] Frequently conjugated without written accents (e.g., *agrio* rather than *agrío*).

Verb	Class (Sub-class)	#	Verb	Class (Sub-class)	#
algodonar	cantar	1	amar	cantar	1
alhajar	cantar	1	amarar	cantar	1
aliar	cantar (enviar)	1-15	amargar	cantar (pagar)	1-2
alicatar	cantar	1	amarillear	cantar	1
alicortar	cantar	1	amarrar	cantar	1
alienar	cantar	1	amartelar	cantar	1
aligerar	cantar	1	amartillar	cantar	1
alimentar	cantar	1	amasar	cantar	1
alinear	cantar	1	amazacotar	cantar	1
aliñar	cantar	1	ambicionar	cantar	1
alisar	cantar	1	ambientar	cantar	1
alistar	cantar	1	amedrentar	cantar	1
aliviar	cantar	1	amenazar	cantar (cazar)	1-4
allanar	cantar	1	amenizar	cantar (cazar)	1-4
allegar	cantar (pagar)	1-2	americanizar	cantar (cazar)	1-4
almacenar	cantar	1	amerizar	cantar (cazar)	1-4
almendrar	cantar	1	ametrallar	cantar	1
almibarar	cantar	1	amigar	cantar (pagar)	1-2
almidonar	cantar	1	amilanar	cantar	1
almohadillar	cantar	1	aminorar	cantar	1
almohazar	cantar (cazar)	1-4	amnistiar	cantar (enviar)	1-15
almorzar	mostrar (forzar)	4B-3	amodorrar(se)	cantar	1
alocar	cantar (tocar)	1-1	amohinar	cantar (amohinar)	1-9
alojar	cantar	1	amojamar	cantar	1
alquilar	cantar	1	amoldar	cantar	1
alterar	cantar	1	amonar(se)	cantar	1
alternar	cantar	1	amonestar	cantar	1
alucinar	cantar	1	amontonar	cantar	1
aludir	subir	3	amoratar(se)	cantar	1
alumbrar	cantar	1	amordazar	cantar (cazar)	1-4
alunizar	cantar (cazar)	1-4	amorriñar(se)	cantar	1
alzar	cantar (cazar)	1-4	amortajar	cantar	1
amadrinar	cantar	1	amortiguar	cantar (averiguar)	1-3
amaestrar	cantar	1	amortizar	cantar (cazar)	1-4
amagar	cantar (pagar)	1-2	amostazar	cantar (cazar)	1-4
amainar	cantar	1	amotinar	cantar	1
amalgamar	cantar	1	amparar	cantar	1
amamantar	cantar	1	ampliar	cantar (enviar)	1-15
amancebar(se)	cantar	1	amplificar	cantar (tocar)	1-1
amanecer	conocer	7A	amputar	cantar	1
amanerar	cantar	1	amueblar	cantar	1
amansar	cantar	1	amuermar	cantar	1
amañar	cantar	1	amurallar	cantar	1

Verb	Class (Sub-class)	#	Verb	Class (Sub-class)	#
analizar	cantar (cazar)	1-4	aparear	cantar	1
anarquizar	cantar (cazar)	1-4	aparecer	conocer	7A
anatematizar	cantar (cazar)	1-4	aparejar	cantar	1
anatomizar	cantar (cazar)	1-4	aparentar	cantar	1
anclar	cantar	1	apartar	cantar	1
andar	andar	35	apasionar	cantar	1
anegar	cantar (pagar)	1-2	apear	cantar	1
anestesiar	cantar	1	apechar	cantar	1
anexionar	cantar	1	apechugar	cantar (pagar)	1-2
angostar	cantar	1	apedrear	cantar	1
angustiar	cantar	1	apegar(se)	cantar (pagar)	1-2
anhelar	cantar	1	apelar	cantar	1
anidar	cantar	1	apellidar	cantar	1
anillar	cantar	1	apelmazar	cantar (cazar)	1-4
animalizar	cantar (cazar)	1-4	apelotonar	cantar	1
animar	cantar	1	apenar	cantar	1
aniñar(se)	cantar	1	apercibir	subir	3
aniquilar	cantar	1	apergaminar(se)	cantar	1
anisar	cantar	1	apesadumbrar	cantar	1
anochecer	conocer	7A	apestar	cantar	1
anonadar	cantar	1	apetecer	conocer	7A
anotar	cantar	1	apiadar	cantar	1
anquilosar	cantar	1	apilar	cantar	1
ansiar	cantar (enviar)	1-15	apiñar	cantar	1
anteceder	comer	2	apisonar	cantar	1
anteponer	poner (suponer)	30-1	aplacar	cantar (tocar)	1-1
anticipar	cantar	1	aplanar	cantar	1
antojar(se)	cantar	1	aplastar	cantar	1
anudar	cantar	1	aplatanar	cantar	1
anular	cantar	1	aplaudir	subir	3
anunciar	cantar	1	aplazar	cantar (cazar)	1-4
añadir	subir	3	aplicar	cantar (tocar)	1-1
añorar	cantar	1	apocar	cantar (tocar)	1-1
apabullar	cantar	1	apocopar	cantar	1
apacentar	pensar	4A	apodar	cantar	1
apaciguar	cantar (averiguar)	1-3	apoderar	cantar	1
apagar	cantar (pagar)	1-2	apolillar	cantar	1
apalabrar	cantar	1	apologizar	cantar (cazar)	1-4
apalancar	cantar (tocar)	1-1	apoltronar(se)	cantar	1
apalear	cantar	1	apoquinar	cantar	1
apañar	cantar	1	aporrear	cantar	1
aparcar	cantar (tocar)	1-1	aportar	cantar	1

Verb	Class (Sub-class)	#	Verb	Class (Sub-class)	#
aposentar	cantar	1	armonizar	cantar (cazar)	1-4
apostar (1)[2]	mostrar	4B	aromatizar	cantar (cazar)	1-4
apostar (2)[3]	cantar	1	arponear	cantar	1
apostatar	cantar	1	arquear	cantar	1
apostillar	cantar	1	arracimar(se)	cantar	1
apostrofar	cantar	1	arraigar	cantar (pagar)	1-2
apoyar	cantar	1	arramblar	cantar	1
apreciar	cantar	1	arramplar	cantar	1
aprehender	comer	2	arrancar	cantar (tocar)	1-1
apremiar	cantar	1	arrasar	cantar	1
aprender	comer	2	arrastrar	cantar	1
apresar	cantar	1	arrear	cantar	1
aprestar	cantar	1	arrebatar	cantar	1
apresurar	cantar	1	arrebolar	cantar	1
apretar	pensar	4A	arrebujar	cantar	1
apretujar	cantar	1	arreciar	cantar	1
aprisionar	cantar	1	arredrar	cantar	1
aprobar	mostrar	4B	arreglar	cantar	1
apropiar	cantar	1	arrellanar(se)	cantar	1
aprovechar	cantar	1	arremangar	cantar (pagar)	1-2
aprovisionar	cantar	1	arremeter	comer	2
aproximar	cantar	1	arremolinar(se)	cantar	1
apuntalar	cantar	1	arrendar	pensar	4A
apuntar	cantar	1	arrepentir(se)	sentir	6A
apuntillar	cantar	1	arrestar	cantar	1
apuñalar	cantar	1	arriar	cantar (enviar)	1-15
apurar	cantar	1	arribar	cantar	1
aquejar	cantar	1	arriesgar	cantar (pagar)	1-2
aquietar	cantar	1	arrimar	cantar	1
aquilatar	cantar	1	arrinconar	cantar	1
arañar	cantar	1	arrobar	cantar	1
arar	cantar	1	arrodillar	cantar	1
arbitrar	cantar	1	arrogar	cantar (pagar)	1-2
arbolar	cantar	1	arrojar	cantar	1
archivar	cantar	1	arrollar	cantar	1
arder	comer	2	arropar	cantar	1
argüir	argüir	18	arrostrar	cantar	1
argumentar	cantar	1	arrugar	cantar (pagar)	1-2
armar	cantar	1	arruinar	cantar	1

[2] To bet.
[3] To station or post.

Verb	Class (Sub-class)	#	Verb	Class (Sub-class)	#
arrullar	cantar	1	asumir	subir	3
arrumbar	cantar	1	asustar	cantar	1
articular	cantar	1	atacar	cantar (tocar)	1-1
asaetear	cantar	1	atajar	cantar	1
asalariar	cantar	1	atañer (DEF)	comer (tañer)	2-5
asaltar	cantar	1	atar	cantar	1
asar	cantar	1	atardecer (DEF)	conocer	7A
ascender	perder	5A	atarugar	cantar (pagar)	1-2
asear	cantar	1	atascar	cantar (tocar)	1-1
asediar	cantar	1	ataviar	cantar (enviar)	1-15
asegurar	cantar	1	atemorizar	cantar (cazar)	1-4
asemejar	cantar	1	atemperar	cantar	1
asentar	pensar	4A	atenazar	cantar (cazar)	1-4
asentir	sentir	6A	atender	perder	5A
aserrar	pensar	4A	atener(se)	tener (obtener)	31-1
asesinar	cantar	1	atentar	cantar	1
asesorar	cantar	1	atenuar	cantar (actuar)	1-14
asestar	cantar	1	aterrar (1)[6]	pensar	4A
aseverar	cantar	1	aterrar (2)[7]	cantar	1
asfaltar	cantar	1	aterrizar	cantar (cazar)	1-4
asfixiar	cantar	1	aterrorizar	cantar (cazar)	1-4
asignar	cantar	1	atesorar	cantar	1
asilar	cantar	1	atestar (1)[8]	pensar	4A
asimilar	cantar	1	atestar (2)[9]	cantar	1
asir	asir	13	atestiguar	cantar (averiguar)	1-3
asistir	subir	3	atiborrar	cantar	1
asociar	cantar	1	atildar	cantar	1
asolar (1)[4]	mostrar	4B	atinar	cantar	1
asolar (2)[5]	cantar	1	atiplar	cantar	1
asomar	cantar	1	atirantar	cantar	1
asombrar	cantar	1	atisbar	cantar	1
aspar	cantar	1	atizar	cantar (cazar)	1-4
asperjar	cantar	1	atocinar	cantar	1
aspirar	cantar	1	atolondrar	cantar	1
asquear	cantar	1	atomizar	cantar (cazar)	1-4
astillar	cantar	1	atontar	cantar	1

[4] To raze, devastate.
[5] To burn up, parch.
[6] To demolish.
[7] To terrify.
[8] To stuff.
[9] To attest.

Verb	Class (Sub-class)	#	Verb	Class (Sub-class)	#
atontolinar	cantar	1	avanzar	cantar (cazar)	1-4
atorar	cantar	1	avasallar	cantar	1
atormentar	cantar	1	avecinar	cantar	1
atornillar	cantar	1	avecindar	cantar	1
atosigar	cantar (pagar)	1-2	avejentar	cantar	1
atracar	cantar (tocar)	1-1	avenir	venir (convenir)	32-1
atraer	traer	33	aventajar	cantar	1
atragantar	cantar	1	aventar	pensar	4A
atrancar	cantar (tocar)	1-1	aventurar	cantar	1
atrapar	cantar	1	avergonzar	mostrar (avergonzar)	4B-6
atrasar	cantar	1	averiar	cantar (enviar)	1-15
atravesar	pensar	4A	averiguar	cantar (averiguar)	1-3
atrever(se)	comer	2	avezar	cantar (cazar)	1-4
atribuir	construir	8	aviar	cantar (enviar)	1-15
atribular	cantar	1	aviejar	cantar	1
atrincherar	cantar	1	avinagrar	cantar	1
atrofiar	cantar	1	avisar	cantar	1
atronar	mostrar	4B	avispar	cantar	1
atropellar	cantar	1	avistar	cantar	1
atufar	cantar	1	avituallar	cantar	1
aturdir	subir	3	avivar	cantar	1
aturullar	cantar	1	avizorar	cantar	1
atusar	cantar	1	ayudar	cantar	1
auditar	cantar	1	ayunar	cantar	1
augurar	cantar	1	azarar	cantar	1
aullar	cantar (aullar)	1-6	azogar	cantar (pagar)	1-2
aumentar	cantar	1	azotar	cantar	1
aunar	cantar (aullar)	1-6	azucarar	cantar	1
aupar	cantar (aullar)	1-6	azufrar	cantar	1
aureolar	cantar	1	azulear	cantar	1
auscultar	cantar	1	azuzar	cantar (cazar)	1-4
ausentar	cantar	1	babear	cantar	1
auspiciar	cantar	1	babosear	cantar	1
autenticar	cantar (tocar)	1-1	bailar	cantar	1
autentificar	cantar (tocar)	1-1	bailotear	cantar	1
autocensurar	cantar	1	bajar	cantar	1
autoeditar	cantar	1	balancear	cantar	1
automatizar	cantar (cazar)	1-4	balar	cantar	1
automedicar(se)	cantar (tocar)	1-1	balbucear	cantar	1
autorizar	cantar (cazar)	1-4	balbucir	subir (abolir)	3-14
autosugestionar(se)	cantar	1	balcanizar	cantar (cazar)	1-4
auxiliar	cantar	1	baldar	cantar	1
avalar	cantar	1	bambolear	cantar	1

Verb	Class (Sub-class)	#	Verb	Class (Sub-class)	#
bandear	cantar	1	bombardear	cantar	1
banderillear	cantar	1	bombear	cantar	1
bañar	cantar	1	bonificar	cantar (tocar)	1-1
baquetear	cantar	1	bordar	cantar	1
barajar	cantar	1	bordear	cantar	1
barnizar	cantar (cazar)	1-4	borrar	cantar	1
barrar	cantar	1	bosquejar	cantar	1
barrenar	cantar	1	bostezar	cantar (cazar)	1-4
barrer	comer	2	botar	cantar	1
barritar	cantar	1	boxear	cantar	1
barruntar	cantar	1	bracear	cantar	1
basar	cantar	1	brear	cantar	1
bascular	cantar	1	bregar	cantar (pagar)	1-2
bastar	cantar	1	bribonear	cantar	1
batallar	cantar	1	brillar	cantar	1
batear	cantar	1	brincar	cantar (tocar)	1-1
batir	subir	3	brindar	cantar	1
bautizar	cantar (cazar)	1-4	bromear	cantar	1
beatificar	cantar (tocar)	1-1	broncear	cantar	1
beber	comer	2	brotar	cantar	1
becar	cantar (tocar)	1-1	brujulear	cantar	1
bendecir	decir (bendecir)	28-2	bruñir	subir (bruñir)	3-6
beneficiar	cantar	1	brutalizar(se)	cantar (cazar)	1-4
berrear	cantar	1	bucear	cantar	1
besar	cantar	1	bufar	cantar	1
bestializar(se)	cantar (cazar)	1-4	bullir	subir (bullir)	3-5
besuquear	cantar	1	burbujear	cantar	1
bifurcar(se)	cantar (tocar)	1-1	burilar	cantar	1
biografiar	cantar (enviar)	1-15	burlar	cantar	1
birlar	cantar	1	burocratizar	cantar (cazar)	1-4
bisar	cantar	1	buscar	cantar (tocar)	1-1
bisbisear	cantar	1	buzonear	cantar	1
biselar	cantar	1	cabalgar	cantar (pagar)	1-2
bizquear	cantar	1	cabecear	cantar	1
blandir	subir	3	caber	caber	23
blanquear	cantar	1	cablear	cantar	1
blasfemar	cantar	1	cablegrafiar	cantar (enviar)	1-15
blasonar	cantar	1	cabrahigar	cantar (cabrahigar)	1-11
blindar	cantar	1	cabrear	cantar	1
bloquear	cantar	1	cabrillear	cantar	1
bobear	cantar	1	cacarear	cantar	1
bogar	cantar (pagar)	1-2	cachear	cantar	1
boicotear	cantar	1	caducar	cantar (tocar)	1-1

Verb	Class (Sub-class)	#	Verb	Class (Sub-class)	#
caer	caer	9	capturar	cantar	1
cagar	cantar (pagar)	1-2	caracolear	cantar	1
calafatear	cantar	1	caracterizar	cantar (cazar)	1-4
calar	cantar	1	caramelizar	cantar (cazar)	1-4
calcar	cantar (tocar)	1-1	carbonatar	cantar	1
calcetar	cantar	1	carbonizar	cantar (cazar)	1-4
calcificar	cantar (tocar)	1-1	carburar	cantar	1
calcinar	cantar	1	carcajear	cantar	1
calcografiar	cantar (enviar)	1-15	carcomer	comer	2
calcular	cantar	1	cardar	cantar	1
caldear	cantar	1	carear	cantar	1
calentar	pensar	4A	carecer	conocer	7A
calibrar	cantar	1	cargar	cantar (pagar)	1-2
calificar	cantar (tocar)	1-1	cariar	cantar	1
caligrafiar	cantar (enviar)	1-15	caricaturizar	cantar (cazar)	1-4
callar	cantar	1	carraspear	cantar	1
callejear	cantar	1	cartear	cantar	1
calmar	cantar	1	cartografiar	cantar (enviar)	1-15
calumniar	cantar	1	casar	cantar	1
calzar	cantar (cazar)	1-4	cascabelear	cantar	1
cambiar	cantar	1	cascar	cantar (tocar)	1-1
camelar	cantar	1	castañetear	cantar	1
caminar	cantar	1	castellanizar	cantar (cazar)	1-4
campar	cantar	1	castigar	cantar (pagar)	1-2
campear	cantar	1	castrar	cantar	1
camuflar	cantar	1	catalanizar	cantar (cazar)	1-4
canalizar	cantar (cazar)	1-4	catalizar	cantar (cazar)	1-4
cancelar	cantar	1	catalogar	cantar (pagar)	1-2
canjear	cantar	1	catapultar	cantar	1
canonizar	cantar (cazar)	1-4	catar	cantar	1
cansar	cantar	1	catear	cantar	1
cantar	cantar	1	categorizar	cantar (cazar)	1-4
canturrear	cantar	1	catequizar	cantar (cazar)	1-4
cañonear	cantar	1	causar	cantar	1
capacitar	cantar	1	cauterizar	cantar (cazar)	1-4
capar	cantar	1	cautivar	cantar	1
capear	cantar	1	cavar	cantar	1
capitalizar	cantar (cazar)	1-4	cavilar	cantar	1
capitanear	cantar	1	cazar	cantar (cazar)	1-4
capitular	cantar	1	cebar	cantar	1
capotar	cantar	1	cecear	cantar	1
capotear	cantar	1	ceder	comer	2
captar	cantar	1	cegar	pensar (negar)	4A-1

Verb	Class (Sub-class)	#	Verb	Class (Sub-class)	#
cejar	cantar	1	chiflar	cantar	1
celar	cantar	1	chillar	cantar	1
celebrar	cantar	1	chinchar	cantar	1
cenar	cantar	1	chinchorrear	cantar	1
censar	cantar	1	chirigotear	cantar	1
censurar	cantar	1	chirriar	cantar (enviar)	1-15
centellear	cantar	1	chismear	cantar	1
centralizar	cantar (cazar)	1-4	chismorrear	cantar	1
centrar	cantar	1	chispear	cantar	1
centrifugar	cantar (pagar)	1-2	chisporrotear	cantar	1
centuplicar	cantar (tocar)	1-1	chistar	cantar	1
ceñir	pedir (ceñir)	6B-3	chivar	cantar	1
cepillar	cantar	1	chocar	cantar (tocar)	1-1
cercar	cantar (tocar)	1-1	chochear	cantar	1
cercenar	cantar	1	choricear	cantar	1
cerciorar	cantar	1	chorrear	cantar	1
cerner	perder	5A	chotear	cantar	1
cernir	discernir	15	chulear	cantar	1
cerrar	pensar	4A	chupar	cantar	1
certificar	cantar (tocar)	1-1	chupetear	cantar	1
cesar	cantar	1	churruscar	cantar (tocar)	1-1
chafar	cantar	1	chutar	cantar	1
chalar	cantar	1	cicatear	cantar	1
chamullar	cantar	1	cicatrizar	cantar (cazar)	1-4
chamuscar	cantar (tocar)	1-1	cifrar	cantar	1
chancear	cantar	1	cimbrear	cantar	1
chancletear	cantar	1	cimentar	pensar	4A
chantajear	cantar	1	cincelar	cantar	1
chapar	cantar	1	cinematografiar	cantar (enviar)	1-15
chapotear	cantar	1	circuncidar	cantar	1
chapucear	cantar	1	circunnavegar	cantar (pagar)	1-2
chapurrear	cantar	1	circunscribir	subir (escribir)	3-11
chapuzar	cantar (cazar)	1-4	circunvalar	cantar	1
chaquetear	cantar	1	ciscar	cantar (tocar)	1-1
charlar	cantar	1	citar	cantar	1
charlatanear	cantar	1	civilizar	cantar (cazar)	1-4
charlotear	cantar	1	cizañar	cantar	1
charolar	cantar	1	clamar	cantar	1
chascar	cantar (tocar)	1-1	clamorear	cantar	1
chasquear	cantar	1	clarear	cantar	1
chatear	cantar	1	clarificar	cantar (tocar)	1-1
chequear	cantar	1	clasificar	cantar (tocar)	1-1
chicolear	cantar	1	claudicar	cantar (tocar)	1-1

Verb	Class (Sub-class)	#	Verb	Class (Sub-class)	#
clausurar	cantar	1	colocar	cantar (tocar)	1-1
clavar	cantar	1	colonizar	cantar (cazar)	1-4
clavetear	cantar	1	colorear	cantar	1
climatizar	cantar (cazar)	1-4	columbrar	cantar	1
clocar	cantar (tocar)	1-1	columpiar	cantar	1
clonar	cantar	1	comadrear	cantar	1
cloquear	cantar	1	comandar	cantar	1
clorar	cantar	1	combar	cantar	1
cloroformizar	cantar (cazar)	1-4	combatir	subir	3
coadyuvar	cantar	1	combinar	cantar	1
coagular	cantar	1	comedir(se)	pedir	6B
coaligar(se)	cantar (pagar)	1-2	comentar	cantar	1
coartar	cantar	1	comenzar	pensar (empezar)	4A-2
cobijar	cantar	1	comer	comer	2
cobrar	cantar	1	comercializar	cantar (cazar)	1-4
cocear	cantar	1	cometer	comer	2
cocer	mover (cocer)	5B-1	comisionar	cantar	1
cocinar	cantar	1	compadecer	conocer	7A
codear	cantar	1	compaginar	cantar	1
codiciar	cantar	1	comparar	cantar	1
codificar	cantar (tocar)	1-1	comparecer	conocer	7A
codirigir	subir (dirigir)	3-2	compartimentar	cantar	1
coercer	comer (vencer)	2-1	compartir	subir	3
coexistir	subir	3	compatibilizar	cantar (cazar)	1-4
coger	comer (coger)	2-2	compeler	comer	2
cohabitar	cantar	1	compendiar	cantar	1
coheredar	cantar	1	compenetrar(se)	cantar	1
cohesionar	cantar	1	compensar	cantar	1
cohibir	subir (prohibir)	3-8	competer	comer	2
coincidir	subir	3	competir	pedir	6B
cojear	cantar	1	compilar	cantar	1
colaborar	cantar	1	complacer	conocer (placer)	7A-2
colacionar	cantar	1	complementar	cantar	1
colapsar	cantar	1	completar	cantar	1
colar	mostrar	4B	complicar	cantar (tocar)	1-1
colear	cantar	1	componer	poner (suponer)	30-1
coleccionar	cantar	1	comportar	cantar	1
colectar	cantar	1	comprar	cantar	1
colectivizar	cantar (cazar)	1-4	comprender	comer	2
colegiar(se)	cantar	1	comprimir	subir	3
colegir	pedir (elegir)	6B-1	comprobar	mostrar	4B
colgar	mostrar (colgar)	4B-2	comprometer	comer	2
colindar	cantar	1	compulsar	cantar	1

Verb	Class (Sub-class)	#	Verb	Class (Sub-class)	#
computadorizar	cantar (cazar)	1-4	configurar	cantar	1
computar	cantar	1	confinar	cantar	1
computarizar	cantar (cazar)	1-4	confirmar	cantar	1
comulgar	cantar (pagar)	1-2	confiscar	cantar (tocar)	1-1
comunicar	cantar (tocar)	1-1	confitar	cantar	1
concatenar	cantar	1	conflagrar	cantar	1
concebir	pedir	6B	confluir	construir	8
conceder	comer	2	conformar	cantar	1
concelebrar	cantar	1	confortar	cantar	1
concentrar	cantar	1	confraternizar	cantar (cazar)	1-4
conceptualizar	cantar (cazar)	1-4	confrontar	cantar	1
conceptuar	cantar (actuar)	1-14	confundir	subir	3
concernir (DEF)	discernir	15	congelar	cantar	1
concertar	pensar	4A	congeniar	cantar	1
conchabar	cantar	1	congestionar	cantar	1
concienciar	cantar	1	conglomerar	cantar	1
conciliar	cantar	1	congraciar	cantar	1
concitar	cantar	1	congratular	cantar	1
concluir	construir	8	congregar	cantar (pagar)	1-2
concordar	mostrar	4B	conjeturar	cantar	1
concretar	cantar	1	conjugar	cantar (pagar)	1-2
concretizar	cantar (cazar)	1-4	conjuntar	cantar	1
conculcar	cantar (tocar)	1-1	conjurar	cantar	1
concurrir	subir	3	conllevar	cantar	1
concursar	cantar	1	conmemorar	cantar	1
condecorar	cantar	1	conmensurar	cantar	1
condenar	cantar	1	conminar	cantar	1
condensar	cantar	1	conmocionar	cantar	1
condescender	perder	5A	conmover	mover	5B
condicionar	cantar	1	conmutar	cantar	1
condimentar	cantar	1	connotar	cantar	1
condoler(se)	mover	5B	conocer	conocer	7A
condonar	cantar	1	conquistar	cantar	1
conducir	conducir	34	consagrar	cantar	1
conectar	cantar	1	conseguir	pedir (seguir)	6B-2
conexionar	cantar	1	consensuar	cantar (actuar)	1-14
confabular	cantar	1	consentir	sentir	6A
confeccionar	cantar	1	conservar	cantar	1
confederar	cantar	1	considerar	cantar	1
conferenciar	cantar	1	consignar	cantar	1
conferir	sentir	6A	consistir	subir	3
confesar	pensar	4A	consolar	mostrar	4B
confiar	cantar (enviar)	1-15	consolidar	cantar	1

Verb	Class (Sub-class)	#	Verb	Class (Sub-class)	#
consonantizar	cantar (cazar)	1-4	controlar	cantar	1
conspirar	cantar	1	conturbar	cantar	1
constar	cantar	1	contusionar	cantar	1
constatar	cantar	1	convalecer	conocer	7A
consternar	cantar	1	convalidar	cantar	1
constipar	cantar	1	convencer	comer (vencer)	2-1
constituir	construir	8	convenir	venir (convenir)	32-1
constreñir	pedir (ceñir)	6B-3	converger	comer (coger)	2-2
construir	construir	8	conversar	cantar	1
consultar	cantar	1	convertir	sentir	6A
consumar	cantar	1	convidar	cantar	1
consumir	subir	3	convivir	subir	3
contabilizar	cantar (cazar)	1-4	convocar	cantar (tocar)	1-1
contactar	cantar	1	convulsionar	cantar	1
contagiar	cantar	1	cooperar	cantar	1
contaminar	cantar	1	coordinar	cantar	1
contar	mostrar	4B	copar	cantar	1
contemplar	cantar	1	copear	cantar	1
contemporizar	cantar (cazar)	1-4	copiar	cantar	1
contender	perder	5A	coproducir	conducir	34
contener	tener (obtener)	31-1	copular	cantar	1
contentar	cantar	1	coquetear	cantar	1
contestar	cantar	1	corear	cantar	1
contextualizar	cantar (cazar)	1-4	coreografiar	cantar (enviar)	1-15
continuar	cantar (actuar)	1-14	cornear	cantar	1
contonear(se)	cantar	1	coronar	cantar	1
contornear	cantar	1	corregir	pedir (elegir)	6B-1
contorsionar(se)	cantar	1	correr	comer	2
contraatacar	cantar (tocar)	1-1	corresponder	comer	2
contradecir	decir (predecir)	28-1	corretear	cantar	1
contraer	traer	33	corroborar	cantar	1
contrahacer	hacer (rehacer)	29-1	corroer	caer (roer)	9-2
contraindicar	cantar (tocar)	1-1	corromper	comer	2
contrapear	cantar	1	cortar	cantar	1
contrapesar	cantar	1	cortejar	cantar	1
contraponer	poner (suponer)	30-1	coscar(se)	cantar (tocar)	1-1
contrariar	cantar (enviar)	1-15	cosechar	cantar	1
contrarrestar	cantar	1	coser	comer	2
contrastar	cantar	1	cosquillear	cantar	1
contratar	cantar	1	costar	mostrar	4B
contravenir	venir (convenir)	32-1	costear	cantar	1
contribuir	construir	8	cotejar	cantar	1
contristar	cantar	1	cotizar	cantar (cazar)	1-4

Verb	Class (Sub-class)	#	Verb	Class (Sub-class)	#
cotorrear	cantar	1	currar	cantar	1
crear	cantar	1	cursar	cantar	1
crecer	conocer	7A	curtir	subir	3
creer	comer (leer)	2-3	curvar	cantar	1
crepitar	cantar	1	custodiar	cantar	1
criar[10]	cantar (enviar)	1-15	damnificar	cantar (tocar)	1-1
cribar	cantar	1	danzar	cantar (cazar)	1-4
crispar	cantar	1	dañar	cantar	1
cristalizar	cantar (cazar)	1-4	dar	dar	25
cristianar	cantar	1	datar	cantar	1
cristianizar	cantar (cazar)	1-4	deambular	cantar	1
criticar	cantar (tocar)	1-1	debatir	subir	3
croar	cantar	1	deber	comer	2
cromar	cantar	1	debilitar	cantar	1
cronometrar	cantar	1	debutar	cantar	1
crucificar	cantar (tocar)	1-1	decaer	caer	9
crujir	subir	3	decantar	cantar	1
cruzar	cantar (cazar)	1-4	decapitar	cantar	1
cuadrar	cantar	1	decepcionar	cantar	1
cuadricular	cantar	1	decidir	subir	3
cuadruplicar	cantar (tocar)	1-1	decir	decir	28
cuajar	cantar	1	declamar	cantar	1
cualificar	cantar (tocar)	1-1	declarar	cantar	1
cuantificar	cantar (tocar)	1-1	declinar	cantar	1
cuartear	cantar	1	decodificar	cantar (tocar)	1-1
cubrir	subir (cubrir)	3-10	decolorar	cantar	1
cuchichear	cantar	1	decomisar	cantar	1
cuestionar	cantar	1	decorar	cantar	1
cuidar	cantar	1	decorticar	cantar (tocar)	1-1
culminar	cantar	1	decrecer	conocer	7A
culpabilizar	cantar (cazar)	1-4	decretar	cantar	1
culpar	cantar	1	dedicar	cantar (tocar)	1-1
cultivar	cantar	1	deducir	conducir	34
culturizar	cantar (cazar)	1-4	defecar	cantar (tocar)	1-1
cumplimentar	cantar	1	defender	perder	5A
cumplir	subir	3	defenestrar	cantar	1
cundir	subir	3	definir	subir	3
curar	cantar	1	deforestar	cantar	1
curiosear	cantar	1	deformar	cantar	1

[10]The new orthographic rules allow alternative forms for the simple past 1s and 3s—*crie/crié, crio/crió*—as well as for the present indicative and subjunctive 2p—*criais/criáis* and *crieis/criéis.*

Verb	Class (Sub-class)	#	Verb	Class (Sub-class)	#
defraudar	cantar	1	depredar	cantar	1
degenerar	cantar	1	deprimir	subir	3
deglutir	subir	3	depurar	cantar	1
degollar	mostrar (agorar)	4B-4	derechizar	cantar (cazar)	1-4
degradar	cantar	1	derivar	cantar	1
degustar	cantar	1	derogar	cantar (pagar)	1-2
deificar	cantar (tocar)	1-1	derramar	cantar	1
dejar	cantar	1	derrapar	cantar	1
delatar	cantar	1	derrengar	cantar (pagar)	1-2
delegar	cantar (pagar)	1-2	derretir	pedir	6B
deleitar	cantar	1	derribar	cantar	1
deletrear	cantar	1	derrocar	cantar (tocar)	1-1
deliberar	cantar	1	derrochar	cantar	1
delimitar	cantar	1	derrotar	cantar	1
delinear	cantar	1	derruir	construir	8
delinquir	subir (delinquir)	3-4	derrumbar	cantar	1
delirar	cantar	1	desabastecer	conocer	7A
demacrar(se)	cantar	1	desabollar	cantar	1
demandar	cantar	1	desabotonar	cantar	1
demarcar	cantar (tocar)	1-1	desabrigar	cantar (pagar)	1-2
demarrar	cantar	1	desabrochar	cantar	1
democratizar	cantar (cazar)	1-4	desacatar	cantar	1
demoler	mover	5B	desacelerar	cantar	1
demorar	cantar	1	desacertar	pensar	4A
demostrar	mostrar	4B	desaclimatar	cantar	1
demudar	cantar	1	desacomodar	cantar	1
denegar	pensar (negar)	4A-1	desaconsejar	cantar	1
denigrar	cantar	1	desacoplar	cantar	1
denominar	cantar	1	desacostumbrar	cantar	1
denostar	mostrar	4B	desacreditar	cantar	1
denotar	cantar	1	desactivar	cantar	1
denunciar	cantar	1	desacuartelar	cantar	1
deparar	cantar	1	desafiar	cantar (enviar)	1-15
departir	subir	3	desafinar	cantar	1
depauperar	cantar	1	desagradar	cantar	1
depender	comer	2	desagraviar	cantar	1
depilar	cantar	1	desaguar	cantar (averiguar)	1-3
deplorar	cantar	1	desahogar	cantar (pagar)	1-2
deponer	poner (suponer)	30-1	desahuciar	cantar	1
deportar	cantar	1	desajustar	cantar	1
depositar	cantar	1	desalar	cantar	1
depravar	cantar	1	desalentar	pensar	4A
depreciar	cantar	1	desalinear	cantar	1

Verb	Class (Sub-class)	#	Verb	Class (Sub-class)	#
desalinizar	cantar (cazar)	1-4	desbarbar	cantar	1
desaliñar	cantar	1	desbarrancar	cantar (tocar)	1-1
desalojar	cantar	1	desbarrar	cantar	1
desalquilar	cantar	1	desbastar	cantar	1
desamortizar	cantar (cazar)	1-4	desbloquear	cantar	1
desamparar	cantar	1	desbocar	cantar (tocar)	1-1
desamueblar	cantar	1	desbordar	cantar	1
desanclar	cantar	1	desbravar	cantar	1
desandar	andar	35	desbrozar	cantar (cazar)	1-4
desangrar	cantar	1	descabalar	cantar	1
desanudar	cantar	1	descabalgar	cantar (pagar)	1-2
desaparecer	conocer	7A	descabellar	cantar	1
desapasionar	cantar	1	descabezar	cantar (cazar)	1-4
desapegar	cantar (pagar)	1-2	descacharrar	cantar	1
desapretar	pensar	4A	descafeinar	cantar (descafeinar)	1-7
desaprobar	mostrar	4B	descalabrar	cantar	1
desaprovechar	cantar	1	descalcificar	cantar (tocar)	1-1
desarbolar	cantar	1	descalificar	cantar (tocar)	1-1
desarmar	cantar	1	descalzar	cantar (cazar)	1-4
desarmonizar	cantar (cazar)	1-4	descamar	cantar	1
desarraigar	cantar (pagar)	1-2	descambiar	cantar	1
desarreglar	cantar	1	descansar	cantar	1
desarrendar	pensar	4A	descaperuzar	cantar (cazar)	1-4
desarrimar	cantar	1	descapotar	cantar	1
desarrollar	cantar	1	descargar	cantar (pagar)	1-2
desarropar	cantar	1	descarnar	cantar	1
desarrugar	cantar (pagar)	1-2	descarriar	cantar (enviar)	1-15
desarticular	cantar	1	descarrilar	cantar	1
desasir	asir	13	descartar	cantar	1
desasistir	subir	3	descasar	cantar	1
desasnar	cantar	1	descascarillar	cantar	1
desasosegar	pensar (negar)	4A-1	descastar	cantar	1
desatar	cantar	1	descender	perder	5A
desatascar	cantar (tocar)	1-1	descentralizar	cantar (cazar)	1-4
desatender	perder	5A	descentrar	cantar	1
desatornillar	cantar	1	descerebrar	cantar	1
desatrancar	cantar (tocar)	1-1	descerrajar	cantar	1
desautorizar	cantar (cazar)	1-4	descifrar	cantar	1
desayunar	cantar	1	desclasificar	cantar (tocar)	1-1
desazonar	cantar	1	desclavar	cantar	1
desbancar	cantar (tocar)	1-1	descocar(se)	cantar (tocar)	1-1
desbarajustar	cantar	1	descodificar	cantar (tocar)	1-1
desbaratar	cantar	1	descolgar	mostrar (colgar)	4B-2

Verb	Class (Sub-class)	#	Verb	Class (Sub-class)	#
descollar	mostrar	4B	desembalar	cantar	1
descolocar	cantar (tocar)	1-1	desembarazar	cantar (cazar)	1-4
descolonizar	cantar (cazar)	1-4	desembarcar	cantar (tocar)	1-1
descompasar	cantar	1	desembargar	cantar (pagar)	1-2
descompensar	cantar	1	desembarrancar	cantar (tocar)	1-1
descomponer	poner (suponer)	30-1	desembarrar	cantar	1
descomprimir	subir	3	desembocar	cantar (tocar)	1-1
desconcertar	pensar	4A	desembolsar	cantar	1
desconchar	cantar	1	desembragar	cantar (pagar)	1-2
desconectar	cantar	1	desembrollar	cantar	1
desconfiar	cantar (enviar)	1-15	desembrujar	cantar	1
descongelar	cantar	1	desembuchar	cantar	1
descongestionar	cantar	1	desempacar	cantar (tocar)	1-1
desconocer	conocer	7A	desempalmar	cantar	1
desconsiderar	cantar	1	desempañar	cantar	1
descontaminar	cantar	1	desempapelar	cantar	1
descontar	mostrar	4B	desempaquetar	cantar	1
descontentar	cantar	1	desemparejar	cantar	1
descontextualizar	cantar (cazar)	1-4	desempatar	cantar	1
descontrolar	cantar	1	desempedrar	pensar	4A
desconvocar	cantar (tocar)	1-1	desempeñar	cantar	1
descorazonar	cantar	1	desempolvar	cantar	1
descorchar	cantar	1	desempotrar	cantar	1
descorrer	comer	2	desenamorar	cantar	1
descoser	comer	2	desencadenar	cantar	1
descoyuntar	cantar	1	desencajar	cantar	1
descreer	comer (leer)	2-3	desencajonar	cantar	1
descremar	cantar	1	desencallar	cantar	1
describir	subir (escribir)	3-11	desencaminar	cantar	1
descuadrar	cantar	1	desencantar	cantar	1
descuajar	cantar	1	desencapotar	cantar	1
descuajeringar	cantar (pagar)	1-2	desencarcelar	cantar	1
descuartizar	cantar (cazar)	1-4	desencasquillar	cantar	1
descubrir	subir (cubrir)	3-10	desenchufar	cantar	1
descuidar	cantar	1	desenclavar	cantar	1
desdecir	decir (predecir)	28-1	desencolar	cantar	1
desdeñar	cantar	1	desencorvar	cantar	1
desdibujar	cantar	1	desencuadernar	cantar	1
desdoblar	cantar	1	desenfadar	cantar	1
desdramatizar	cantar (cazar)	1-4	desenfocar	cantar (tocar)	1-1
desear	cantar	1	desenfrenar	cantar	1
desecar	cantar (tocar)	1-1	desenfundar	cantar	1
desechar	cantar	1	desenfurruñar	cantar	1

Verb	Class (Sub-class)	#	Verb	Class (Sub-class)	#
desenganchar	cantar	1	desforrar	cantar	1
desengañar	cantar	1	desgajar	cantar	1
desengrasar	cantar	1	desgañitar(se)	cantar	1
desenhebrar	cantar	1	desgarrar	cantar	1
desenjaular	cantar	1	desgasificar	cantar (tocar)	1-1
desenladrillar	cantar	1	desgastar	cantar	1
desenlazar	cantar (cazar)	1-4	desglosar	cantar	1
desenmarañar	cantar	1	desgraciar	cantar	1
desenmascarar	cantar	1	desgranar	cantar	1
desenraizar	cantar (enraizar)	1-12	desgravar	cantar	1
desenredar	cantar	1	desguarnecer	conocer	7A
desenrollar	cantar	1	desguazar	cantar (cazar)	1-4
desenroscar	cantar (tocar)	1-1	deshabitar	cantar	1
desensibilizar	cantar (cazar)	1-4	deshacer	hacer	29
desensillar	cantar	1	deshelar	pensar	4A
desentablillar	cantar	1	desheredar	cantar	1
desentender(se)	perder	5A	deshidratar	cantar	1
desenterrar	pensar	4A	deshilachar	cantar	1
desentoldar	cantar	1	deshilvanar	cantar	1
desentonar	cantar	1	deshinchar	cantar	1
desentrañar	cantar	1	deshojar	cantar	1
desentrenar	cantar	1	deshollinar	cantar	1
desentumecer	conocer	7A	deshonrar	cantar	1
desenvainar	cantar	1	deshuesar	cantar	1
desenvolver	mover (volver)	5B-4	deshumanizar	cantar (cazar)	1-4
desequilibrar	cantar	1	designar	cantar	1
desertar	cantar	1	desigualar	cantar	1
desertificar	cantar (tocar)	1-1	desilusionar	cantar	1
desertizar	cantar (cazar)	1-4	desimantar	cantar	1
desescombrar	cantar	1	desincrustar	cantar	1
desesperar	cantar	1	desinfectar	cantar	1
desestabilizar	cantar (cazar)	1-4	desinflar	cantar	1
desestimar	cantar	1	desinformar	cantar	1
desfalcar	cantar (tocar)	1-1	desinhibir	subir	3
desfallecer	conocer	7A	desinsectar	cantar	1
desfasar	cantar	1	desintegrar	cantar	1
desfavorecer	conocer	7A	desinteresar(se)	cantar	1
desfigurar	cantar	1	desintoxicar	cantar (tocar)	1-1
desfilar	cantar	1	desistir	subir	3
desflecar	cantar (tocar)	1-1	deslavazar	cantar (cazar)	1-4
desflorar	cantar	1	deslegalizar	cantar (cazar)	1-4
desfogar	cantar (pagar)	1-2	deslegitimar	cantar	1
desfondar	cantar	1	desleír	pedir (reír)	6B-4

Verb	Class (Sub-class)	#	Verb	Class (Sub-class)	#
desliar	cantar (enviar)	1-15	desocupar	cantar	1
desligar	cantar (pagar)	1-2	desodorizar	cantar (cazar)	1-4
deslindar	cantar	1	desoír	oír	10
deslizar	cantar (cazar)	1-4	desojar	cantar	1
deslomar	cantar	1	desollar	mostrar	4B
deslucir	lucir	7B	desorbitar	cantar	1
deslumbrar	cantar	1	desordenar	cantar	1
desmadejar	cantar	1	desorejar	cantar	1
desmadrar	cantar	1	desorganizar	cantar (cazar)	1-4
desmagnetizar	cantar (cazar)	1-4	desorientar	cantar	1
desmandar	cantar	1	desosar	mostrar (desosar)	4B-5
desmantelar	cantar	1	desovar	cantar	1
desmaquillar	cantar	1	desovillar	cantar	1
desmarcar	cantar (tocar)	1-1	desoxidar	cantar	1
desmayar	cantar	1	despabilar	cantar	1
desmejorar	cantar	1	despachar	cantar	1
desmelenar	cantar	1	despachurrar	cantar	1
desmembrar	pensar	4A	despampanar	cantar	1
desmentir	sentir	6A	despanzurrar	cantar	1
desmenuzar	cantar (cazar)	1-4	desparasitar	cantar	1
desmerecer	conocer	7A	desparejar	cantar	1
desmigajar	cantar	1	desparramar	cantar	1
desmigar	cantar (pagar)	1-2	despatarrar	cantar	1
desmilitarizar	cantar (cazar)	1-4	despechugar	cantar (pagar)	1-2
desmineralizar(se)	cantar (cazar)	1-4	despedazar	cantar (cazar)	1-4
desmitificar	cantar (tocar)	1-1	despedir	pedir	6B
desmochar	cantar	1	despegar	cantar (pagar)	1-2
desmontar	cantar	1	despeinar	cantar	1
desmoralizar	cantar (cazar)	1-4	despejar	cantar	1
desmoronar	cantar	1	despellejar	cantar	1
desmotivar	cantar	1	despelotar	cantar	1
desmovilizar	cantar (cazar)	1-4	despenalizar	cantar (cazar)	1-4
desnacionalizar	cantar (cazar)	1-4	despendolar(se)	cantar	1
desnatar	cantar	1	despeñar	cantar	1
desnaturalizar	cantar (cazar)	1-4	despepitar	cantar	1
desnivelar	cantar	1	desperdiciar	cantar	1
desnortar(se)	cantar	1	desperdigar	cantar (pagar)	1-2
desnucar	cantar (tocar)	1-1	desperezar(se)	cantar (cazar)	1-4
desnuclearizar	cantar (cazar)	1-4	despersonalizar	cantar (cazar)	1-4
desnudar	cantar	1	despertar	pensar	4A
desnutrir(se)	subir	3	despiezar	cantar (cazar)	1-4
desobedecer	conocer	7A	despilfarrar	cantar	1
desobstruir	construir	8	despiojar	cantar	1

Verb	Class (Sub-class)	#	Verb	Class (Sub-class)	#
despistar	cantar	1	destinar	cantar	1
desplanchar	cantar	1	destituir	construir	8
desplantar	cantar	1	destornillar	cantar	1
desplazar	cantar (cazar)	1-4	destrenzar	cantar (cazar)	1-4
desplegar	pensar (negar)	4A-1	destripar	cantar	1
desplomar	cantar	1	destronar	cantar	1
desplumar	cantar	1	destrozar	cantar (cazar)	1-4
despoblar	mostrar	4B	destruir	construir	8
despojar	cantar	1	desubicar	cantar (tocar)	1-1
despolitizar	cantar (cazar)	1-4	desunir	subir	3
desportillar	cantar	1	desusar	cantar	1
desposar	cantar	1	desvalijar	cantar	1
desposeer	comer (leer)	2-3	desvalorizar	cantar (cazar)	1-4
despotricar	cantar (tocar)	1-1	desvanecer	conocer	7A
despreciar	cantar	1	desvariar	cantar (enviar)	1-15
desprender	comer	2	desvelar	cantar	1
despreocupar(se)	cantar	1	desvencijar	cantar	1
desprestigiar	cantar	1	desvendar	cantar	1
despresurizar	cantar (cazar)	1-4	desvergonzar(se)	mostrar (avergonzar)	4B-6
desprivatizar	cantar (cazar)	1-4	desvestir	pedir	6B
desprogramar	cantar	1	desviar	cantar (enviar)	1-15
desproveer[11]	comer (leer)	2-3	desvincular	cantar	1
despuntar	cantar	1	desvirgar	cantar (pagar)	1-2
desquiciar	cantar	1	desvirtuar	cantar (actuar)	1-14
desquitar	cantar	1	desvitalizar	cantar (cazar)	1-4
desratizar	cantar (cazar)	1-4	desvivir(se)	subir	3
desriñonar	cantar	1	detallar	cantar	1
desrizar	cantar (cazar)	1-4	detectar	cantar	1
destacar	cantar (tocar)	1-1	detener	tener (obtener)	31-1
destapar	cantar	1	detentar	cantar	1
destaponar	cantar	1	deteriorar	cantar	1
destejer	comer	2	determinar	cantar	1
destellar	cantar	1	detestar	cantar	1
destemplar	cantar	1	detraer	traer	33
destensar	cantar	1	devaluar	cantar (actuar)	1-14
desteñir	pedir (ceñir)	6B-3	devanar	cantar	1
desternillar(se)	cantar	1	devastar	cantar	1
desterrar	pensar	4A	devengar	cantar (pagar)	1-2
destetar	cantar	1	devenir	venir (convenir)	32-1
destilar	cantar	1	devolver	mover (volver)	5B-4

[11] Past participle: *desprovisto/desproveído*.

Verb	Class (Sub-class)	#	Verb	Class (Sub-class)	#
devorar	cantar	1	diseminar	cantar	1
diagnosticar	cantar (tocar)	1-1	disentir	sentir	6A
diagramar	cantar	1	diseñar	cantar	1
dializar	cantar (cazar)	1-4	disertar	cantar	1
dialogar	cantar (pagar)	1-2	disfrazar	cantar (cazar)	1-4
dibujar	cantar	1	disfrutar	cantar	1
dictaminar	cantar	1	disgregar	cantar (pagar)	1-2
dictar	cantar	1	disgustar	cantar	1
diezmar	cantar	1	disimilar	cantar	1
difamar	cantar	1	disimular	cantar	1
diferenciar	cantar	1	disipar	cantar	1
diferir	sentir	6A	dislocar	cantar (tocar)	1-1
dificultar	cantar	1	disminuir	construir	8
difuminar	cantar	1	disociar	cantar	1
difundir	subir	3	disolver	mover (resolver)	5B-3
digerir	sentir	6A	disparar	cantar	1
digitalizar	cantar (cazar)	1-4	disparatar	cantar	1
dignar(se)	cantar	1	dispensar	cantar	1
dignificar	cantar (tocar)	1-1	dispersar	cantar	1
dilapidar	cantar	1	disponer	poner (suponer)	30-1
dilatar	cantar	1	disputar	cantar	1
diligenciar	cantar	1	distanciar	cantar	1
dilucidar	cantar	1	distar	cantar	1
diluir	construir	8	distender	perder	5A
diluviar (DEF)	cantar	1	distinguir	subir (distinguir)	3-3
dimanar	cantar	1	distorsionar	cantar	1
dimitir	subir	3	distraer	traer	33
dinamitar	cantar	1	distribuir	construir	8
dinamizar	cantar (cazar)	1-4	disuadir	subir	3
diplomar	cantar	1	divagar	cantar (pagar)	1-2
diptongar	cantar (pagar)	1-2	divergir	subir (dirigir)	3-2
dirigir	subir (dirigir)	3-2	diversificar	cantar (tocar)	1-1
dirimir	subir	3	divertir	sentir	6A
discernir	discernir	15	dividir	subir	3
disciplinar	cantar	1	divinizar	cantar (cazar)	1-4
discordar	mostrar	4B	divisar	cantar	1
discrepar	cantar	1	divorciar	cantar	1
discriminar	cantar	1	divulgar	cantar (pagar)	1-2
disculpar	cantar	1	doblar	cantar	1
discurrir	subir	3	doblegar	cantar (pagar)	1-2
discutir	subir	3	doctorar	cantar	1
disecar	cantar (tocar)	1-1	documentar	cantar	1
diseccionar	cantar	1	dogmatizar	cantar (cazar)	1-4

Verb	Class (Sub-class)	#	Verb	Class (Sub-class)	#
doler	mover	5B	elidir	subir	3
domar	cantar	1	eliminar	cantar	1
domeñar	cantar	1	elogiar	cantar	1
domesticar	cantar (tocar)	1-1	elucidar	cantar	1
domiciliar	cantar	1	elucubrar	cantar	1
dominar	cantar	1	eludir	subir	3
donar	cantar	1	emanar	cantar	1
dopar	cantar	1	emancipar	cantar	1
dorar	cantar	1	emascular	cantar	1
dormir	dormir	6C	embadurnar	cantar	1
dormitar	cantar	1	embalar	cantar	1
dosificar	cantar (tocar)	1-1	embaldosar	cantar	1
dotar	cantar	1	embalsamar	cantar	1
dragar	cantar (pagar)	1-2	embalsar	cantar	1
dramatizar	cantar (cazar)	1-4	embarazar	cantar (cazar)	1-4
drenar	cantar	1	embarcar	cantar (tocar)	1-1
driblar	cantar	1	embargar	cantar (pagar)	1-2
drogar	cantar (pagar)	1-2	embarrancar	cantar (tocar)	1-1
duchar	cantar	1	embarrar	cantar	1
dudar	cantar	1	embarullar	cantar	1
dulcificar	cantar (tocar)	1-1	embaucar	cantar (tocar)	1-1
duplicar	cantar (tocar)	1-1	embazar	cantar (cazar)	1-4
durar	cantar	1	embeber	comer	2
echar	cantar	1	embelesar	cantar	1
eclipsar	cantar	1	embellecer	conocer	7A
economizar	cantar (cazar)	1-4	embestir	pedir	6B
edificar	cantar (tocar)	1-1	embetunar	cantar	1
editar	cantar	1	emblanquecer	conocer	7A
educar	cantar (tocar)	1-1	embobar	cantar	1
edulcorar	cantar	1	embolsar	cantar	1
efectuar	cantar (actuar)	1-14	emborrachar	cantar	1
ejecutar	cantar	1	emborrascar	cantar (tocar)	1-1
ejemplarizar	cantar (cazar)	1-4	emborronar	cantar	1
ejemplificar	cantar (tocar)	1-1	emboscar	cantar (tocar)	1-1
ejercer	comer (vencer)	2-1	embotar	cantar	1
ejercitar	cantar	1	embotellar	cantar	1
elaborar	cantar	1	embotijar	cantar	1
electrificar	cantar (tocar)	1-1	embozar	cantar (cazar)	1-4
electrizar	cantar (cazar)	1-4	embragar	cantar (pagar)	1-2
electrocutar	cantar	1	embravecer	conocer	7A
electrolizar	cantar (cazar)	1-4	embrear	cantar	1
elegir	pedir (elegir)	6B-1	embriagar	cantar (pagar)	1-2
elevar	cantar	1	embridar	cantar	1

Verb	Class (Sub-class)	#	Verb	Class (Sub-class)	#
embrollar	cantar	1	emperrar(se)	cantar	1
embromar	cantar	1	empezar	pensar (empezar)	4A-2
embrujar	cantar	1	empinar	cantar	1
embrutecer	conocer	7A	empitonar	cantar	1
embuchar	cantar	1	emplastecer	conocer	7A
embutir	subir	3	emplazar	cantar (cazar)	1-4
emerger	comer (coger)	2-2	emplear	cantar	1
emigrar	cantar	1	emplomar	cantar	1
emitir	subir	3	emplumar	cantar	1
emocionar	cantar	1	empobrecer	conocer	7A
empacar	cantar (tocar)	1-1	empollar	cantar	1
empachar	cantar	1	empolvar	cantar	1
empadronar	cantar	1	emponzoñar	cantar	1
empalagar	cantar (pagar)	1-2	emporcar	mostrar (trocar)	4B-1
empalar	cantar	1	empotrar	cantar	1
empalidecer	conocer	7A	emprender	comer	2
empalmar	cantar	1	empujar	cantar	1
empanar	cantar	1	empuñar	cantar	1
empantanar	cantar	1	emular	cantar	1
empañar	cantar	1	emulsionar	cantar	1
empapar	cantar	1	enajenar	cantar	1
empapelar	cantar	1	enaltecer	conocer	7A
empapuzar	cantar (cazar)	1-4	enamorar	cantar	1
empaquetar	cantar	1	enamoriscar(se)	cantar (tocar)	1-1
emparedar	cantar	1	enarbolar	cantar	1
emparejar	cantar	1	enarcar	cantar (tocar)	1-1
emparentar[12]	pensar	4A	enardecer	conocer	7A
empastar	cantar	1	enarenar	cantar	1
empatar	cantar	1	encabalgar	cantar (pagar)	1-2
empavonar	cantar	1	encabestrar	cantar	1
empecer	conocer	7A	encabezar	cantar (cazar)	1-4
empecinar(se)	cantar	1	encabritar(se)	cantar	1
empedrar	pensar	4A	encabronar	cantar	1
empeller	comer (empeller)	2-4	encadenar	cantar	1
empeñar	cantar	1	encajar	cantar	1
empeorar	cantar	1	encajonar	cantar	1
empequeñecer	conocer	7A	encalar	cantar	1
emperejilar	cantar	1	encallar	cantar	1
emperifollar	cantar	1	encallecer	conocer	7A

---

[12] Can also be conjugated without diphthongs, like *cantar*.

Verb	Class (Sub-class)	#	Verb	Class (Sub-class)	#
encallejonar	cantar	1	encizañar	cantar	1
encamar	cantar	1	enclaustrar	cantar	1
encaminar	cantar	1	enclavar	cantar	1
encanar(se)	cantar	1	encocorar	cantar	1
encandilar	cantar	1	encofrar	cantar	1
encanecer	conocer	7A	encoger	comer (coger)	2-2
encanijar	cantar	1	encolar	cantar	1
encantar	cantar	1	encolerizar	cantar (cazar)	1-4
encanutar	cantar	1	encomendar	pensar	4A
encañonar	cantar	1	encomiar	cantar	1
encapotar	cantar	1	enconar	cantar	1
encaprichar(se)	cantar	1	encontrar	mostrar	4B
encapsular	cantar	1	encopetar	cantar	1
encapuchar	cantar	1	encorajinar	cantar	1
encaramar	cantar	1	encorbatar	cantar	1
encarar	cantar	1	encordar	mostrar	4B
encarcelar	cantar	1	encorsetar	cantar	1
encarecer	conocer	7A	encorvar	cantar	1
encargar	cantar (pagar)	1-2	encrespar	cantar	1
encariñar	cantar	1	encuadernar	cantar	1
encarnar	cantar	1	encuadrar	cantar	1
encarnizar	cantar (cazar)	1-4	encubrir	subir (cubrir)	3-10
encarpetar	cantar	1	encuestar	cantar	1
encarrilar	cantar	1	encumbrar	cantar	1
encartar	cantar	1	encurtir	subir	3
encartonar	cantar	1	endemoniar	cantar	1
encasillar	cantar	1	enderezar	cantar (cazar)	1-4
encasquetar	cantar	1	endeudar(se)	cantar	1
encasquillar	cantar	1	endilgar	cantar (pagar)	1-2
encastrar	cantar	1	endiñar	cantar	1
encausar	cantar	1	endiosar	cantar	1
encauzar	cantar (cazar)	1-4	endomingar(se)	cantar (pagar)	1-2
encebollar	cantar	1	endosar	cantar	1
encelar	cantar	1	endulzar	cantar (cazar)	1-4
enceldar	cantar	1	endurecer	conocer	7A
encenagar	cantar (pagar)	1-2	enemistar	cantar	1
encender	perder	5A	enervar	cantar	1
encerar	cantar	1	enfadar	cantar	1
encerrar	pensar	4A	enfajar	cantar	1
encestar	cantar	1	enfangar	cantar (pagar)	1-2
encharcar	cantar (tocar)	1-1	enfatizar	cantar (cazar)	1-4
enchufar	cantar	1	enfermar	cantar	1
encintar	cantar	1	enfervorizar	cantar (cazar)	1-4

Verb	Class (Sub-class)	#	Verb	Class (Sub-class)	#
enfilar	cantar	1	enjoyar	cantar	1
enflaquecer	conocer	7A	enjuagar	cantar (pagar)	1-2
enfocar	cantar (tocar)	1-1	enjugar	cantar (pagar)	1-2
enfoscar	cantar (tocar)	1-1	enjuiciar	cantar	1
enfrascar(se)	cantar (tocar)	1-1	enladrillar	cantar	1
enfrentar	cantar	1	enlatar	cantar	1
enfriar	cantar (enviar)	1-15	enlazar	cantar (cazar)	1-4
enfundar	cantar	1	enlodar	cantar	1
enfurecer	conocer	7A	enloquecer	conocer	7A
enfurruñar(se)	cantar	1	enlosar	cantar	1
engalanar	cantar	1	enlucir	lucir	7B
enganchar	cantar	1	enlutar	cantar	1
engañar	cantar	1	enmadrar(se)	cantar	1
engarabitar	cantar	1	enmarañar	cantar	1
engarzar	cantar (cazar)	1-4	enmarcar	cantar (tocar)	1-1
engastar	cantar	1	enmascarar	cantar	1
engatusar	cantar	1	enmendar	pensar	4A
engendrar	cantar	1	enmohecer	conocer	7A
englobar	cantar	1	enmoquetar	cantar	1
engolar	cantar	1	enmudecer	conocer	7A
engolfar	cantar	1	ennegrecer	conocer	7A
engolosinar	cantar	1	ennoblecer	conocer	7A
engomar	cantar	1	ennoviar(se)	cantar	1
engominar(se)	cantar	1	enojar	cantar	1
engordar	cantar	1	enorgullecer	conocer	7A
engranar	cantar	1	enquistar	cantar	1
engrandecer	conocer	7A	enrabietar	cantar	1
engrasar	cantar	1	enraizar	cantar (enraizar)	1-12
engreír	pedir (reír)	6B-4	enrarecer	conocer	7A
engrescar	cantar (tocar)	1-1	enredar	cantar	1
engrosar	cantar	1	enrejar	cantar	1
enguachinar	cantar	1	enriquecer	conocer	7A
enguantar	cantar	1	enrocar	cantar (tocar)	1-1
enguarrar	cantar	1	enrojecer	conocer	7A
engullir	subir (bullir)	3-5	enrolar	cantar	1
engurruñar	cantar	1	enrollar	cantar	1
enharinar	cantar	1	enronquecer	conocer	7A
enhebrar	cantar	1	enroscar	cantar (tocar)	1-1
enjabonar	cantar	1	ensalzar	cantar (cazar)	1-4
enjaezar	cantar (cazar)	1-4	ensamblar	cantar	1
enjalbegar	cantar (pagar)	1-2	ensanchar	cantar	1
enjaretar	cantar	1	ensangrentar	pensar	4A
enjaular	cantar	1	ensañar	cantar	1

Verb	Class (Sub-class)	#	Verb	Class (Sub-class)	#
ensartar	cantar	1	entresacar	cantar (tocar)	1-1
ensayar	cantar	1	entretener	tener (obtener)	31-1
enseñar	cantar	1	entrever	ver (prever)	14-1
enseñorear(se)	cantar	1	entrevistar	cantar	1
ensillar	cantar	1	entristecer	conocer	7A
ensimismar(se)	cantar	1	entrometer	comer	2
ensoberbecer	conocer	7A	entroncar	cantar (tocar)	1-1
ensombrecer	conocer	7A	entronizar	cantar (cazar)	1-4
ensordecer	conocer	7A	entubar	cantar	1
ensortijar	cantar	1	entumecer	conocer	7A
ensuciar	cantar	1	enturbiar	cantar	1
entablar	cantar	1	entusiasmar	cantar	1
entablillar	cantar	1	enumerar	cantar	1
entallar	cantar	1	enunciar	cantar	1
entarimar	cantar	1	envainar	cantar	1
entelar	cantar	1	envalentonar	cantar	1
entender	perder	5A	envanecer	conocer	7A
entenebrecer	conocer	7A	envarar	cantar	1
enterar	cantar	1	envasar	cantar	1
enternecer	conocer	7A	envejecer	conocer	7A
enterrar	pensar	4A	envenenar	cantar	1
entibiar	cantar	1	enviar	cantar (enviar)	1-15
entintar	cantar	1	enviciar	cantar	1
entoldar	cantar	1	envidar	cantar	1
entonar	cantar	1	envidiar	cantar	1
entontecer	conocer	7A	envilecer	conocer	7A
entornar	cantar	1	enviudar	cantar	1
entorpecer	conocer	7A	envolver	mover (volver)	5B-4
entrampar	cantar	1	enyesar	cantar	1
entrañar	cantar	1	enzarzar	cantar (cazar)	1-4
entrar	cantar	1	epatar	cantar	1
entreabrir	subir (abrir)	3-9	epilogar	cantar (pagar)	1-2
entrechocar	cantar (tocar)	1-1	equidistar	cantar	1
entrecomillar	cantar	1	equilibrar	cantar	1
entrecortar	cantar	1	equipar	cantar	1
entrecruzar	cantar (cazar)	1-4	equiparar	cantar	1
entregar	cantar (pagar)	1-2	equivaler	valer	12
entrelazar	cantar (cazar)	1-4	equivocar	cantar (tocar)	1-1
entrelucir	lucir	7B	erguir	sentir (erguir)	6A-1
entremeter	comer	2	erigir	subir (dirigir)	3-2
entremezclar	cantar	1	erisipelar	cantar	1
entrenar	cantar	1	erizar	cantar (cazar)	1-4
entreoír	oír	10	erosionar	cantar	1

Verb	Class (Sub-class)	#	Verb	Class (Sub-class)	#
erotizar	cantar (cazar)	1-4	escotar	cantar	1
erradicar	cantar (tocar)	1-1	escribir	subir (escribir)	3-11
errar	pensar (errar)	4A-3	escriturar	cantar	1
eructar	cantar	1	escrutar	cantar	1
esbozar	cantar (cazar)	1-4	escuchar	cantar	1
escabechar	cantar	1	escudar	cantar	1
escabullir	subir (bullir)	3-5	escudriñar	cantar	1
escacharrar	cantar	1	esculpir	subir	3
escachifollar	cantar	1	escupir	subir	3
escalar	cantar	1	escurrir	subir	3
escaldar	cantar	1	esforzar	mostrar (forzar)	4B-3
escalfar	cantar	1	esfumar	cantar	1
escalonar	cantar	1	esgrimir	subir	3
escamar	cantar	1	eslabonar	cantar	1
escamotear	cantar	1	esmaltar	cantar	1
escampar	cantar	1	esmerar	cantar	1
escanciar	cantar	1	esmerilar	cantar	1
escandalizar	cantar (cazar)	1-4	espabilar	cantar	1
escanear	cantar	1	espachurrar	cantar	1
escapar	cantar	1	espaciar	cantar	1
escaquear(se)	cantar	1	espantar	cantar	1
escarbar	cantar	1	españolear	cantar	1
escarchar	cantar	1	españolizar	cantar (cazar)	1-4
escardar	cantar	1	esparcir	subir (fruncir)	3-1
escarificar	cantar (tocar)	1-1	especializar	cantar (cazar)	1-4
escarmentar	pensar	4A	especificar	cantar (tocar)	1-1
escarnecer	conocer	7A	especular	cantar	1
escasear	cantar	1	espejar	cantar	1
escatimar	cantar	1	espeluznar	cantar	1
escayolar	cantar	1	esperanzar	cantar (cazar)	1-4
escenificar	cantar (tocar)	1-1	esperar	cantar	1
escindir	subir	3	espesar	cantar	1
esclarecer	conocer	7A	espetar	cantar	1
esclavizar	cantar (cazar)	1-4	espiar	cantar (enviar)	1-15
esclerosar	cantar	1	espichar	cantar	1
esclerotizar	cantar (cazar)	1-4	espigar	cantar (pagar)	1-2
escobar	cantar	1	espirar	cantar	1
escocer	mover (cocer)	5B-1	espiritualizar	cantar (cazar)	1-4
escoger	comer (coger)	2-2	espolear	cantar	1
escolarizar	cantar (cazar)	1-4	espolvorear	cantar	1
escoltar	cantar	1	esponjar	cantar	1
esconder	comer	2	esponsorizar	cantar (cazar)	1-4
escorar	cantar	1	esposar	cantar	1

Verb	Class (Sub-class)	#	Verb	Class (Sub-class)	#
esprintar	cantar	1	estornudar	cantar	1
espulgar	cantar (pagar)	1-2	estragar	cantar (pagar)	1-2
espumar	cantar	1	estrangular	cantar	1
espurrear	cantar	1	estraperlear	cantar	1
esputar	cantar	1	estratificar	cantar (tocar)	1-1
esquejar	cantar	1	estrechar	cantar	1
esquematizar	cantar (cazar)	1-4	estrellar	cantar	1
esquiar	cantar (enviar)	1-15	estremecer	conocer	7A
esquilar	cantar	1	estrenar	cantar	1
esquilmar	cantar	1	estreñir	pedir (ceñir)	6B-3
esquinar	cantar	1	estresar	cantar	1
esquivar	cantar	1	estriar	cantar (enviar)	1-15
estabilizar	cantar (cazar)	1-4	estribar	cantar	1
establecer	conocer	7A	estropear	cantar	1
estabular	cantar	1	estructurar	cantar	1
estacionar	cantar	1	estrujar	cantar	1
estafar	cantar	1	estucar	cantar (tocar)	1-1
estallar	cantar	1	estuchar	cantar	1
estampar	cantar	1	estudiar	cantar	1
estampillar	cantar	1	estuprar	cantar	1
estancar	cantar (tocar)	1-1	eternizar	cantar (cazar)	1-4
estandarizar	cantar (cazar)	1-4	etimologizar	cantar (cazar)	1-4
estar	estar	20	etiquetar	cantar	1
estatalizar	cantar (cazar)	1-4	europeizar	cantar (europeizar)	1-13
estatuir	construir	8	evacuar	cantar	1
estenografiar	cantar (enviar)	1-15	evadir	subir	3
estercolar	cantar	1	evaluar	cantar (actuar)	1-14
estereotipar	cantar	1	evangelizar	cantar (cazar)	1-4
esterilizar	cantar (cazar)	1-4	evaporar	cantar	1
estibar	cantar	1	evidenciar	cantar	1
estigmatizar	cantar (cazar)	1-4	evitar	cantar	1
estilar	cantar	1	evocar	cantar (tocar)	1-1
estilizar	cantar (cazar)	1-4	evolucionar	cantar	1
estimar	cantar	1	exacerbar	cantar	1
estimular	cantar	1	exagerar	cantar	1
estipular	cantar	1	exaltar	cantar	1
estirajar	cantar	1	examinar	cantar	1
estirar	cantar	1	exasperar	cantar	1
estocar	cantar (tocar)	1-1	excarcelar	cantar	1
estofar	cantar	1	excavar	cantar	1
estomagar	cantar (pagar)	1-2	exceder	comer	2
estoquear	cantar	1	exceptuar	cantar (actuar)	1-14
estorbar	cantar	1	excitar	cantar	1

Verb	Class (Sub-class)	#	Verb	Class (Sub-class)	#
exclamar	cantar	1	expropiar	cantar	1
exclaustrar	cantar	1	expugnar	cantar	1
excluir	construir	8	expulsar	cantar	1
excomulgar	cantar (pagar)	1-2	expurgar	cantar (pagar)	1-2
excretar	cantar	1	extasiar	cantar (enviar)	1-15
exculpar	cantar	1	extender	perder	5A
excusar	cantar	1	extenuar	cantar (actuar)	1-14
execrar	cantar	1	exteriorizar	cantar (cazar)	1-4
exfoliar	cantar	1	exterminar	cantar	1
exhalar	cantar	1	extinguir	subir (distinguir)	3-3
exhibir	subir	3	extirpar	cantar	1
exhortar	cantar	1	extorsionar	cantar	1
exhumar	cantar	1	extractar	cantar	1
exigir	subir (dirigir)	3-2	extraditar	cantar	1
exiliar	cantar	1	extraer	traer	33
eximir	subir	3	extralimitar(se)	cantar	1
existir	subir	3	extranjerizar	cantar (cazar)	1-4
exonerar	cantar	1	extrañar	cantar	1
exorbitar	cantar	1	extrapolar	cantar	1
exorcizar	cantar (cazar)	1-4	extraviar	cantar (enviar)	1-15
expandir	subir	3	extremar	cantar	1
expansionar	cantar	1	exudar	cantar	1
expatriar	cantar (enviar)	1-15	exultar	cantar	1
expectorar	cantar	1	eyacular	cantar	1
expedientar	cantar	1	fabricar	cantar (tocar)	1-1
expedir	pedir	6B	fabular	cantar	1
expeler	comer	2	facilitar	cantar	1
expender	comer	2	facturar	cantar	1
experimentar	cantar	1	facultar	cantar	1
expiar	cantar (enviar)	1-15	faenar	cantar	1
expirar	cantar	1	fagocitar	cantar	1
explayar	cantar	1	fajar	cantar	1
explicar	cantar (tocar)	1-1	faldear	cantar	1
explicitar	cantar	1	fallar	cantar	1
explicotear(se)	cantar	1	fallecer	conocer	7A
explorar	cantar	1	falsear	cantar	1
explosionar	cantar	1	falsificar	cantar (tocar)	1-1
explotar	cantar	1	faltar	cantar	1
expoliar	cantar	1	familiarizar	cantar (cazar)	1-4
exponer	poner (suponer)	30-1	fanatizar	cantar (cazar)	1-4
exportar	cantar	1	fanfarronear	cantar	1
expresar	cantar	1	fantasear	cantar	1
exprimir	subir	3	fardar	cantar	1

Verb	Class (Sub-class)	#	Verb	Class (Sub-class)	#
farfullar	cantar	1	flechar	cantar	1
farolear	cantar	1	fletar	cantar	1
fascinar	cantar	1	flexibilizar	cantar (cazar)	1-4
fastidiar	cantar	1	flexionar	cantar	1
fatigar	cantar (pagar)	1-2	flirtear	cantar	1
favorecer	conocer	7A	flojear	cantar	1
fechar	cantar	1	florear	cantar	1
fecundar	cantar	1	florecer	conocer	7A
federar	cantar	1	flotar	cantar	1
felicitar	cantar	1	fluctuar	cantar (actuar)	1-14
fenecer	conocer	7A	fluidificar	cantar (tocar)	1-1
feriar	cantar	1	fluir[14]	construir	8
fermentar	cantar	1	fluorar	cantar	1
fertilizar	cantar (cazar)	1-4	focalizar	cantar (cazar)	1-4
festejar	cantar	1	foguear	cantar	1
festonear	cantar	1	foliar	cantar	1
fiar[13]	cantar (enviar)	1-15	follar	cantar	1
fichar	cantar	1	fomentar	cantar	1
figurar	cantar	1	fondear	cantar	1
fijar	cantar	1	forcejear	cantar	1
filetear	cantar	1	forestar	cantar	1
filiar	cantar	1	forjar	cantar	1
filmar	cantar	1	formalizar	cantar (cazar)	1-4
filosofar	cantar	1	formar	cantar	1
filtrar	cantar	1	formatear	cantar	1
finalizar	cantar (cazar)	1-4	formular	cantar	1
financiar	cantar	1	fornicar	cantar (tocar)	1-1
fingir	subir (dirigir)	3-2	forrajear	cantar	1
finiquitar	cantar	1	forrar	cantar	1
firmar	cantar	1	fortalecer	conocer	7A
fiscalizar	cantar (cazar)	1-4	fortificar	cantar (tocar)	1-1
fisgar	cantar (pagar)	1-2	forzar	mostrar (forzar)	4B-3
fisgonear	cantar	1	fosforescer	conocer	7A
flagelar	cantar	1	fosilizar(se)	cantar (cazar)	1-4
flambear	cantar	1	fotocopiar	cantar	1
flamear	cantar	1	fotografiar	cantar (enviar)	1-15
flanquear	cantar	1	fotosintetizar	cantar (cazar)	1-4
flaquear	cantar	1	fracasar	cantar	1

[13] The new orthographic rules allow alternative forms for the simple past 1s and 3s—*fie/fié, fio/fió*—as well as for the present indicative and subjunctive 2p—*fiais/fiáis* and *fieis/fiéis*.

[14] The new orthographic rules allow alternative forms for the simple past 1s—*flui/fluí*—as well as for the present indicative 2p—*fluis/fluís*.

Verb	Class (Sub-class)	#	Verb	Class (Sub-class)	#
fraccionar	cantar	1	ganar	cantar	1
fracturar	cantar	1	gandulear	cantar	1
fragmentar	cantar	1	gangrenar(se)	cantar	1
fraguar	cantar (averiguar)	1-3	gansear	cantar	1
franquear	cantar	1	gañir	subir (bruñir)	3-6
frasear	cantar	1	garabatear	cantar	1
fraternizar	cantar (cazar)	1-4	garantizar	cantar (cazar)	1-4
frecuentar	cantar	1	gargajear	cantar	1
fregar	pensar (negar)	4A-1	gargarizar	cantar (cazar)	1-4
fregotear	cantar	1	garrapatear	cantar	1
freír[15]	pedir (reír)	6B-4	garrapiñar	cantar	1
frenar	cantar	1	gasear	cantar	1
fresar	cantar	1	gasificar	cantar (tocar)	1-1
friccionar	cantar	1	gastar	cantar	1
frisar	cantar	1	gatear	cantar	1
frivolizar	cantar (cazar)	1-4	gemir	pedir	6B
frotar	cantar	1	generalizar	cantar (cazar)	1-4
fructificar	cantar (tocar)	1-1	generar	cantar	1
fruncir	subir (fruncir)	3-1	germanizar	cantar (cazar)	1-4
frustrar	cantar	1	germinar	cantar	1
fugar	cantar (pagar)	1-2	gestar	cantar	1
fulgurar	cantar	1	gesticular	cantar	1
fulminar	cantar	1	gestionar	cantar	1
fumar	cantar	1	gibar	cantar	1
fumigar	cantar (pagar)	1-2	gimotear	cantar	1
funcionar	cantar	1	girar	cantar	1
fundamentar	cantar	1	gitanear	cantar	1
fundar	cantar	1	glasear	cantar	1
fundir	subir	3	globalizar	cantar (cazar)	1-4
fusilar	cantar	1	gloriar	cantar (enviar)	1-15
fusionar	cantar	1	glorificar	cantar (tocar)	1-1
fustigar	cantar (pagar)	1-2	glosar	cantar	1
gafar	cantar	1	gobernar	pensar	4A
galantear	cantar	1	golear	cantar	1
galardonar	cantar	1	golfear	cantar	1
gallardear	cantar	1	golosear	cantar	1
gallear	cantar	1	golpear	cantar	1
galopar	cantar	1	golpetear	cantar	1
galvanizar	cantar (cazar)	1-4	gorgoritear	cantar	1
gamberrear	cantar	1	gorgotear	cantar	1

[15] Past participle: *frito/freído*.

Verb	Class (Sub-class)	#	Verb	Class (Sub-class)	#
gorjear	cantar	1	habitar	cantar	1
gorronear	cantar	1	habituar	cantar (actuar)	1-14
gotear	cantar	1	hablar	cantar	1
gozar	cantar (cazar)	1-4	hacer	hacer	29
grabar	cantar	1	hacinar	cantar	1
graduar	cantar (actuar)	1-14	halagar	cantar (pagar)	1-2
gramaticalizar(se)	cantar (cazar)	1-4	hallar	cantar	1
granar	cantar	1	haraganear	cantar	1
granizar (DEF)	cantar (cazar)	1-4	hartar	cantar	1
granjear	cantar	1	hastiar	cantar (enviar)	1-15
granular	cantar	1	hebraizar	cantar (enraizar)	1-12
grapar	cantar	1	hechizar	cantar (cazar)	1-4
gratificar	cantar (tocar)	1-1	heder	perder	5A
gratinar	cantar	1	helar	pensar	4A
gravar	cantar	1	helenizar	cantar (cazar)	1-4
gravitar	cantar	1	henchir	pedir	6B
graznar	cantar	1	hendir	discernir	15
grillar(se)	cantar	1	heñir	pedir (ceñir)	6B-3
gripar	cantar	1	heredar	cantar	1
grisear	cantar	1	herir	sentir	6A
gritar	cantar	1	hermanar	cantar	1
gruñir	subir (bruñir)	3-6	hermosear	cantar	1
guardar	cantar	1	herniar(se)	cantar	1
guarecer	conocer	7A	herrar	pensar	4A
guarnecer	conocer	7A	herrumbrar	cantar	1
guarnicionar	cantar	1	hervir	sentir	6A
guarrear	cantar	1	hibernar	cantar	1
guasear(se)	cantar	1	hidratar	cantar	1
guerrear	cantar	1	higienizar	cantar (cazar)	1-4
guerrillear	cantar	1	hilar	cantar	1
guiar[16]	cantar (enviar)	1-15	hilvanar	cantar	1
guillotinar	cantar	1	himplar	cantar	1
guiñar	cantar	1	hincar	cantar (tocar)	1-1
guipar	cantar	1	hinchar	cantar	1
guisar	cantar	1	hipar	cantar	1
gulusmear	cantar	1	hipertrofiar(se)	cantar	1
gustar	cantar	1	hipnotizar	cantar (cazar)	1-4
haber	haber	21	hipotecar	cantar (tocar)	1-1
habilitar	cantar	1	hispanizar	cantar (cazar)	1-4

---

[16] The new orthographic rules allow alternative forms for the simple past 1s and 3s—*guie/guié, guio/guió*—as well as for the present indicative and subjunctive 2p—*guiais/guiáis* and *guieis/guiéis*.

Verb	Class (Sub-class)	#	Verb	Class (Sub-class)	#
historiar	cantar	1	idolatrar	cantar	1
hocicar	cantar (tocar)	1-1	ignorar	cantar	1
hojaldrar	cantar	1	igualar	cantar	1
hojear	cantar	1	ilegalizar	cantar (cazar)	1-4
holgar	mostrar (colgar)	4B-2	ilegitimar	cantar	1
holgazanear	cantar	1	iluminar	cantar	1
hollar	mostrar	4B	ilusionar	cantar	1
homenajear	cantar	1	ilustrar	cantar	1
homogeneizar	cantar (cazar)	1-4	imaginar	cantar	1
homologar	cantar (pagar)	1-2	imantar	cantar	1
hondear	cantar	1	imbricar	cantar (tocar)	1-1
honrar	cantar	1	imbuir	construir	8
horadar	cantar	1	imitar	cantar	1
hormiguear	cantar	1	impacientar	cantar	1
hornear	cantar	1	impactar	cantar	1
horripilar	cantar	1	impartir	subir	3
horrorizar	cantar (cazar)	1-4	impedir	pedir	6B
hospedar	cantar	1	impeler	comer	2
hospitalizar	cantar (cazar)	1-4	imperar	cantar	1
hostiar	cantar	1	impermeabilizar	cantar (cazar)	1-4
hostigar	cantar (pagar)	1-2	impersonalizar	cantar (cazar)	1-4
hostilizar	cantar (cazar)	1-4	implantar	cantar	1
hozar	cantar (cazar)	1-4	implementar	cantar	1
huir[17]	construir	8	implicar	cantar (tocar)	1-1
humanizar	cantar (cazar)	1-4	implorar	cantar	1
humar	cantar	1	imponer	poner (suponer)	30-1
humear	cantar	1	importar	cantar	1
humedecer	conocer	7A	importunar	cantar	1
humidificar	cantar (tocar)	1-1	imposibilitar	cantar	1
humillar	cantar	1	impostar	cantar	1
hundir	subir	3	imprecar	cantar (tocar)	1-1
hurgar	cantar (pagar)	1-2	impregnar	cantar	1
huronear	cantar	1	impresionar	cantar	1
hurtar	cantar	1	imprimir	subir (imprimir)	3-12
husmear	cantar	1	improvisar	cantar	1
idealizar	cantar (cazar)	1-4	impugnar	cantar	1
idear	cantar	1	impulsar	cantar	1
identificar	cantar (tocar)	1-1	imputar	cantar	1
idiotizar	cantar (cazar)	1-4	inaugurar	cantar	1

[17] The new orthographic rules allow alternative forms for the simple past 1s—*hui/huí*—as well as for the present indicative 2p—*huis/huís*.

Verb	Class (Sub-class)	#	Verb	Class (Sub-class)	#
incapacitar	cantar	1	infiltrar	cantar	1
incardinar	cantar	1	inflamar	cantar	1
incautar(se)	cantar	1	inflar	cantar	1
incendiar	cantar	1	infligir	subir (dirigir)	3-2
incensar	pensar	4A	influenciar	cantar	1
incentivar	cantar	1	influir	construir	8
incidir	subir	3	informar	cantar	1
incinerar	cantar	1	informatizar	cantar (cazar)	1-4
incitar	cantar	1	infrautilizar	cantar (cazar)	1-4
inclinar	cantar	1	infravalorar	cantar	1
incluir	construir	8	infringir	subir (dirigir)	3-2
incomodar	cantar	1	infundir	subir	3
incomunicar	cantar (tocar)	1-1	ingeniar	cantar	1
incordiar	cantar	1	ingerir	sentir	6A
incorporar	cantar	1	ingresar	cantar	1
incrementar	cantar	1	inhabilitar	cantar	1
increpar	cantar	1	inhalar	cantar	1
incriminar	cantar	1	inhibir	subir	3
incrustar	cantar	1	inhumar	cantar	1
incubar	cantar	1	inicializar	cantar (cazar)	1-4
inculcar	cantar (tocar)	1-1	iniciar	cantar	1
incumbir	subir	3	injerir	sentir	6A
incumplir	subir	3	injertar	cantar	1
incurrir	subir	3	injuriar	cantar	1
incursionar	cantar	1	inmigrar	cantar	1
indagar	cantar (pagar)	1-2	inmiscuir	construir	8
indemnizar	cantar (cazar)	1-4	inmolar	cantar	1
independizar	cantar (cazar)	1-4	inmortalizar	cantar (cazar)	1-4
indicar	cantar (tocar)	1-1	inmovilizar	cantar (cazar)	1-4
indigestar(se)	cantar	1	inmunizar	cantar (cazar)	1-4
indignar	cantar	1	inmutar	cantar	1
indisciplinar(se)	cantar	1	innovar	cantar	1
indisponer	poner (suponer)	30-1	inocular	cantar	1
individualizar	cantar (cazar)	1-4	inquietar	cantar	1
inducir	conducir	34	inquirir	adquirir	17
indultar	cantar	1	insalivar	cantar	1
industrializar	cantar (cazar)	1-4	inscribir	subir (escribir)	3-11
infamar	cantar	1	inseminar	cantar	1
infantilizar	cantar (cazar)	1-4	insensibilizar	cantar (cazar)	1-4
infartar	cantar	1	insertar	cantar	1
infectar	cantar	1	insinuar	cantar (actuar)	1-14
inferir	sentir	6A	insistir	subir	3
infestar	cantar	1	insolentar	cantar	1

Verb	Class (Sub-class)	#	Verb	Class (Sub-class)	#
jaranear	cantar	1	laquear	cantar	1
jarrear	cantar	1	largar	cantar (pagar)	1-2
jaspear	cantar	1	lastimar	cantar	1
jerarquizar	cantar (cazar)	1-4	lastrar	cantar	1
jeringar	cantar (pagar)	1-2	lateralizar	cantar (cazar)	1-4
joder	comer	2	latinizar	cantar (cazar)	1-4
jorobar	cantar	1	latir	subir	3
jubilar	cantar	1	laurear	cantar	1
judaizar	cantar (enraizar)	1-12	lavar	cantar	1
juerguear(se)	cantar	1	lavotear	cantar	1
jugar	jugar	16	laxar	cantar	1
juguetear	cantar	1	leer	comer (leer)	2-3
juntar	cantar	1	legalizar	cantar (cazar)	1-4
juramentar	cantar	1	legar	cantar (pagar)	1-2
jurar	cantar	1	legislar	cantar	1
justificar	cantar (tocar)	1-1	legitimar	cantar	1
justipreciar	cantar	1	legrar	cantar	1
juzgar	cantar (pagar)	1-2	lesionar	cantar	1
kilometrar	cantar	1	levantar	cantar	1
labializar	cantar (cazar)	1-4	levar	cantar	1
laborar	cantar	1	levitar	cantar	1
labrar	cantar	1	lexicalizar	cantar (cazar)	1-4
lacar	cantar (tocar)	1-1	liar[18]	cantar (enviar)	1-15
lacerar	cantar	1	libar	cantar	1
lacrar	cantar	1	liberalizar	cantar (cazar)	1-4
lactar	cantar	1	liberar	cantar	1
ladear	cantar	1	libertar	cantar	1
ladrar	cantar	1	librar	cantar	1
ladrillar	cantar	1	licenciar	cantar	1
lagrimear	cantar	1	licitar	cantar	1
laicizar	cantar (cazar)	1-4	licuar	cantar	1
lamentar	cantar	1	liderar	cantar	1
lamer	comer	2	lidiar	cantar	1
laminar	cantar	1	ligar	cantar (pagar)	1-2
lampar	cantar	1	lijar	cantar	1
lancear	cantar	1	limar	cantar	1
languidecer	conocer	7A	limitar	cantar	1
lanzar	cantar (cazar)	1-4	limosnear	cantar	1
lapidar	cantar	1	limpiar	cantar	1

---

[18] The new orthographic rules allow alternative forms for the simple past 1s and 3s—*lie/lié, lio/lió*—as well as for the present indicative and subjunctive 2p—*liais/liáis* and *lieis/liéis*.

Verb	Class (Sub-class)	#	Verb	Class (Sub-class)	#
maquinizar	cantar (cazar)	1-4	mencionar	cantar	1
maravillar	cantar	1	mendigar	cantar (pagar)	1-2
marcar	cantar (tocar)	1-1	menear	cantar	1
marchar	cantar	1	menguar	cantar (averiguar)	1-3
marchitar	cantar	1	menoscabar	cantar	1
marear	cantar	1	menospreciar	cantar	1
marginar	cantar	1	menstruar	cantar (actuar)	1-14
maridar	cantar	1	mensualizar	cantar (cazar)	1-4
martillar	cantar	1	mentalizar	cantar (cazar)	1-4
martillear	cantar	1	mentar	pensar	4A
martirizar	cantar (cazar)	1-4	mentir	sentir	6A
masacrar	cantar	1	menudear	cantar	1
masajear	cantar	1	mercadear	cantar	1
mascar	cantar (tocar)	1-1	mercantilizar	cantar (cazar)	1-4
masculinizar	cantar (cazar)	1-4	mercar	cantar (tocar)	1-1
mascullar	cantar	1	merecer	conocer	7A
masificar	cantar (tocar)	1-1	merendar	pensar	4A
masticar	cantar (tocar)	1-1	mermar	cantar	1
masturbar	cantar	1	merodear	cantar	1
matar	cantar	1	mesar	cantar	1
matasellar	cantar	1	mestizar	cantar (cazar)	1-4
materializar	cantar (cazar)	1-4	mesurar	cantar	1
maternizar	cantar (cazar)	1-4	metabolizar	cantar (cazar)	1-4
matizar	cantar (cazar)	1-4	metaforizar	cantar (cazar)	1-4
matricular	cantar	1	metalizar	cantar (cazar)	1-4
matrimoniar	cantar	1	metamorfosear	cantar	1
maullar	cantar (aullar)	1-6	meteorizar	cantar (cazar)	1-4
maximizar	cantar (cazar)	1-4	meter	comer	2
mear	cantar	1	metodizar	cantar (cazar)	1-4
mecanizar	cantar (cazar)	1-4	mezclar	cantar	1
mecanografiar	cantar (enviar)	1-15	microfilmar	cantar	1
mecer	comer (vencer)	2-1	migar	cantar (pagar)	1-2
mechar	cantar	1	militar	cantar	1
mediar	cantar	1	militarizar	cantar (cazar)	1-4
mediatizar	cantar (cazar)	1-4	mimar	cantar	1
medicar	cantar (tocar)	1-1	minar	cantar	1
medicinar	cantar	1	mineralizar	cantar (cazar)	1-4
medir	pedir	6B	miniaturizar	cantar (cazar)	1-4
meditar	cantar	1	minimizar	cantar (cazar)	1-4
medrar	cantar	1	ministrar	cantar	1
mejorar	cantar	1	minusvalorar	cantar	1
mellar	cantar	1	mirar	cantar	1
memorizar	cantar (cazar)	1-4	mistificar	cantar (tocar)	1-1

Verb	Class (Sub-class)	#	Verb	Class (Sub-class)	#
mitificar	cantar (tocar)	1-1	multar	cantar	1
mitigar	cantar (pagar)	1-2	multicopiar	cantar	1
mixtificar	cantar (tocar)	1-1	multiplicar	cantar (tocar)	1-1
mocar	cantar (tocar)	1-1	municipalizar	cantar (cazar)	1-4
modelar	cantar	1	murar	cantar	1
moderar	cantar	1	murmurar	cantar	1
modernizar	cantar (cazar)	1-4	musicar	cantar (tocar)	1-1
modificar	cantar (tocar)	1-1	musitar	cantar	1
modular	cantar	1	mustiar	cantar	1
mofar	cantar	1	mutar	cantar	1
mojar	cantar	1	mutilar	cantar	1
moldar	cantar	1	nacer	conocer	7A
moldear	cantar	1	nacionalizar	cantar (cazar)	1-4
moler	mover	5B	nadar	cantar	1
molestar	cantar	1	narcotizar	cantar (cazar)	1-4
momificar	cantar (tocar)	1-1	narrar	cantar	1
mondar	cantar	1	nasalizar	cantar (cazar)	1-4
monitorizar	cantar (cazar)	1-4	naturalizar	cantar (cazar)	1-4
monologar	cantar (pagar)	1-2	naufragar	cantar (pagar)	1-2
monopolizar	cantar (cazar)	1-4	navegar	cantar (pagar)	1-2
monoptongar	cantar (pagar)	1-2	necesitar	cantar	1
montar	cantar	1	negar	pensar (negar)	4A-1
monumentalizar	cantar (cazar)	1-4	negociar	cantar	1
moquear	cantar	1	negrear	cantar	1
moralizar	cantar (cazar)	1-4	neurotizar	cantar (cazar)	1-4
morar	cantar	1	neutralizar	cantar (cazar)	1-4
morder	mover	5B	nevar	pensar	4A
mordisquear	cantar	1	ningunear	cantar	1
morigerar	cantar	1	niñear	cantar	1
morir	dormir (morir)	6C-1	niquelar	cantar	1
mortificar	cantar (tocar)	1-1	nivelar	cantar	1
mosconear	cantar	1	nombrar	cantar	1
mosquear	cantar	1	nominar	cantar	1
mostrar	mostrar	4B	noquear	cantar	1
motear	cantar	1	normalizar	cantar (cazar)	1-4
motejar	cantar	1	notar	cantar	1
motivar	cantar	1	notificar	cantar (tocar)	1-1
motorizar	cantar (cazar)	1-4	novelar	cantar	1
mover	mover	5B	nublar	cantar	1
movilizar	cantar (cazar)	1-4	nuclearizar	cantar (cazar)	1-4
mudar	cantar	1	numerar	cantar	1
mugir	subir (dirigir)	3-2	nutrir	subir	3
mullir	subir (bullir)	3-5	obcecar	cantar (tocar)	1-1

Verb	Class (Sub-class)	#	Verb	Class (Sub-class)	#
obedecer	conocer	7A	opositar	cantar	1
objetar	cantar	1	oprimir	subir	3
objetivar	cantar	1	optar	cantar	1
obligar	cantar (pagar)	1-2	optimar	cantar	1
obliterar	cantar	1	optimizar	cantar (cazar)	1-4
obnubilar	cantar	1	orar	cantar	1
obrar	cantar	1	ordenar	cantar	1
obsequiar	cantar	1	ordeñar	cantar	1
observar	cantar	1	orear	cantar	1
obsesionar	cantar	1	organizar	cantar (cazar)	1-4
obstaculizar	cantar (cazar)	1-4	orientar	cantar	1
obstar	cantar	1	originar	cantar	1
obstinar(se)	cantar	1	orillar	cantar	1
obstruir	construir	8	orinar	cantar	1
obtener	tener (obtener)	31-1	orlar	cantar	1
obturar	cantar	1	ornamentar	cantar	1
obviar	cantar	1	ornar	cantar	1
ocasionar	cantar	1	orquestar	cantar	1
ociar	cantar	1	osar	cantar	1
ocluir	construir	8	oscilar	cantar	1
ocultar	cantar	1	oscurecer	conocer	7A
ocupar	cantar	1	ostentar	cantar	1
ocurrir	subir	3	otear	cantar	1
odiar	cantar	1	otorgar	cantar (pagar)	1-2
ofender	comer	2	ovacionar	cantar	1
ofertar	cantar	1	ovalar	cantar	1
oficializar	cantar (cazar)	1-4	ovar	cantar	1
oficiar	cantar	1	ovillar	cantar	1
ofrecer	conocer	7A	ovular	cantar	1
ofrendar	cantar	1	oxidar	cantar	1
ofuscar	cantar (tocar)	1-1	oxigenar	cantar	1
oír	oír	10	pacer	conocer	7A
ojear	cantar	1	pacificar	cantar (tocar)	1-1
oler	mover (oler)	5B-2	pactar	cantar	1
olfatear	cantar	1	padecer	conocer	7A
olisquear	cantar	1	pagar	cantar (pagar)	1-2
olvidar	cantar	1	paginar	cantar	1
omitir	subir	3	paladear	cantar	1
ondear	cantar	1	palatalizar	cantar (cazar)	1-4
ondular	cantar	1	paliar	cantar	1
operar	cantar	1	palidecer	conocer	7A
opinar	cantar	1	palmar	cantar	1
oponer	poner (suponer)	30-1	palmear	cantar	1

Verb	Class (Sub-class)	#
palmotear	cantar	1
palpar	cantar	1
palpitar	cantar	1
panificar	cantar (tocar)	1-1
papear	cantar	1
parabolizar	cantar (cazar)	1-4
parafrasear	cantar	1
paralizar	cantar (cazar)	1-4
parangonar	cantar	1
parapetar(se)	cantar	1
parar	cantar	1
parcelar	cantar	1
parchear	cantar	1
parcializar	cantar (cazar)	1-4
parecer	conocer	7A
parir	subir	3
parlamentar	cantar	1
parlar	cantar	1
parlotear	cantar	1
parodiar	cantar	1
parpadear	cantar	1
parrandear	cantar	1
participar	cantar	1
particularizar	cantar (cazar)	1-4
partir	subir	3
pasar	cantar	1
pasear	cantar	1
pasmar	cantar	1
pastar	cantar	1
pasteurizar	cantar (cazar)	1-4
pastorear	cantar	1
patalear	cantar	1
patear	cantar	1
patentar	cantar	1
patentizar	cantar (cazar)	1-4
patinar	cantar	1
patrocinar	cantar	1
patrullar	cantar	1
pausar	cantar	1
pautar	cantar	1
pavimentar	cantar	1
pavonear	cantar	1
pecar	cantar (tocar)	1-1

Verb	Class (Sub-class)	#
pechar	cantar	1
pedalear	cantar	1
pedir	pedir	6B
pedorrear	cantar	1
pegar	cantar (pagar)	1-2
pegotear	cantar	1
peinar	cantar	1
pelar	cantar	1
pelear	cantar	1
peligrar	cantar	1
pellizcar	cantar (tocar)	1-1
pelotear	cantar	1
penalizar	cantar (cazar)	1-4
penar	cantar	1
pender	comer	2
pendonear	cantar	1
penetrar	cantar	1
pensar	pensar	4A
pensionar	cantar	1
peraltar	cantar	1
percatar(se)	cantar	1
percibir	subir	3
percutir	subir	3
perder	perder	5A
perdonar	cantar	1
perdurar	cantar	1
perecer	conocer	7A
peregrinar	cantar	1
perennizar	cantar (cazar)	1-4
perfeccionar	cantar	1
perfilar	cantar	1
perforar	cantar	1
perfumar	cantar	1
pergeñar	cantar	1
periclitar	cantar	1
peritar	cantar	1
perjudicar	cantar (tocar)	1-1
perjurar	cantar	1
perlar	cantar	1
permanecer	conocer	7A
permitir	subir	3
permutar	cantar	1
pernoctar	cantar	1

Verb	Class (Sub-class)	#	Verb	Class (Sub-class)	#
perorar	cantar	1	piratear	cantar	1
perpetrar	cantar	1	piropear	cantar	1
perpetuar	cantar (actuar)	1-14	pirrar(se)	cantar	1
perseguir	pedir (seguir)	6B-2	piruetear	cantar	1
perseverar	cantar	1	pisar	cantar	1
persignar	cantar	1	pisotear	cantar	1
persistir	subir	3	pitar	cantar	1
personalizar	cantar (cazar)	1-4	pitorrear(se)	cantar	1
personar(se)	cantar	1	pivotar	cantar	1
personificar	cantar (tocar)	1-1	placer	conocer (placer)	7A-2
persuadir	subir	3	plagar	cantar (pagar)	1-2
pertenecer	conocer	7A	plagiar	cantar	1
pertrechar	cantar	1	planchar	cantar	1
perturbar	cantar	1	planear	cantar	1
pervertir	sentir	6A	planificar	cantar (tocar)	1-1
pervivir	subir	3	plantar	cantar	1
pesar	cantar	1	plantear	cantar	1
pescar	cantar (tocar)	1-1	plantificar	cantar (tocar)	1-1
pespuntear	cantar	1	plañir	subir (bruñir)	3-6
pestañear	cantar	1	plasmar	cantar	1
petar	cantar	1	plastificar	cantar (tocar)	1-1
petardear	cantar	1	platear	cantar	1
peticionar	cantar	1	platicar	cantar (tocar)	1-1
petrificar	cantar (tocar)	1-1	plegar	pensar (negar)	4A-1
piafar	cantar	1	pleitear	cantar	1
piar[19]	cantar (enviar)	1-15	plisar	cantar	1
picar	cantar (tocar)	1-1	pluralizar	cantar (cazar)	1-4
picotear	cantar	1	poblar	mostrar	4B
pifiar	cantar	1	podar	cantar	1
pigmentar	cantar	1	poder	poder	26
pillar	cantar	1	podrir[20]	subir (pudrir)	3-13
pilotar	cantar	1	poetizar	cantar (cazar)	1-4
pimplar	cantar	1	polarizar	cantar (cazar)	1-4
pincelar	cantar	1	polemizar	cantar (cazar)	1-4
pinchar	cantar	1	policromar	cantar	1
pintar	cantar	1	polinizar	cantar (cazar)	1-4
pintarrajear	cantar	1	politizar	cantar (cazar)	1-4
pinzar	cantar (cazar)	1-4	polucionar	cantar	1
pirar(se)	cantar	1	ponderar	cantar	1

[19] The new orthographic rules allow alternative forms for the simple past 1s and 3s—*pie/pié, pio/pió*—as well as for the present indicative and subjunctive 2p—*piais/piáis* and *pieis/piéis*.

[20] Conjugation identical to that of *pudrir* apart from infinitive.

Verb	Class (Sub-class)	#	Verb	Class (Sub-class)	#
poner	poner	30	preguntar	cantar	1
pontificar	cantar (tocar)	1-1	prejuzgar	cantar (pagar)	1-2
popularizar	cantar (cazar)	1-4	preludiar	cantar	1
pordiosear	cantar	1	premeditar	cantar	1
porfiar	cantar (enviar)	1-15	premiar	cantar	1
pormenorizar	cantar (cazar)	1-4	prendar	cantar	1
portar	cantar	1	prender	comer	2
portear	cantar	1	prensar	cantar	1
posar	cantar	1	preñar	cantar	1
poseer	comer (leer)	2-3	preocupar	cantar	1
posesionar	cantar	1	preparar	cantar	1
posibilitar	cantar	1	preponderar	cantar	1
posicionar	cantar	1	presagiar	cantar	1
positivar	cantar	1	prescindir	subir	3
posponer	poner (suponer)	30-1	prescribir	subir (escribir)	3-11
postergar	cantar (pagar)	1-2	preseleccionar	cantar	1
postinear	cantar	1	presenciar	cantar	1
postrar	cantar	1	presentar	cantar	1
postular	cantar	1	presentir	sentir	6A
potabilizar	cantar (cazar)	1-4	preservar	cantar	1
potar	cantar	1	presidir	subir	3
potenciar	cantar	1	presintonizar	cantar (cazar)	1-4
practicar	cantar (tocar)	1-1	presionar	cantar	1
precaver	comer	2	prestar	cantar	1
preceder	comer	2	prestigiar	cantar	1
preciar	cantar	1	presumir	subir	3
precintar	cantar	1	presuponer	poner (suponer)	30-1
precipitar	cantar	1	presupuestar	cantar	1
precisar	cantar	1	presurizar	cantar (cazar)	1-4
preconcebir	pedir	6B	pretender	comer	2
preconizar	cantar (cazar)	1-4	pretextar	cantar	1
predatar	cantar	1	prevalecer	conocer	7A
predecir	decir (predecir)	28-1	prevaricar	cantar (tocar)	1-1
predestinar	cantar	1	prevenir	venir (convenir)	32-1
predeterminar	cantar	1	prever	ver (prever)	14-1
predicar	cantar (tocar)	1-1	primar	cantar	1
predisponer	poner (suponer)	30-1	pringar	cantar (pagar)	1-2
predominar	cantar	1	priorizar	cantar (cazar)	1-4
preexistir	subir	3	privar	cantar	1
preferir	sentir	6A	privatizar	cantar (cazar)	1-4
prefigurar	cantar	1	privilegiar	cantar	1
prefijar	cantar	1	probar	mostrar	4B
pregonar	cantar	1	proceder	comer	2

Verb	Class (Sub-class)	#	Verb	Class (Sub-class)	#
procesar	cantar	1	prosificar	cantar (tocar)	1-1
proclamar	cantar	1	prosperar	cantar	1
procrear	cantar	1	prosternar(se)	cantar	1
procurar	cantar	1	prostituir	construir	8
prodigar	cantar (pagar)	1-2	protagonizar	cantar (cazar)	1-4
producir	conducir	34	proteger	comer (coger)	2-2
profanar	cantar	1	protestar	cantar	1
proferir	sentir	6A	proveer[21]	comer (leer)	2-3
profesar	cantar	1	provenir	venir (convenir)	32-1
profesionalizar	cantar (cazar)	1-4	provocar	cantar (tocar)	1-1
profetizar	cantar (cazar)	1-4	proyectar	cantar	1
profundizar	cantar (cazar)	1-4	psicoanalizar	cantar (cazar)	1-4
programar	cantar	1	publicar	cantar (tocar)	1-1
progresar	cantar	1	publicitar	cantar	1
prohibir	subir (prohibir)	3-8	pudrir	subir (pudrir)	3-13
proliferar	cantar	1	puentear	cantar	1
prologar	cantar (pagar)	1-2	pugnar	cantar	1
prolongar	cantar (pagar)	1-2	pujar	cantar	1
promediar	cantar	1	pulimentar	cantar	1
prometer	comer	2	pulir	subir	3
promocionar	cantar	1	pulsar	cantar	1
promover	mover	5B	pulular	cantar	1
promulgar	cantar (pagar)	1-2	pulverizar	cantar (cazar)	1-4
pronosticar	cantar (tocar)	1-1	puntear	cantar	1
pronunciar	cantar	1	puntualizar	cantar (cazar)	1-4
propagar	cantar (pagar)	1-2	puntuar	cantar (actuar)	1-14
propalar	cantar	1	punzar	cantar (cazar)	1-4
propasar	cantar	1	purgar	cantar (pagar)	1-2
propender	comer	2	purificar	cantar (tocar)	1-1
propiciar	cantar	1	putear	cantar	1
propinar	cantar	1	quebrantar	cantar	1
proponer	poner (suponer)	30-1	quebrar	pensar	4A
proporcionar	cantar	1	quedar	cantar	1
propugnar	cantar	1	quemar	cantar	1
propulsar	cantar	1	querellar(se)	cantar	1
prorratear	cantar	1	querer	querer	27
prorrogar	cantar (pagar)	1-2	quintuplicar	cantar (tocar)	1-1
prorrumpir	subir	3	quitar	cantar	1
proscribir	subir (escribir)	3-11	rabiar	cantar	1
proseguir	pedir (seguir)	6B-2	racanear	cantar	1

[21] Past participle: *provisto/proveído*.

Verb	Class (Sub-class)	#	Verb	Class (Sub-class)	#
racionalizar	cantar (cazar)	1-4	reanudar	cantar	1
racionar	cantar	1	reaparecer	conocer	7A
radiar	cantar	1	rearmar	cantar	1
radicalizar	cantar (cazar)	1-4	reasegurar	cantar	1
radicar	cantar (tocar)	1-1	reavivar	cantar	1
radiodifundir	subir	3	rebajar	cantar	1
radiografiar	cantar (enviar)	1-15	rebanar	cantar	1
radiotelegrafiar	cantar (enviar)	1-15	rebañar	cantar	1
raer	caer (raer)	9-1	rebasar	cantar	1
rajar	cantar	1	rebatir	subir	3
ralentizar	cantar (cazar)	1-4	rebelar(se)	cantar	1
rallar	cantar	1	reblandecer	conocer	7A
ramificar	cantar (tocar)	1-1	rebobinar	cantar	1
ramonear	cantar	1	rebordear	cantar	1
rapar	cantar	1	rebosar	cantar	1
raptar	cantar	1	rebotar	cantar	1
rarificar	cantar (tocar)	1-1	rebozar	cantar (cazar)	1-4
rasar	cantar	1	rebrotar	cantar	1
rascar	cantar (tocar)	1-1	rebuscar	cantar (tocar)	1-1
rasgar	cantar (pagar)	1-2	rebuznar	cantar	1
rasguear	cantar	1	recabar	cantar	1
raspar	cantar	1	recaer	caer	9
rastrear	cantar	1	recalar	cantar	1
rastrillar	cantar	1	recalcar	cantar (tocar)	1-1
rastrojar	cantar	1	recalentar	pensar	4A
rasurar	cantar	1	recalificar	cantar (tocar)	1-1
ratificar	cantar (tocar)	1-1	recamar	cantar	1
rayar	cantar	1	recambiar	cantar	1
razonar	cantar	1	recapacitar	cantar	1
reabrir	subir (abrir)	3-9	recapitular	cantar	1
reabsorber	comer	2	recargar	cantar (pagar)	1-2
reaccionar	cantar	1	recatar	cantar	1
reactivar	cantar	1	recauchutar	cantar	1
readaptar	cantar	1	recaudar	cantar	1
readmitir	subir	3	recelar	cantar	1
reafirmar	cantar	1	recetar	cantar	1
reagrupar	cantar	1	rechazar	cantar (cazar)	1-4
reajustar	cantar	1	rechinar	cantar	1
realizar	cantar (cazar)	1-4	rechistar	cantar	1
realojar	cantar	1	recibir	subir	3
realquilar	cantar	1	reciclar	cantar	1
realzar	cantar (cazar)	1-4	recidivar	cantar	1
reanimar	cantar	1	recitar	cantar	1

Verb	Class (Sub-class)	#	Verb	Class (Sub-class)	#
reclamar	cantar	1	recusar	cantar	1
reclinar	cantar	1	redactar	cantar	1
recluir	construir	8	redefinir	subir	3
reclutar	cantar	1	redimir	subir	3
recobrar	cantar	1	redistribuir	construir	8
recocer	mover (cocer)	5B-1	redoblar	cantar	1
recochinear(se)	cantar	1	redondear	cantar	1
recoger	comer (coger)	2-2	reducir	conducir	34
recolectar	cantar	1	redundar	cantar	1
recomendar	pensar	4A	reduplicar	cantar (tocar)	1-1
recomenzar	pensar (empezar)	4A-2	reedificar	cantar (tocar)	1-1
recomer(se)	comer	2	reeditar	cantar	1
recompensar	cantar	1	reeducar	cantar (tocar)	1-1
recomponer	poner (suponer)	30-1	reelaborar	cantar	1
reconcentrar	cantar	1	reeligir	pedir (elegir)	6B-1
reconciliar	cantar	1	reembarcar	cantar (tocar)	1-1
reconcomer(se)	comer	2	reembolsar	cantar	1
reconducir	conducir	34	reemplazar	cantar (cazar)	1-4
reconfirmar	cantar	1	reencarnar	cantar	1
reconfortar	cantar	1	reencontrar	mostrar	4B
reconocer	conocer	7A	reencuadernar	cantar	1
reconquistar	cantar	1	reenganchar	cantar	1
reconsiderar	cantar	1	reensayar	cantar	1
reconstituir	construir	8	reenviar	cantar (enviar)	1-15
reconstruir	construir	8	reescribir	subir (escribir)	3-11
recontar	mostrar	4B	reestrenar	cantar	1
reconvenir	venir (convenir)	32-1	reestructurar	cantar	1
reconvertir	sentir	6A	reexaminar	cantar	1
recopilar	cantar	1	reexpedir	pedir	6B
recordar	mostrar	4B	reexportar	cantar	1
recorrer	comer	2	referir	sentir	6A
recortar	cantar	1	refinar	cantar	1
recoser	comer	2	reflejar	cantar	1
recostar	mostrar	4B	reflexionar	cantar	1
recrear	cantar	1	reflorecer	conocer	7A
recriminar	cantar	1	reflotar	cantar	1
recrudecer	conocer	7A	refluir	construir	8
rectificar	cantar (tocar)	1-1	refocilar	cantar	1
recuadrar	cantar	1	reforestar	cantar	1
recubrir	subir (cubrir)	3-10	reformar	cantar	1
recular	cantar	1	reforzar	mostrar (forzar)	4B-3
recuperar	cantar	1	refractar	cantar	1
recurrir	subir	3	refregar	pensar (negar)	4A-1

Verb	Class (Sub-class)	#
refreír[22]	pedir (reír)	6B-4
refrenar	cantar	1
refrendar	cantar	1
refrescar	cantar (tocar)	1-1
refrigerar	cantar	1
refugiar	cantar	1
refulgir	subir (dirigir)	3-2
refundir	subir	3
refunfuñar	cantar	1
refutar	cantar	1
regalar	cantar	1
regañar	cantar	1
regar	pensar (negar)	4A-1
regatear	cantar	1
regenerar	cantar	1
regentar	cantar	1
regionalizar	cantar (cazar)	1-4
regir	pedir (elegir)	6B-1
registrar	cantar	1
reglamentar	cantar	1
reglar	cantar	1
regocijar	cantar	1
regodear(se)	cantar	1
regresar	cantar	1
regular	cantar	1
regularizar	cantar (cazar)	1-4
regurgitar	cantar	1
rehabilitar	cantar	1
rehacer	hacer (rehacer)	29-1
rehogar	cantar (pagar)	1-2
rehuir[23]	construir	8
rehumedecer	conocer	7A
rehundir	subir (reunir)	3-7
rehusar	cantar (rehusar)	1-8
reimplantar	cantar	1
reimportar	cantar	1
reimprimir	subir (imprimir)	3-12
reinar	cantar	1
reincidir	subir	3
reincorporar	cantar	1

Verb	Class (Sub-class)	#
reingresar	cantar	1
reiniciar	cantar	1
reinscribir	subir (escribir)	3-11
reinsertar	cantar	1
reinstalar	cantar	1
reintegrar	cantar	1
reinvertir	sentir	6A
reír	pedir (reír)	6B-4
reiterar	cantar	1
reivindicar	cantar (tocar)	1-1
rejonear	cantar	1
rejuvenecer	conocer	7A
relacionar	cantar	1
relajar	cantar	1
relamer	comer	2
relampaguear	cantar	1
relanzar	cantar (cazar)	1-4
relatar	cantar	1
relativizar	cantar (cazar)	1-4
releer	comer (leer)	2-3
relegar	cantar (pagar)	1-2
relevar	cantar	1
religar	cantar (pagar)	1-2
relinchar	cantar	1
rellenar	cantar	1
relucir	lucir	7B
relumbrar	cantar	1
remachar	cantar	1
remangar	cantar (pagar)	1-2
remansar(se)	cantar	1
remar	cantar	1
remarcar	cantar (tocar)	1-1
remasterizar	cantar (cazar)	1-4
rematar	cantar	1
rembolsar	cantar	1
remedar	cantar	1
remediar	cantar	1
rememorar	cantar	1
remendar	pensar	4A
remeter	comer	2

[22] Past participle: *refrito/refreído*.
[23] In conjugations where stem syllable is stressed, *ehu → ehú* (as for 1-8 *rehusar*).

Verb	Class (Sub-class)	#	Verb	Class (Sub-class)	#
remitir	subir	3	reportar	cantar	1
remodelar	cantar	1	reposar	cantar	1
remojar	cantar	1	repostar	cantar	1
remolcar	cantar (tocar)	1-1	reprender	comer	2
remolonear	cantar	1	representar	cantar	1
remontar	cantar	1	reprimir	subir	3
remorder	mover	5B	reprobar	mostrar	4B
remover	mover	5B	reprocesar	cantar	1
remozar	cantar (cazar)	1-4	reprochar	cantar	1
remplazar	cantar (cazar)	1-4	reproducir	conducir	34
remunerar	cantar	1	reptar	cantar	1
renacer	conocer	7A	repudiar	cantar	1
rendir	pedir	6B	repugnar	cantar	1
renegar	pensar (negar)	4A-1	repujar	cantar	1
renegociar	cantar	1	repulir	subir	3
renombrar	cantar	1	reputar	cantar	1
renovar	mostrar	4B	requebrar	pensar	4A
renquear	cantar	1	requerir	sentir	6A
rentabilizar	cantar (cazar)	1-4	requisar	cantar	1
renunciar	cantar	1	resaltar	cantar	1
reñir	pedir (ceñir)	6B-3	resarcir	subir (fruncir)	3-1
reordenar	cantar	1	resbalar	cantar	1
reorganizar	cantar (cazar)	1-4	rescatar	cantar	1
reparar	cantar	1	rescindir	subir	3
repartir	subir	3	rescribir	subir (escribir)	3-11
repasar	cantar	1	resecar	cantar (tocar)	1-1
repatear	cantar	1	resentir(se)	sentir	6A
repatriar	cantar (enviar)	1-15	reseñar	cantar	1
repeinar	cantar	1	reservar	cantar	1
repeler	comer	2	resetear	cantar	1
repensar	pensar	4A	resfriar	cantar (enviar)	1-15
repercutir	subir	3	resguardar	cantar	1
repescar	cantar (tocar)	1-1	residir	subir	3
repetir	pedir	6B	resignar	cantar	1
repicar	cantar (tocar)	1-1	resinar	cantar	1
repintar	cantar	1	resistir	subir	3
repiquetear	cantar	1	resolver	mover (resolver)	5B-3
replantar	cantar	1	resonar	mostrar	4B
replantear	cantar	1	resoplar	cantar	1
replegar	pensar (negar)	4A-1	respaldar	cantar	1
replicar	cantar (tocar)	1-1	respetar	cantar	1
repoblar	mostrar	4B	respingar	cantar (pagar)	1-2
reponer	poner (suponer)	30-1	respirar	cantar	1

Verb	Class (Sub-class)	#	Verb	Class (Sub-class)	#
ronzar	cantar (cazar)	1-4	saquear	cantar	1
roscar	cantar (tocar)	1-1	satinar	cantar	1
rotar	cantar	1	satirizar	cantar (cazar)	1-4
rotular	cantar	1	satisfacer	hacer (satisfacer)	29-2
roturar	cantar	1	saturar	cantar	1
rozar	cantar (cazar)	1-4	sazonar	cantar	1
ruborizar	cantar (cazar)	1-4	secar	cantar (tocar)	1-1
rubricar	cantar (tocar)	1-1	seccionar	cantar	1
rugir	subir (dirigir)	3-2	secretar	cantar	1
rular	cantar	1	secretear	cantar	1
rumiar	cantar	1	secuenciar	cantar	1
rumorear	cantar	1	secuestrar	cantar	1
runrunear	cantar	1	secularizar	cantar (cazar)	1-4
rutilar	cantar	1	secundar	cantar	1
saber	saber	22	sedar	cantar	1
sablear	cantar	1	sedimentar	cantar	1
saborear	cantar	1	seducir	conducir	34
sabotear	cantar	1	segar	pensar (negar)	4A-1
sacar	cantar (tocar)	1-1	segmentar	cantar	1
saciar	cantar	1	segregar	cantar (pagar)	1-2
sacralizar	cantar (cazar)	1-4	seguir	pedir (seguir)	6B-2
sacramentar	cantar	1	seleccionar	cantar	1
sacrificar	cantar (tocar)	1-1	sellar	cantar	1
sacudir	subir	3	sembrar	pensar	4A
sajar	cantar	1	semejar	cantar	1
salar	cantar	1	sensibilizar	cantar (cazar)	1-4
saldar	cantar	1	sentar	pensar	4A
salir	salir	11	sentenciar	cantar	1
salivar	cantar	1	sentir	sentir	6A
salmodiar	cantar	1	señalar	cantar	1
salpicar	cantar (tocar)	1-1	señalizar	cantar (cazar)	1-4
salpimentar	pensar	4A	separar	cantar	1
saltar	cantar	1	sepultar	cantar	1
saltear	cantar	1	ser	ser	19
saludar	cantar	1	serenar	cantar	1
salvaguardar	cantar	1	seriar	cantar	1
salvar	cantar	1	sermonear	cantar	1
sanar	cantar	1	serpentear	cantar	1
sancionar	cantar	1	serrar	pensar	4A
sanear	cantar	1	servir	pedir	6B
sangrar	cantar	1	sesear	cantar	1
santificar	cantar (tocar)	1-1	sesgar	cantar (pagar)	1-2
santiguar	cantar (averiguar)	1-3	sestear	cantar	1

Verb	Class (Sub-class)	#	Verb	Class (Sub-class)	#
sextuplicar	cantar (tocar)	1-1	sobresaltar	cantar	1
significar	cantar (tocar)	1-1	sobrescribir	subir (escribir)	3-11
silabear	cantar	1	sobreseer	comer (leer)	2-3
silbar	cantar	1	sobrestimar	cantar	1
silenciar	cantar	1	sobrevalorar	cantar	1
siluetear	cantar	1	sobrevenir	venir (convenir)	32-1
simbolizar	cantar (cazar)	1-4	sobrevivir	subir	3
simpatizar	cantar (cazar)	1-4	sobrevolar	mostrar	4B
simplificar	cantar (tocar)	1-1	socarrar	cantar	1
simular	cantar	1	socavar	cantar	1
simultanear	cantar	1	sociabilizar	cantar (cazar)	1-4
sincerar	cantar	1	socializar	cantar (cazar)	1-4
sincopar	cantar	1	socorrer	comer	2
sincronizar	cantar (cazar)	1-4	sofisticar	cantar (tocar)	1-1
sindicar	cantar (tocar)	1-1	soflamar	cantar	1
singularizar	cantar (cazar)	1-4	sofocar	cantar (tocar)	1-1
sintetizar	cantar (cazar)	1-4	sofreír[24]	pedir (reír)	6B-4
sintonizar	cantar (cazar)	1-4	sojuzgar	cantar (pagar)	1-2
sisar	cantar	1	solapar	cantar	1
sisear	cantar	1	solazar	cantar (cazar)	1-4
sistematizar	cantar (cazar)	1-4	soldar	mostrar	4B
sitiar	cantar	1	solear	cantar	1
situar	cantar (actuar)	1-14	solemnizar	cantar (cazar)	1-4
sobar	cantar	1	soler (DEF)[25]	mover	5B
sobetear	cantar	1	solfear	cantar	1
sobornar	cantar	1	solicitar	cantar	1
sobrar	cantar	1	solidarizar(se)	cantar (cazar)	1-4
sobrealimentar	cantar	1	solidificar	cantar (tocar)	1-1
sobreañadir	subir	3	soliloquiar	cantar	1
sobrecargar	cantar (pagar)	1-2	soliviantar	cantar	1
sobrecoger	comer (coger)	2-2	sollozar	cantar (cazar)	1-4
sobredimensionar	cantar	1	soltar	mostrar	4B
sobreexcitar	cantar	1	solucionar	cantar	1
sobrehilar	cantar (descafeinar)	1-7	solventar	cantar	1
sobrellevar	cantar	1	somatizar	cantar (cazar)	1-4
sobre(e)ntender	perder	5A	sombrear	cantar	1
sobrepasar	cantar	1	someter	comer	2
sobreponer	poner (suponer)	30-1	sonar	mostrar	4B
sobresalir	salir	11	sondar	cantar	1

[24] Past participle: *sofrito/sofreído*.
[25] Exists in all six persons but not used in future, conditional, or imperative.

Verb	Class (Sub-class)	#	Verb	Class (Sub-class)	#
sondear	cantar	1	subyacer	conocer (yacer)	7A-1
sonorizar	cantar (cazar)	1-4	subyugar	cantar (pagar)	1-2
sonreír	pedir (reír)	6B-4	succionar	cantar	1
sonrojar	cantar	1	suceder	comer	2
sonsacar	cantar (tocar)	1-1	sucumbir	subir	3
soñar	mostrar	4B	sudar	cantar	1
sopapear	cantar	1	sufragar	cantar (pagar)	1-2
sopar	cantar	1	sufrir	subir	3
sopesar	cantar	1	sugerir	sentir	6A
soplar	cantar	1	sugestionar	cantar	1
soportar	cantar	1	suicidar(se)	cantar	1
sorber	comer	2	sujetar	cantar	1
sorprender	comer	2	sulfatar	cantar	1
sortear	cantar	1	sulfurar	cantar	1
sosegar	pensar (negar)	4A-1	sumar	cantar	1
soslayar	cantar	1	sumariar	cantar	1
sospechar	cantar	1	sumergir	subir (dirigir)	3-2
sostener	tener (obtener)	31-1	suministrar	cantar	1
soterrar	pensar	4A	sumir	subir	3
sovietizar	cantar (cazar)	1-4	supeditar	cantar	1
suavizar	cantar (cazar)	1-4	superabundar	cantar	1
subalternar	cantar	1	superar	cantar	1
subarrendar	pensar	4A	superponer	poner (suponer)	30-1
subastar	cantar	1	supervalorar	cantar	1
subcontratar	cantar	1	supervisar	cantar	1
subdelegar	cantar (pagar)	1-2	suplantar	cantar	1
subdividir	subir	3	suplicar	cantar (tocar)	1-1
subestimar	cantar	1	suplir	subir	3
subir	subir	3	suponer	poner (suponer)	30-1
subjetivar	cantar	1	suprimir	subir	3
sublevar	cantar	1	supurar	cantar	1
sublimar	cantar	1	surcar	cantar (tocar)	1-1
subordinar	cantar	1	surgir	subir (dirigir)	3-2
subrayar	cantar	1	surtir	subir	3
subrogar	cantar (pagar)	1-2	suscitar	cantar	1
subsanar	cantar	1	suscribir	subir (escribir)	3-11
subsidiar	cantar	1	suspender	comer	2
subsistir	subir	3	suspirar	cantar	1
subsumir	subir	3	sustanciar	cantar	1
subtitular	cantar	1	sustantivar	cantar	1
subvencionar	cantar	1	sustentar	cantar	1
subvenir	venir (convenir)	32-1	sustituir	construir	8
subvertir	sentir	6A	sustraer	traer	33

Verb	Class (Sub-class)	#	Verb	Class (Sub-class)	#
susurrar	cantar	1	televisar	cantar	1
suturar	cantar	1	temblar	pensar	4A
tabicar	cantar (tocar)	1-1	temblequear	cantar	1
tablear	cantar	1	temer	comer	2
tabular	cantar	1	temperar	cantar	1
tachar	cantar	1	templar	cantar	1
tachonar	cantar	1	temporizar	cantar (cazar)	1-4
taconear	cantar	1	tender	perder	5A
tajar	cantar	1	tener	tener	31
taladrar	cantar	1	tensar	cantar	1
talar	cantar	1	tensionar	cantar	1
tallar	cantar	1	tentar	pensar	4A
tambalear	cantar	1	teñir	pedir (ceñir)	6B-3
tamborilear	cantar	1	teologizar	cantar (cazar)	1-4
tamizar	cantar (cazar)	1-4	teorizar	cantar (cazar)	1-4
tanguear	cantar	1	terciar	cantar	1
tantear	cantar	1	tergiversar	cantar	1
tañer	comer (tañer)	2-5	terminar	cantar	1
tapar	cantar	1	terraplenar	cantar	1
tapear	cantar	1	tersar	cantar	1
tapiar	cantar	1	testar	cantar	1
tapizar	cantar (cazar)	1-4	testificar	cantar (tocar)	1-1
taponar	cantar	1	testimoniar	cantar	1
taquigrafiar	cantar (enviar)	1-15	tildar	cantar	1
taracear	cantar	1	timar	cantar	1
tarar	cantar	1	timbrar	cantar	1
tararear	cantar	1	tintar	cantar	1
tardar	cantar	1	tintinear	cantar	1
tarifar	cantar	1	tipificar	cantar (tocar)	1-1
tarjetear(se)	cantar	1	tiranizar	cantar (cazar)	1-4
tartajear	cantar	1	tirar	cantar	1
tartamudear	cantar	1	tiritar	cantar	1
tasar	cantar	1	tirotear	cantar	1
tatarear	cantar	1	titilar	cantar	1
tatuar	cantar (actuar)	1-14	titubear	cantar	1
teatralizar	cantar (cazar)	1-4	titular	cantar	1
techar	cantar	1	titularizar	cantar (cazar)	1-4
teclear	cantar	1	tiznar	cantar	1
tecnificar	cantar (tocar)	1-1	tocar	cantar (tocar)	1-1
tejer	comer	2	toldar	cantar	1
teledirigir	subir (dirigir)	3-2	tolerar	cantar	1
telefonear	cantar	1	tomar	cantar	1
telegrafiar	cantar (enviar)	1-15	tonificar	cantar (tocar)	1-1

Verb	Class (Sub-class)	#	Verb	Class (Sub-class)	#
tonsurar	cantar	1	transparentar	cantar	1
tontear	cantar	1	transpirar	cantar	1
topar	cantar	1	transportar	cantar	1
toquetear	cantar	1	trapacear	cantar	1
torcer	mover (cocer)	5B-1	trapichear	cantar	1
torear	cantar	1	traquetear	cantar	1
tornar	cantar	1	trasbordar	cantar	1
tornasolar	cantar	1	trascender	perder	5A
tornear	cantar	1	trasegar	pensar (negar)	4A-1
torpedear	cantar	1	trashumar	cantar	1
torrar	cantar	1	trasladar	cantar	1
torturar	cantar	1	traslucir	lucir	7B
toser	comer	2	trasmutar	cantar	1
tostar	mostrar	4B	trasnochar	cantar	1
totalizar	cantar (cazar)	1-4	traspapelar	cantar	1
trabajar	cantar	1	traspasar	cantar	1
trabar	cantar	1	trasplantar	cantar	1
traducir	conducir	34	trasponer	poner (suponer)	30-1
traer	traer	33	trasquilar	cantar	1
traficar	cantar (tocar)	1-1	trastabillar	cantar	1
tragar	cantar (pagar)	1-2	trastear	cantar	1
traicionar	cantar	1	trastocar	cantar (tocar)	1-1
trajear	cantar	1	trastornar	cantar	1
trajinar	cantar	1	trasvasar	cantar	1
tramar	cantar	1	tratar	cantar	1
tramitar	cantar	1	traumatizar	cantar (cazar)	1-4
trampear	cantar	1	travestir	pedir	6B
trancar	cantar (tocar)	1-1	trazar	cantar (cazar)	1-4
tranquilizar	cantar (cazar)	1-4	tremolar	cantar	1
transbordar	cantar	1	trenzar	cantar (cazar)	1-4
transcribir	subir (escribir)	3-11	trepanar	cantar	1
transcurrir	subir	3	trepar	cantar	1
transferir	sentir	6A	trepidar	cantar	1
transfigurar	cantar	1	tributar	cantar	1
transformar	cantar	1	tricotar	cantar	1
transfundir	subir	3	trillar	cantar	1
transgredir	subir (abolir)	3-14	trinar	cantar	1
transigir	subir (dirigir)	3-2	trincar	cantar (tocar)	1-1
transitar	cantar	1	trinchar	cantar	1
transliterar	cantar	1	triplicar	cantar (tocar)	1-1
transmigrar	cantar	1	triptongar	cantar (pagar)	1-2
transmitir	subir	3	tripular	cantar	1
transmutar	cantar	1	triturar	cantar	1

Verb	Class (Sub-class)	#	Verb	Class (Sub-class)	#
versar	cantar	1	volcar	mostrar (trocar)	4B-1
versificar	cantar (tocar)	1-1	volear	cantar	1
vertebrar	cantar	1	voltear	cantar	1
verter	perder	5A	volver	mover (volver)	5B-4
vestir	pedir	6B	vomitar	cantar	1
vetar	cantar	1	vosear	cantar	1
vetear	cantar	1	votar	cantar	1
viabilizar	cantar (cazar)	1-4	vulcanizar	cantar (cazar)	1-4
viajar	cantar	1	vulgarizar	cantar (cazar)	1-4
vibrar	cantar	1	vulnerar	cantar	1
viciar	cantar	1	xerocopiar	cantar	1
vidriar	cantar	1	xerografiar	cantar (enviar)	1-15
vigilar	cantar	1	yacer	conocer (yacer)	7A-1
vigorizar	cantar (cazar)	1-4	yantar	cantar	1
vilipendiar	cantar	1	yermar	cantar	1
vincular	cantar	1	yodurar	cantar	1
vindicar	cantar (tocar)	1-1	yugular	cantar	1
violar	cantar	1	yuxtaponer	poner (suponer)	30-1
violentar	cantar	1	zafar	cantar	1
virar	cantar	1	zaherir	sentir	6A
virilizar(se)	cantar (cazar)	1-4	zamarrear	cantar	1
visar	cantar	1	zambullir	subir (bullir)	3-5
visibilizar	cantar (cazar)	1-4	zampar	cantar	1
visionar	cantar	1	zanganear	cantar	1
visitar	cantar	1	zanjar	cantar	1
vislumbrar	cantar	1	zapar	cantar	1
visualizar	cantar (cazar)	1-4	zapatear	cantar	1
vitorear	cantar	1	zapear	cantar	1
vitrificar	cantar (tocar)	1-1	zarandear	cantar	1
vituperar	cantar	1	zarpar	cantar	1
vivaquear	cantar	1	zascandilear	cantar	1
vivificar	cantar (tocar)	1-1	zigzaguear	cantar	1
vivir	subir	3	zonificar	cantar (tocar)	1-1
vocalizar	cantar (cazar)	1-4	zorrear	cantar	1
vocear	cantar	1	zozobrar	cantar	1
vociferar	cantar	1	zumbar	cantar	1
volar	mostrar	4B	zurcir	subir (fruncir)	3-1
volatilizar	cantar (cazar)	1-4	zurrar	cantar	1

Selected References

Alarcos Llorach, Emilio. 1999. *Gramática de la lengua española*. Madrid: Real Academia Española (Espasa Calpe).

Borrego, J., Asencio, J. G., and Prieto, E. 1992. *El subjuntivo. Valores y usos*. Madrid: Sociedad General Española de Librería.

Freysselinard, Eric. 1998. *Ser y estar. Le verbe être en espagnol*. Paris: Ophrys.

Gómez Torrego, Leonardo. 2000. *Ortografía de uso del español actual*. Madrid: Ediciones SM.

Lathrop, Thomas A. 2003. *The Evolution of Spanish*. Univ. of Delaware: Juan de la Cuesta. (Also available in Spanish translation.)

Moliner, María. 1998. *Diccionario de uso del español*. Madrid: Editorial Gredos. (Also available on CD-ROM.)

Penny, Ralph. 1991. *A History of the Spanish Language*. Cambridge: Cambridge University Press. (Also available in Spanish translation.)

Porto Dapena, José Álvaro. 1991. *Del indicativo al subjuntivo. Valores y usos de los modos del verbo*. Madrid: Arco/Libros.

Real Academia Española. 2001. *Diccionario de la lengua española*. Madrid: Espasa Calpe. (Also available at: <www.rae.es>.)

———. [2004]. *Diccionario panhispánico de dudas*. Online: <www.rae.es>.

———. 1999. *Ortografía de la Lengua Española*. Madrid: Espasa Calpe.

VOX Diccionario para la enseñanza de la lengua española. 1997. Barcelona: Bibliograf.